1001 Beds

Sean!

Great to work together. I look forward to more adventures

love
Tim

OTHER BOOKS BY TIM MILLER:

Shirts & Skin

Body Blows: Six Performances

1001 *Beds*

Performances, Essays, and Travels

Tim Miller

Edited by
Glen Johnson

The University of Wisconsin Press

The University of Wisconsin Press
1930 Monroe Street
Madison, Wisconsin 53711

www.wisc.edu/wisconsinpress/

3 Henrietta Street
London WC2E 8LU, England

1   3   5   4   2

Printed in the United States of America

Library of Congress Cataloging-in-Publication Data
Miller, Tim, 1958–
1001 beds: performances, essays, and travels /
Tim Miller; edited by Glen Johnson.
p.   cm. — (Living out)
Includes bibliographical references.
ISBN-13: 978-0-299-21690-0 (hard cover: alk. paper)
ISBN-13: 978-0-299-21694-8 (pbk.: alk. paper)
1. Miller, Tim, 1958–   2. Gay men—United States—Biography.
3. Performance artists—United States—Biography.
I. Title: One thousand one beds.   II. Johnson, Glen.
III. Title.   IV. Series.
HQ75.8M55 A3   2006
700.92—dc22   2005032878

To my partner,

ALISTAIR McCARTNEY,

in gratitude for the love that fills
our bed,
our home,
our life . . .

Contents

Part 3: Culture War

Part 4: The Teacher

Part 5: Us

    TIM MILLER and ALISTAIR MCCARTNEY

Contents

Editor's Introduction

GLEN JOHNSON

Art and Culture

Tim Miller had an ambiguous place in *The American Century*, a huge installation of "Art and Culture" that filled New York's Whitney Museum of American Art during 1999 and 2000. The exhibition's curators recognized the importance of the solo performance art of the century's final decades, but they registered ambivalence about how to place Tim Miller, one of the founders and most successful practitioners of this vibrant contemporary form. Tim Miller's contribution to the American century was represented by a two-minute video loop of the "get hard" litany from *My Queer Body* (1992), in which a naked Tim exhorts his penis—unsuccessfully, as scripted—to rise to a sexual political gesture. Tim Miller performed nonstop on video, but not in the exhibition area devoted to "Video and Performance." Instead, he appeared inside a curious tunnel-shaped enclosure jutting out at an angle from the back wall of the museum's second floor and labeled "The Culture Wars." The tunnel provided good artistic company, including Robert Mapplethorpe's "Man in a Polyester Suit," a Dona Ann McAdams photo of Annie Sprinkle, and an excerpt from Marlon Riggs's documentary *Tongues Untied*. But it also included footage of Patrick J. Buchanan exhorting the 1992 Republican National Convention to fight "a cultural war," as well as a news photo of homophobic demonstrators affiliated with the Reverend Fred Phelps and his "God Hates Fags" crusade. Within *The American Century,* among the artworks but not quite of them, Tim Miller in the tunnel became part of a "cultural site."

Falling back on the archaic distinction between art and culture that other parts of its exhibition countered, the Whitney Museum's segregation and labeling of Tim Miller's work in many ways epitomizes his career within the contentious America of recent decades. The museum's signage implied a need to shield young museum goers from an artist dealing with homosexuality and known for performing naked, though this explanation was hardly consistent with the ample supply of genitalia and other sexual content on view in open exhibition areas. Skittishness was understandable in a political environment where museums, like Tim Miller and other "controversial" (meaning gay) artists, had been targeted in the name of "family values." Beyond timidity, the Whitney's enclosure reflected uncertainty about the role of activism in art. RoseLee Goldberg wrote in the *American Century* exhibition catalog that "many artists reclaimed performance as a mechanism for grassroots activism, and in the hands of Tim Miller or the late David Wojnarowicz, . . . it became the most effective means to publicize political and social issues." Although the exhibition was able to do some justice to feminist performers, for the most part it bracketed activist performance as a "mechanism" or "means" to goals outside the realm of art. Contemporary solo performers who were displayed outside the tunnel— from Meredith Monk, Laurie Anderson, and Bruce Nauman to Matthew Barney—were those whose accomplishments could be addressed in more purely aesthetic terms.

1001 Beds defines Tim Miller's place as a citizen artist in the contemporary United States through a wide range of his writings, including performance scripts, essays, interviews, and journal entries. For a quarter-century, Miller has worked at the intersection of performance, politics, and identity, using his personal experience to focus entertaining but pointed explorations of life as a gay American man, part of a community both assertive and beleaguered in a deeply homophobic and increasingly divided political culture. The result is a distinctive body of work of unique value. Taking advantage of the quick responsiveness and portability of solo performance, Miller has brought current issues to audiences throughout the United States as well as in Europe, Australia, and Japan. His political interventions have ranged from a performance at a hospital vigil during the AIDS funding crisis to demonstrations outside national political conventions, into the twenty-first century, when he has been the only theater artist regularly touring work dealing with immigration and "gay marriage" issues. As a teacher and as founder and curator of performance venues, he has been a central figure in the growth of performance art and the exploration of its potentials, both artistic and political. His visibility and success as an activist artist led to his being targeted by the radical Right during the 1990s, a culture-wars episode whose effects shadow the arts in America to this day. Taken together, the writings collected here constitute a professional autobiography of this activist artist, one of the creators of a crucial contemporary art form and a tireless advocate for the American dream of political equality for all citizens.

Politics and Performance

When Tim Miller arrived in New York at the age of nineteen as an apprentice postmodern dancer, his political awareness and his professional ambitions were intense but still largely separate. His interest in American politics arose precociously: growing up in Whittier, California, hometown of Richard Nixon, he assumed that he too would someday be president. But his growing awareness of himself as a gay man in a homophobic nation channeled his aspirations away from elective office and toward oppositional politics and the activist community. His move from California to New York in 1978 was shadowed by the growth of right-wing conservatism and propelled by the political murder in San Francisco of Harvey Milk, the nation's first openly gay elected official. After two years spent tentatively exploring his artistic vocation and activist issues in the neighborhoods of Manhattan's Lower East Side, the young dancer was "fueled and challenged" toward a new form of activist performance by the 1980 election to the presidency of Ronald Reagan. Reagan had been governor of California during Miller's childhood, and the triumph of the Right's agendas fronted by Reagan presented "a crisis period for artists, a crisis that has not abated since." In his first major solo work, *Postwar* of 1982, Miller staged a scene where he was beaten up by a dancer in a Reagan mask. His opposition to Reaganism soon came to focus on the president's silence as AIDS devastated the gay male community, leading Miller to the militant ACT UP (the AIDS Coalition to Unleash Power) movement, whose participatory ethos and confrontational tactics became, as he told Steven Durland in the 1991 interview printed here, "the single most influential thing in my life."

The stylized battle with Reagan in *Postwar* was transformed into the activist performer's real confrontation with power. The confrontation became even sharper as President Reagan's willful neglect of the AIDS crisis was followed by the overt homophobia of the first Bush administration, which launched an agenda to intimidate the arts community and silence activist performers including Tim Miller. In 1992, Miller demonstrated with ACT UP outside the Republican National Convention in Houston, while Reagan protege Buchanan added "culture war" to the national vocabulary. The Republican defeat that year by Bill Clinton renewed progressive hopes, which were reflected also by Miller's anticipatory celebration in *My Queer Body* of the inauguration of a black lesbian president. But the culture war continued. A dozen years after Buchanan's speech, with the Right again in control of the federal government, the struggle for equal rights for gay and lesbian Americans had moved to marriage license bureaus and immigration offices—and to the performance spaces where Miller's *Us* pushed for national legal acknowledgment of gay relationships, even as President George W. Bush called for

Tim-Reagan dance from Postwar, 1982. Photo © Paula Court.

expanding the homophobic Defense of Marriage Act (signed by Clinton) into a constitutional amendment.

Since the 1980s, Miller's work has emphasized a participatory ethos that invites his audience—sitting in a theater, collaborating in a performance workshop, or demonstrating before a federal building, a public hospital, a marriage bureau—to use the space of performance both to raise awareness and to empower change. In his theatrical works this notion regularly takes him—sometimes naked—into the audience. The melding into performance of personal experience, bodily self-assertion, a communal ideal, and political goals characterizes the selections collected in *1001 Beds*. His belief in the power of performance to effect change infuses these essays, manifestoes, journal entries, transcriptions of performance pieces, and the full text of *Us,* his funny and furious work addressing the official homophobia of U.S. immigration policies and laws that deny gay partners any of the rights granted heterosexual couples. Discrimination against gay families became the main focus of Miller's work years before the U.S. Supreme Court's overturning of sodomy laws in 2003 reenergized gay communities and moved to the forefront of national discussion the legal status of same-sex couples. His 1999 work *Glory Box* first addressed the dilemma of Miller and his Australian partner, Alistair McCartney, who face separation or exile from the United States unless these laws are reformed. Characteristically, personal experience developed into activism as Miller and McCartney joined with other binational couples to publicize and lobby. More than any previous Miller work, *Us* became part of a comprehensive activist strategy inside theaters and outside.

As he has done for two decades, Tim Miller in *Us* deploys his personal experience as a touchstone for addressing social issues, mixing "juicy autobiographical bits" with passionate and humorous insights into both the pleasures of gay life and the "nasty injustices that queer folk face." The material in *1001 Beds* gives insight into his process of turning myriad experiences and memories into narratives that are then crafted into essays and performance pieces. The arrangement of the selections follows Miller's professional trajectory, from performance pieces in the early 1980s that focused on the power and politics of the nuclear family and of relationships with lovers, through the overtly political works fueled by Miller's street activism and urging audiences to confront with him the daily injustices of gay people's lives. In both form and content, *1001 Beds* represents the hallmarks of Miller's work. Episodic and at times fragmentary, the material weaves Miller's own stories with those of friends, lovers, colleagues, and students while it addresses questions of social justice for gay men, lesbians, and other members of the diverse communities that make up the United States. The selections in this book overlap and revisit particular stories and events to present Miller as a vital American cultural figure.

These works exemplify Tim Miller's love of language and wordplay, such as his puns on *writes,* civil *rights,* and the marriage *rites* that are so much a part of contemporary political discourse as well as of Miller's performances and essays. The range of works included here also highlights the deep engagement with American history and culture that runs through Miller's work and underlies his critique of American politics. Miller's desire to "figure out all this America stuff" informs his work from the early *Postwar,* which traced the Miller family's history through social changes and the nuclear threat of post–World War II America, through the text of *Democracy in America,* the multimedia ensemble piece he created for the 1984 Next Wave Festival at the Brooklyn Academy of Music, to the joyous yet bittersweet role that Miller's love of American musical theater plays in *Us.* He has lent his voice, his body, and his art to the growing assertiveness of gay men and lesbians, part of a profound continuing social change empowering women and ethnic, sexual, and cultural minorities. Miller's fascination with American identity, his own and that of the country at large, provides for greater understanding of his anger at a federal government that has almost always come down on the homophobic side of issues involving the lives of its gay citizens. *1001 Beds* reveals how firmly this artist's idealism is rooted in American values and the American dream, lending poignancy to *Us,* where he faces forced exile from what *Glory Box* calls "my pathetic, frustrating, hate-filled, when-will-we-grow-up, annoying and ever beloved country."

Since 1979, Miller has helped to define the genre of solo performance as a "quintessentially American art." He cofounded two of the most important American venues for alternative performances, Performance Space 122 in New York and Highways Performance Space in Santa Monica, California. These venues are dedicated to the transformative potential of performance, showcasing innovative solo performers and training and supporting emerging artists, experimental theater and dance troupes, and socially conscious art. Founded in 1979 by Charlie Moulton, Charles Dennis, Peter Rose, and Tim Miller, PS 122 is housed in a former public school in New York's East Village, historically an immigrant and working-class neighborhood that has attracted young artists and radical thinkers. It has been a central force in the burgeoning of the East Village as a site for cultural and performance venues. At PS 122 in 1980, Miller organized "Men Together," the first festival of gay male performance art in the United States. After returning to the West Coast, Miller cofounded Highways in 1989 with Linda Frye Burnham, serving as its artistic director throughout the 1990s. At Highways in particular, he developed the gay men's performance workshops that both built community and fueled Miller's own works, eventually expanding to venues throughout the United States as well as in Britain. Both PS 122 and Highways have tapped into the divergent artistic energies specific to their local communities—the experimental volatility of New York's downtown arts scene and Los Angeles's community-based, politicized arts movements. PS 122 and Highways have physically actualized Miller's aspirations for community building through performance.

Tim Miller's performing life has spanned four continents but has always centered on these two artistic homes, one within sight of the East River and the other blocks from the Pacific Ocean. Both his art and his activism share this bicoastal dimension. When he arrived in New York in 1978 after a year's detour to the University of Washington, the nineteen-year-old dancer brought with him notions formed by feminist performance in his native Los Angeles—"the personal, the small, the healing"—as well as scars from the murder of his first political idol, the gay San Francisco supervisor Harvey Milk. In New York Miller intended to study dance with Merce Cunningham, but what he found there was not what he expected. As Miller puts it, at that time the New York art world affected "postmodern cool"—"images without politics, gesture without social action." Miller soon "got myself into trouble" by publicly criticizing established gay artists like Cunningham and Robert Wilson for political apathy around gay issues. But he found alternative inspiration in the emerging downtown scene and artists like Spalding Gray and the Wooster Group, for whom art was inextricably personal and political. Enthusiastically embracing that scene, Miller within a few years had become the "golden boy" of New York performance art. As he recalls in the essay-interview "Professional Autobiography," accolades and international success came quickly—too quickly, he later came to believe, though his high profile gave him the opportunity to experiment widely with the content and form of solo, duo, and ensemble performances. When Miller came to rethink his approach to performance in the wake of dissatisfaction with the large-scale, elaborate, and poorly received *Democracy in America,* the elements were in place for a new synthesis that has marked his career ever since. Moving back to California in 1986, he brought with him the verbal exuberance and virtuosity of movement he had honed in New York, and in Los Angeles he reconnected with the art of "social context, coming from cultural communities, . . . where the artist is also a social creature . . . and a social activist."

The earliest writings in *1001 Beds* are permeated with the young performer's concern that his developing art should be socially aware, artistically gratifying, accessible, and critically successful. As he moved into more explicitly political works, these tensions coalesced for him into two key principles: that "performance is by nature a social act, a public act," and that the strongest element of his work is its personal specificity, his own "strange cosmology which begins to take life on stage, dynamically and passionately." Back in Los Angeles, Miller worked among community-focused artists who defined themselves as citizen activists. This included street activism: as he says in "Professional Autobiography," artists who dealt with homelessness or AIDS "better also be functional" in trying to resolve those crises. Miller joined ACT UP, an organization of individuals putting their bodies on the line against the inaction of government and the medical establishment in the AIDS pandemic. ACT UP's tactics forced attention on the stories of those lost to an epidemic not yet even publicly mentioned by the country's president. Miller joined in protests and in organizing demonstrations in Los Angeles and throughout the United States. Of these actions, two were especially important to him. The weeklong vigil in 1989 at the Los Angeles County Hospital demanding an AIDS ward was, as Miller notes, a case where activists achieved direct tangible success, even at the cost of being roughed up by police. Equally important, if less clearly successful, was the "Art Attack" mock-arrest of the Los Angeles Federal Building in 1990 during which demonstrators protested attempts by right-wingers in government to suppress artistic expression; Miller was among the twenty-eight who were arrested for real. When on tour outside of Los Angeles, Miller connected with local ACT UP chapters, which became his primary national community.

Miller's ACT UP–inspired performances showed not only increased militancy but also a more explicit, joyous exploration of the male body and sexuality. The nature of these late 1980s works gave Miller a high profile and brought him into the sights of a concerted attack, spearheaded by the congressional Right led by Senator Jesse Helms and with the connivance of the Bush administration, on artists dealing provocatively with sexuality. Government-sanctioned repression initially focused on visual artists, including Robert Mapplethorpe and Andres Serrano, and on the museums that showed their works, resulting in canceled exhibitions, lawsuits, and a chilling effect on institutions once bold enough to showcase innovative and controversial art.

The most protracted high-profile case of censorship occurred at the National Endowment for the Arts. A decade and a half after it began, the "NEA Four" episode still provides the label with which Miller is most frequently identified. In 1990, after moving successfully through the NEA's established peer-review process, in which a committee of artists selects projects for funding based on their merits, performance grants to Tim Miller, Holly Hughes, John Fleck, and Karen Finley were killed by the chair of the NEA, Bush appointee John Frohnmayer. Three of the NEA Four artists were gay or lesbian, and all four dealt with sexual themes. A subsequent lawsuit brought to light what had been obvious from the start: that Frohnmayer acted in direct response to pressure from the Bush White

House, thereby violating the independence from political interference guaranteed by the NEA's charter. Miller's earlier anger at the Reagan administration over AIDS was matched by his outrage toward the Bush government for violating the mission of the NEA, the American spirit of freedom of expression, and his own rights as a citizen artist. In his defiant July 4, 1990, "Artist's Declaration of Independence," President Bush became "King George," reincarnating the monarch whose earlier infringement of Americans' rights inspired the 1776 Declaration of Independence and the American Revolution.

Though always an enthusiastic provocateur, Miller did not choose his designated role in the culture war. He engaged it with customary intensity, but his part was uncharacteristically reactive and symbolic. Useful as notoriety can sometimes be, it inevitably oversimplifies and limits an artist. Once targeted, Miller could anticipate protesters outside, and spies inside, any theater, as well as garbled or false reports of his performances. In the environment generated by right-wing smear tactics, no less a personage than Robert Brustein, founding director of Yale Repertory and American Repertory Theatres, wrote in the *New Republic* that Tim Miller "proudly displayed his erect organ" onstage. Brustein had never seen Miller perform. When I questioned him about this falsehood, which is at best a gross caricature of the "get hard" verbal litany in *My Queer Body* (the same segment later chosen by the Whitney Museum to represent Miller's work), Brustein replied that he had "read it somewhere." In such a cultural climate, Tim Miller quickly came to regard the NEA fracas as a distraction from more important work.

In his comments on the culture war, Miller has consistently observed that, stressful and constricting as the attacks were on established artists like himself, the most pernicious effect was on young performers and the institutions providing opportunities for their work to be seen. This was no facile observation: throughout his career, Miller has devoted major portions of his time and energy to training and encouraging young artists and to promoting venues where their work can be seen. In the 1990s, while regularly under political attack, Miller channeled additional energy into his teaching. Beyond long- and short-term university positions, he conducted performance workshops for apprentice actors, academics, theater professionals, seminarians, and, especially, gay men who may or may not aspire to artistic careers. Expanding techniques honed as artistic director of Highways to other venues on three continents, his gay men's workshops ranged from one-day affairs, typically held at spaces where Miller was performing in the evenings, to more extended undertakings that eventuated in public performances created by workshop members. The workshops were symbiotic with Miller's own performances: beginning with *My Queer Body* and extending to *Us,* many of Miller's stories took shape from exercises he did alongside workshop participants.

In the 1990s, harassment by the homophobic Right was a fact of professional life for Tim Miller, even as the political climate shifted with the election of Bill Clinton. Like many artists, Miller worked for the Clinton ticket. He was slated to perform at a 1992 Clinton fundraiser for the gay community, but his appearance was quashed out of fear that the notoriety of the NEA Four case would be used to attack the candidate. Although Miller continued to support Clinton, that bit of shiftiness proved to be prophetic. Following the 1992 election, the NEA Four's lawsuit was settled, in effect awarding them the grants withheld by Frohnmayer. The matter did not end there, however, because the Clinton Justice Department unaccountably appealed a circuit court ruling that struck down the congressional "decency" clause that had been used against the artists. In 1998, the United States Supreme Court reversed that ruling, 8–1 (both Clinton appointees in the majority), and "decency" remains the law of the land, delimiting projects that can receive government funding. Making the "indecent" label stick was President Clinton's ironic parting gift to the NEA Four.

For all the caricaturing and sensationalizing that the culture war engendered, Miller's work is profoundly rooted in American ideals of freedom, equality, justice—and decency. He can be excused a touch of egotism in calling himself "a Jimmy Stewart–type queer persona," since—as with the U.S. senator played by Stewart in *Mr. Smith Goes to Washington*—the combination of idealism and anger voiced in Miller's works is fueled by repeated betrayal of those ideals. As early as 1984, Jacki Appel noted that Miller differs from most of his contemporaries in that his characteristic mode is indignation rather than irony. Indignation is the mirror image of hope, and both are products of idealism. Often angry, Miller's writings are expressions of a hopeful activist determination to realize American ideals. *Us,* whose complete script appears in this book, expresses his demand for the simple right to marry his Australian-born partner and settle with him into the life of an American family. While Miller's works have expounded the pleasures and dangers of gay sex and the male body, they have also highlighted the sweetness and vulnerability of love. This last characteristic gives *Us* added potency in the current struggle to define marriage in the United States, appealing to Americans both within and beyond the gay and lesbian community.

Of all the national political events in Tim Miller's lifetime, the election of 2000 was the most directly relevant to him, because Democratic candidate Al Gore endorsed the cause for which Miller had been working for years: immigration rights for same-sex couples. The defeat of Gore (at the hands of the same Supreme Court that had upheld the "decency" clause against the NEA Four) contributed to the more determined activism that infuses the text of *Us* and surrounds its performances. Miller has been able to celebrate some victories—most notably, performing *Us* in Austin on the day in 2003 when the Supreme Court overturned Texas's sodomy law. But eighteen months later, anti–"gay marriage" referenda were used in eleven states to bring out votes to keep the Bush administration in power. Eight of the eleven successful referenda also banned civil unions for gay and lesbian couples. The simple goal of full equality remains elusive, so in *1001 Beds,* which concludes this collection of his writings, Tim Miller looks forward to another twenty years taking his activist performances to audiences throughout the United States and the world.

The Shape of a Career

This book's comprehensive picture of Tim Miller as artist, teacher, and citizen activist counters the lingering effects of culture-war rhetoric that ignores the range of his activities and oversimplifies his art. The ongoing American culture war is fundamentally about access—about whose stories get heard fully and in their integrity. The notoriety that the Whitney Museum's *American Century* exhibit emphasized underlines the importance of understanding Miller as more than a "cultural site"—the need to see him as a creative artist at the intersection of performance, activism, and gay identity. National politics, gay issues, activist performance, and—holding all together—the experience of an American gay man trying to make a life, a community, and a family in a culture still legally and officially homophobic—that matrix defines Tim Miller's artistic career and this book.

The five sections of *1001 Beds* are topical and roughly chronological. An essay from 1999, "Memory and Facing the Future," serves as prologue. All of the book's selections demonstrate the belief stated in "Memory and Facing the Future," that writing one's story is "a fierce act of imagining the future." The material that follows—from performances, interviews in which he discusses his creative process, essays on pedagogy, and selections from his journals—resonates with his power to use the personal and particular to speak to the communal: "I perform stories of who I have been in order to imagine who I might become—who we might become."

The opening section, "New York Years," recounts the period between 1978 and 1986, during which Tim Miller discovered his art form and developed his distinctive voice. Arriving in New York City at the age of nineteen, he soon was drawn to the emerging forms of performance in the downtown theater scene. This section includes material Miller introduced at PS 122, the venue he cofounded in 1979 and the site in 1980 of both his first full-evening solo perform-ance, *Pretty Boy/Big Bldg/Grand Mal,* and the first-ever festival of gay male performance, "Men Together," which he curated. His skills in improvisation and interacting with an audience were fostered by a series of Monday-night informal performing events started on his twenty-second birthday in September 1980. Among the selections, "Performance N.Y.C." is a 1981 riff on themes from Miller's earliest pieces. "Floor It!" a short performance work, conveys the anarchic creative spirit of the early years at PS 122.

Over the next four years, while Miller was developing solo and small-scale collaborative works, he also created a series of ambitious, large-scale multimedia works for choreographed ensembles: *Postwar* (1982; an earlier version was called *Survival Tactic*), *Cost of Living* (1983), and the grant-supported and relatively lavishly budgeted *Democracy in America* (1984). A spin-off from *Democracy in America* was a short book by the same title, produced in collaboration with photographer Dona Ann McAdams, who would photograph almost every subsequent Miller work. This section includes fourteen "sto-ries" from Miller's and McAdams's book. Poorly received (Miller himself refers to it as a "mess"), *Democracy in America* caused Miller to rethink how he conceived his art and what he wanted it to accom-plish, leading him to hone the more intimate solo and duo perform-ance style that he had developed at PS 122.

An important example was *Live Boys,* created in March 1981 with Miller's partner, dancer John Bernd, following their initial collabora-tion for the "Men Together" gay performance festival the previous November. *Live Boys* continues their complicated love story, which concluded in a final episode performed in August 1981, though it res-onates through Miller's subsequent solo work, particularly *Naked Breath* (1994). *Live Boys* is also the first theater piece to refer to AIDS, more than a year before the disease was identified and named: for that reason, David Gere has written, this work "cries out to be recon-jured and seen anew." In the three *Live Boys* episodes, Miller and

Bernd chronicled the joys and conflicts and, finally, the dissolution of their relationship. In the wake of Miller's dissatisfaction with *Democracy in America,* the solo works and *Live Boys* provided the models for subsequent work. The first fruit was *Buddy Systems* (1985), which combined solo segments and collaboration with Douglas Sadownick, who became Tim Miller's lover and collaborator in various ways for more than a dozen years. The "New York Years" section includes two excerpts from *Buddy Systems,* which premiered in California shortly before Miller and Sadownick relocated to Los Angeles and marks the conclusion of his nine years in New York.

During his time in New York, Tim Miller was involved in a range of activist movements—anti-nuclear and anti-gentrification demonstrations, the People's Convention during the 1980 Democratic National Convention, and agitation for gay liberation. These involvements paralleled his performing activities but remained largely separate from them. Goal-driven political activities, including gay rights, are mostly absent from his performance works of the time. As an organizing principle, politics is found during this period almost exclusively in Miller's large-scale works, where it takes the form of a generalized Left-populist idealism. Gay experience was, of course, the essence of Miller's and Bernd's *Live Boys* series as well as of Miller's and Sadownick's *Buddy Systems.* Still, the focus in both collaborative works is personal politics: the give and take of relationships, issues of commitment. Miller had not yet found an integrating principle to bring together his personal experience as a gay man, his political ideals, his activist impulses, and his performing art.

That step is recounted in the second section of *1001 Beds,* "Activism," which focuses mainly on the later 1980s. That half-decade crystallized Miller's sense of himself as an activist-artist and of performance as an ideal vehicle to promote social goals. Two factors were enormously influential in redirecting his thinking and activity. First was his return to Los Angeles in 1986, where he immersed himself in a multicultural performing environment, joining with Linda Frye Burnham in 1989 to found Highways Performance Space. The second, overwhelming factor was the AIDS crisis and, in particular, Miller's involvement in ACT UP. From a somewhat tentative, though excited, initial contact with ACT UP in 1987, Miller progressed from raising money to organizing several high-profile actions. One of these, the "Art Attack" protest at the Los Angeles Federal Building in 1990, provides the background for Miller's "Civil Disobedience Weekend," which is printed here. The "Activism" section also includes materials from various sources that depict Tim Miller's political commitments and his thinking about the role of performance art in promoting social change. The section opens with "Professional Autobiography," an interview-essay from 1990 in which Miller recounts the influence of the politically sophisticated, ethnically diverse, and historically informed Los Angeles performing scene and details his philosophical and ideological approach to performance, finding his voice as "a politicized gay activist, gay cultural person, AIDS activist, American citizen." Entries from Miller's journals recount his involvement in ACT UP over a seven-year period, a topic further developed in a 1990 interview with Linda Frye Burnham. A more directly personal note is struck in Miller's account of his and Douglas Sadownick's first AIDS tests in 1990.

Not included here is "Preaching to the Converted," which Tim Miller wrote in 1995 in collaboration with David Román. This important essay provides a theoretical, historically based rationale for "work that is explicitly directed toward a queer audience and performed in a community-based or queer-friendly venue." "Preaching to the Converted" also provides the authors' thoughts on matters such as the importance of Protestant preaching as a precursor for American performance art. "Preaching to the Converted" was published in *Theater Journal* (1995) and reprinted in *The Queerest Art: Essays on Lesbian and Gay Theater* (2002), listed in the bibliography.

Demonstrations such as the "Art Attack" and performances such as "Civil Disobedience Weekend" gave Tim Miller the high visibility that led directly to the 1990 NEA Four episode. The "Culture War" section of *1001 Beds* prints materials from the NEA Four battles and related skirmishes. The "Artist's Statement" from Tim Miller's grant application to the National Endowment for the Arts is accompanied by excerpts from his deposition in the lawsuit that followed the politically motivated rejection of his and three other recommended grants. The deposition reveals, among other things, that an Endowment staffer, anticipating what might happen given the Bush administration's politicization of the NEA, attempted to have the statement rewritten. The quashing of grants came just before America's Independence Day, an irony that Miller seized on in his July 4, 1990, "Artist's Declaration of Independence" against "King George" Bush. His perspective one year into the subsequent eight-year episode is provided by a 1991 interview with Steven Durland, originally done as part of an "Offensive Plays" feature in the journal *The Drama Review*. And two unpublished "Supreme Court Reports" from 1998 recount Miller's reaction to oral arguments and the final decision in the NEA Four case, which affirmed the congressional "decency" clause. Beyond the specific NEA case, the essay "The Battle of Chattanooga" gives a sense of what it is like to be targeted for harassment by extremists both inside and outside the government. This essay riffs on Miller's interest in the Civil War, as he takes a side trip to the battleground outside Chattanooga and faces an uncivil protest against his work outside the theater where he is performing.

Selections in "The Teacher" show Tim Miller's increased commitment to gay male performance as a means of self-discovery and community expression in the midst of the culture war. "Embodied Pedagogy," a 1998 essay published here for the first time, provides details of Miller's workshop methods as well as what he wants these undertakings to accomplish for participants. This essay focuses mainly on Miller's work with apprentice actors, such as his students in the MFA program at UCLA. The workshops specifically for gay men highlight a central theme of all his work, that self-acceptance, including acceptance of one's body, must underlie self-assertion and political awareness. That theme is key to "Suck, Spit, Chew, Swallow," an extended essay that brings together all elements of his pedagogy in recounting a two-week intensive workshop in Birmingham, England, that eventuated in a public performance.

Miller's vocation as teacher and mentor has been influenced by his religious sense, which is often manifested in his teaching practices. From the start of his performing career, Miller regarded religion as one of his key subjects: the word *faith* appears in the earliest-dated item in this volume, "Performance N.Y.C." For Miller, religious commitment characteristically points toward social action. A particularly intense period of religious thinking for Miller came in 1989 and 1990, through his association with the activist Episcopal priest Malcolm Boyd. The most visible manifestation of this renewed spiritual engagement was a pair of performance sermons during Easter season at an Episcopal parish in Santa Monica. Miller wrote about this experience in "Jesus and the Queer Performance Artist," which incorporates material from the performance sermons. This essay ties Tim Miller's religious consciousness both to childhood influences (always a powerful force in his work) and to meditation on Jesus as a model activist performer. Although its emphasis is on individual spirituality and commitment, the essay also indirectly anticipates the debates that have increasingly roiled church institutions in subsequent years, concerning gay ordination, blessing of unions, and other matters related to homosexuality and religion. In the mid-1990s and again in 2005, Miller taught performance courses for seminarians at the Claremont School of Theology. In recent years, his specific church-focused activities have declined in number, but his sense of teaching as a mission has remained.

Us

The turn of the millennium brought a national political focus on "gay marriage"—that phrase serving as shorthand for a range of issues involving legal status and legal protections for same-sex relationships. This discussion accelerated and became increasingly politicized following the 2003 U.S. Supreme Court decision overturning sodomy laws, subsequent court rulings concerning same-sex marriages, thousands of gay wedding ceremonies, President George W. Bush's advocacy of a constitutional amendment banning gay marriage, and attempts to foment a voter backlash in the run-up to the 2004 elections. As he has been for two decades, Tim Miller is in the vanguard of activism. Characteristically, his commitment derives from a mixture of principle, patriotism, and personal experience. Miller's relationship with the Australian writer Alistair McCartney, which began in 1994, plunged them into the labyrinth of U.S. immigration policy, a particularly aggressive manifestation of government hostility toward same-sex relationships. For more than a half-dozen years, Miller and McCartney have lived in the trigger-sights of a policy that would force them to leave the United States in order to preserve their relationship. With characteristic vigor, Miller threw his energy into the issue, demonstrating, lobbying, exhorting, and making common cause with hundreds of binational couples facing deportation. As AIDS did in works of the 1980s and early 1990s, the immigration issue became the starting point for major performances: *Glory Box* (1999) and *Us* (2003). The latter forms the centerpiece of this concluding section of *1001 Beds*. It is accompanied by an interview with John Gentile, which in discussing the composition and structure of *Us* provides Miller's most extended account of his working methods. This concluding section is introduced by "Oklahomo!" which celebrates the Supreme Court decision and introduces Miller's love of American musical theater that is central to *Us*. Following is the script of *Carnal Garage,* a 1997 collaboration with Alistair McCartney. Recounting the nervous exhilaration of their developing love, *Carnal Garage* makes a trilogy with the other partner works printed in this book, *Live Boys* and *Buddy Systems.* It ends with a metaphorical marriage ritual, anticipating *Us* and its extended creative statement on the dilemmas of relationships in the contemporary United States. Also included is "Tokyo Tim," from 2003, which recounts his first performances in Asia.

The book concludes with the essay that provides its title. "1001 Beds" considers the physical and personal toll of a life spent as a traveling performer activist, then explains why the effort is worthwhile, indeed imperative, for Tim Miller. The essay ends with an expression of confidence that this peripatetic life performing, teaching, and pushing for change has had, and is having, positive effects on the body politic.

To reach the figure of 1001 beds slept in, Miller anticipates another two decades of performing on the road. In his forties, his career is dynamic and ongoing. The materials that conclude this book nevertheless can be seen as a culmination—perhaps something of a full circle—for the themes and directions charted throughout. The punning title of *Us* brings together in one syllable the personal, community, and national political strands that interweave Tim Miller's work from its beginnings, as well as the contents of this book: *Us* as a committed relationship, *Us* as the community of gay men and lesbians, *Us* as the American nation. There is pathos in the fact that the personal, artistic, and political integrity of his voice is reciprocated by Miller's homeland with grinding slowness at best. *Us* is an angry work, which is consistent with his political focus, since indignation flows from frustrated idealism and provides the energy for activism. His anger never stands alone: as often before in Miller's works, (almost) the last word of *Us* is "hope." But it is a fragile hope that remains in unresolved tension with the performance's simple question to our country: "What's wrong with Us?" For now, the task is simply making room for these American families to exist. Nevertheless, if the prospect of a gay-positive America seems, despite everything, less remote than it did when Tim Miller began performing a quarter-century ago, he can—and justifiably does—claim some of the credit. As he writes in "Memory and Facing the Future": "I have always used the memories of things passed to rewrite the ending of what is to come." In the process he has created a vital body of work that points directions toward a more just future.

Prologue

Tim Miller on the roof of his Mulberry Street apartment, New York, 1987. Photo © Tom Brazil.

Memory and Facing the Future

In the immense court of my memory . . . I come to meet myself.
Saint Augustine, *The Confessions*

As someone who has spent my whole adult life writing and performing stories from my experience, the gnarly terrain of memoir is both a favorite comfy chair and a particularly scary attic room. I have bounced between both the exquisite pleasures and pitfalls that are inevitably part of the encounter with one's life and memory. I have put myself (and, of course, my boyfriends) through the most detailed public revelations of the psychic, emotional, and sexual autobiographical narratives to which the flesh is heir. I sometimes have to remind myself that not everyone could tolerate their lives being on display like this. Most people sensibly maintain some pretty fixed boundaries about what is and is not available for public consumption. To "rim and tell" loudmouths like me, these boundaries just function as a tempting dare to dive into what I hope might be a deeper, more naked truth.

I have kept a journal consistently since I was in fifth grade. The fact that I first picked up a spiral notebook at the age of ten and began writing daily about what happened to me is every bit as important a detail about who I am as the fact that when I was fourteen I realized that I was gay and that it was my fate to love the boy next door. I would hazard that my need as a young boy-child to document my story was tightly bound up with the inchoate inkling that I would soon also have to rewrite *their* story, the heterosexual

3

narrative! Long before I began dressing like Oscar Wilde when I was fifteen, the impulse to write my memoir was my first declaration to the world that I was here and before too long would also be queer.

My favorite book during that revelatory Wildean sophomore year of high school was the *Confessions* of Jean Jacques Rousseau. (This should have tipped everyone off right then that I was destined to be a naked performance artist!) I suppose I was inspired by Rousseau's urgent need in his *Confessions* to spill all the beans: his obsessive masturbation, his penchant for indecent exposure in public parks, and so on. I learned that as salubrious as it is to spew those garbanzos in the privacy of your own three-ring binder, it's even better to spread them out à la carte for all to see. Since the moment I did my first feverish scribblings in my gay boy's adolescent journal, the crazed scrawl as panicky as a seismograph after an 8.1 earthquake, I have always seen writing about my life to be a fundamental act of knowing myself, of claiming space, and of simple survival. The act of remembering and sharing that memory with others became a crucial way to survive the shit that the world would strew in my path. I figured that if Rousseau's autobiographical ranting could start the French Revolution, my own might at least get me through high school so I could finally find a boyfriend.

Speaking of boyfriends, I have been writing a lot these days about my relationship with my lover, Alistair. Since he is from Australia, an antipodal land where people are not "blessed" by U.S. citizenship, for many years we have been dealing with the septic tank of homophobic INS rules and regulations that determine how we can make a life together. This is quite a challenge on top of negotiating the garden-variety difficulties that any two men have in trying to relate to each other. Since I keep trying to stay true to my crazy notion that I should always write about what is most truly on the front burner in my life, I am naturally trying to get down on paper in the book I'm currently writing the steak tartar of feelings that this existential binational relationship is bringing up. Alistair and I have had to fling ourselves around the globe trying to get papers in order so that our love for each other could find a place to grow. You can forget such luxuries as wall-to-wall carpeting and a room with a view. We just want to be in the same time zone!

This sometimes overwhelming international dilemma has tapped me back into a kind of faith I had as a tortured gay teenager, that if I wrote about the hard stuff in my life, it just might make the situation better. During the rigors of individuating as a gay boy in hate-filled America, I had somehow begun to believe that the act of writing about life might be a way to find the potential to transform it. If the truth be told, I think I have never stopped believing this. Writing about my life has always carried the potential for liberation. Maybe the writing cure could now help me once again to get a lock on a very chaotic situation, the nagging fear that at some point Alistair will be forced to leave the country. This can really cut through a lot of writer's block. I'm writing as fast as I can before his visa expires! I have never really lost this trust that the act of writing down my story somehow could alchemically affect how the story might end.

A moment ago I took a break from writing these words and stepped outside the house that Alistair and I share in Venice Beach. I decided that rather than dutifully try to meet my deadline, it was more important that I should spy on Alistair in his office, a small writing cabana next to our gurgling hot tub. Leaving my office with the computer humming its annoyance with my bad work habits, I made a quick detour to the kitchen for a reduced-fat granola bar (empty calories have been proven crucial to the memoir-writing process!) and turned the light off by the fridge before sneaking outdoors and down to the ugly powder-blue tile the previous owner of the house put down over his failed grass lawn. Alistair's face is right behind the window of his writing fort. His mouth tenses as he searches for the right word, the exact association, the accessed feeling for the memoir that he is writing about his childhood. Several images on the bulletin board on the wall behind him frame Alistair's face: a beautiful Sicilian boy, now long dead, photographed by Baron Von Gloeden; an image of Patti Smith in concert; a bold blood-red printout from one of the many websites dedicated to Rimbaud. He brushes some hair off his forehead, perhaps thinking, "I'm not sure that I really like this long hair hanging in my face, but I know that Tim fetishizes the look, so I can live with it."

He is probably writing from his own memory about the time when a magpie swooped down on him as a child, or about the first time that he came, or about a father who was so distant that he might as well have not existed. Whatever he is writing about, I can see it wander across his face. I, a literary Peeping Tom, try to see what's going on with him so that I can then snare that moment and drag it kicking and screaming back into the house to write about it. I will do this to try to make sense of my chaotic life and to share what sense I may find there with an unsuspecting reader. This act of writing memoir is how Alistair is also doing his part to solve, for the present at least, our immigration problem. Alistair and I are able to be together in the United States because he has a student visa to do an MFA in creative nonfiction at Antioch University in Los Angeles. So, you see, this subject is near and dear to me, because the act of writing memoir is both the practical and the psychic mechanism for Alistair and me to share our lives together.

Peeking (all right, spying) at Alistair as he types away feels a lot like when I try to look at my own life so as to write about it. I take off my shoes, sneak up on myself very quietly. I don't want to scare myself off. I pull out my machete and start to hack away at the tangled vines that block my view. I make decisions, have attacks of selective memory. Sometimes I am too easy on myself; the next moment I describe some ordinary selfish moment more brutally than it probably deserves.

As I look at Alistair writing away in his hut thousands of miles away from the land where he grew up, how can I hope in my own writing to get at the knotty tendons of how complex our real life is? Every time I try to write down anything from my memory, I am pulling the words out through a shrinking device that makes the feelings and the experience and the joys and the shit seem all vaguely squeezed, like trying to coax the last bit of toothpaste (or KY for that matter!) out of the tube and onto your trembling toothbrush (or tumescent red-purple cock). Like Pepé Le Pew forever caught in the grasp of a Warner Brothers cartoon laundry wringer, I am in trouble every time I start to write down what has gone on in my life.

How can I describe the fall of even a single hair on Alistair's forehead and hope to get anywhere near the ballpark of how tender and hard we can be with one another? When I write about the experiences and feelings that have come up from being in love with a man from another country, while living in a society that puts no value on such relationships, how can I get under the covers with the hurt that such a situation brings up inside me? Lately I often find myself crying at the drop of a hat whenever I actually allow myself to feel the pain of the fact that my partnership with Alistair is totally negated by my own country's immigration laws, part of the platter of rights every heterosexual takes for granted. These tears are definitely welcome to this tightly wound WASP, and their salt is quite precious to me. Any arrangement of subjects and verbs I might find to describe this reality may well be insufficient by comparison to the actual wet feeling of the thing, yet I know I must keep trying to find these words, write them, fling them from the stage and the page, or I will go fucking nuts from anger and fear.

When I tell the stories from my life, I hope I can be at least a tiny bit as authentic and surprising as those tears that creep down my face when I least expect them, when something reminds me of this situation Alistair and I face. I want those tears to get the page wet and tell their own story of how much joy and hurt there is in loving a man from another land. Pushing beyond my bad writing habits (my Mixmaster metaphors, attraction to puns, and shameless hyperbole, for starters), I want to find the words that might invite you into this place where I live. I write these stories in the hope that someone else just might understand what it has felt like to walk around in my smelly shoes. On a good day, I can hold these stories in the palm of my palm, in a clear light, toward you.

I know that the words I squeeze out of the tube and onto the page will never be as true or wet as the messy experiences lived from day to day. There is such a sweet hopelessness in trying to write from your life, a built-in certainty that whatever you cull will not be as layered or true as what you go through in a single day. Inevitably, the act of writing will distill, edit, change, compress, compact, alter, disguise, enhance, and reduce the raw mess of living. But parallel to that is another magic trick at work. As real as those perils are, the writing of memoir can also hone, expose, reveal, connect, and dig up something from inside me that I can use to build a future.

I have a big story to tell right now. It fills my memory. It's a story of how I met a man from another land and how I want to be with him. But my country, which I both love and hate, doesn't allow such things. I need to tell this story or I will go crazy. When I write my story, I can howl out the rage I feel at both our medieval government and my own shortcomings as a man and a lover. I can draw attention to the injustice. As I write this story, it becomes a completely necessary act of looking at the past as a means of negotiating a more empowered and grounded relationship in an uncertain future. Each in our own way, Alistair and I are writing our memoirs of what has happened as a way of creating a future together.

I have a completely unsubstantiated faith that if I write this story, I may be able to affect how the story will end. I have always used the memories of things passed to rewrite the ending of what is to come. I have done this from that first moment that I picked up my spiral binder at the edge of ten and somehow knew that the queer boy star of my story was not going to end up hanging by his neck from a beam in our family's detached suburban garage. I write these stories of who I have been to imagine who I might become. Writing memoir is a fierce act of imagining the future.

Part 1

New York Years

"It's me—Tim Miller—jumping, and Barry Davison pushing the lawnmower. This was 1982, my first trip out of the U.S. to perform. I was twenty-three years old and performing at the Dance Umbrella Festival at the Institute for Contemporary Art in London. I had done very few photo shoots before and I remember photographer Chris Harris's reassuring and sweet and feisty and fun energy as he made me jump again and again being chased by that damn lawnmower! I look at this picture now. Chris has died. My friend Barry, who performed a lot with me in my early work, would die of AIDS a few years after this photo was taken. When I performed in London in 2002, twenty years on from this photo, I sat with Val Bourne, director of Dance Umbrella, and she talked about Chris's death and that day with his camera at the ICA rushed back, a reminder of the painful impermanence of life and performance." Photo courtesy of Chris HA Theatre Museum Collection, Victoria and Albert Museum.

Performance N.Y.C.

Jim Miller's interest in what was beginning to be known as performance art launched his move to New York in 1978 at the age of nineteen. Although in many ways continuing to think of himself primarily as a dancer, he began improvising performances at PS 122, and by mid-1980 he was presenting full-length solo works. This previously unpublished essay from the autumn of 1981 recounts elements of Jim Miller's first year of performances. It was intended as a free-form illustrated lecture, with photos by Kirk Winslow. Jim's lawnmower dance was incorporated in Postwar *(1982), along with the Miller family history and the theme of the atom bomb. The motif of body spray-painting would reappear in* Live Boys *and* Buddy Systems. *The essay's final paragraph enunciates a major theme, the fear of sudden annihilation from above, which is found in various political, theological, and sociological forms throughout Miller's works.*

Today I wrote a nice song called the Hamburger Song. I can't sing it now but it's a very good song, about keeping going even after the big bombs fall and you've got no more teeth and we have to cling to the simple things. I love hamburgers. I had one tonight at the Polish restaurant on Second Avenue. It had the nicest piece of individually wrapped Kraft American cheese on it, nice square and safe.

This is a picture of me from a performance work at the Kitchen in NYC. My name is spraypainted with black Rustoleum on my chest. If you paint your name on your chest then you can point to it to help you remember and understand who you are in the world and the way things work. And if you understand your name then maybe you can understand other words too and the big ideas of our time. Behind me in the picture are more words painted on the wall. These words talk about going to the beach and about my mom driving in our Rambler station wagon to the hospital to have me. I was born in Pasadena but then I grew up in East Whittier and slept under a picture of Dick Nixon. And came to NYC when I was nineteen. I love New York. This is my home now. I just had my twenty-third birthday. So I've been here almost four years now. It's cold out tonight in NYC. Cream of Wheat weather. Gotta find a new boyfriend before it gets too cold. But maybe not this year. . . .

I'm very busy these days. I wanna be famous and have enough money to buy black cowboy boots and lots of different kinds of cheese. I'm very busy these days. Making a big piece called "Postwar." That's where the hamburger song comes in. I'm making this piece now and everything starts when I run in a circle as fast as I can think and then my heart beats and beats and I breathe and breathe and when I perform I run run run and run and almost step on people's shoes in the audience and they feel the wind as I run by. 1945. 1946. 1947. 1948. 1949. 1950. 1951. 1952. 1953. 1954. 1955. 1956. 1957. 1958. That's me. 9/22/58. All those years go by and so many babies got born, all my friends born in those years, and if we hadn't dropped the big bomb on Japan my Dad would have had to invade and he might have gotten killed and I never would have been born. My mom always used tell me this whenever we talked about the atom bomb, like at Thanksgiving or Xmas or whenever the subject came up. . . .

I'm very interested in history. I like dates and the way they connect to my dates. . . . It must be cold. Gotta find a new boyfriend before it gets too cold.

My Mom got into the Rambler station wagon and my Dad drove her to St. Luke's Hospital to have the last baby. On Monday. I love Mondays. That's the day I was born. So I took off my shirt and then painted my name on my chest in black Rustoleum and lean and throw my head over as far as I can go and oh oh oh one nice moment there on one leg arms back back somewhere behind my head. You could buy a whole house for fourteen thousand dollars. They even came with one tree in the front yard.

I have dreams about lawnmowers. Mowing the front and back yard. Mowing the neighbor's yard. Mowing across this big nation. Mowing a state at a time. Mowing a nice easy square state like Kansas. Mowing a hard state like Maryland. Mowing a tiny state like Rhode Island only takes an afternoon. Mowing Alaska can take a lot longer. Then when I'm done mowing all the states I start mowing indoors. Mowing the bedroom. Mowing the kitchen. Mowing the den. Mowing the performance space. Mowing the theater. Mowing the rock club. Mowing the opera house. . . . I've been performing a lawnmower dance for a year or so. A friend of mine named Barry who thinks he's the child of J.F.K. and Marilyn Monroe mows the space and I dance and dance and the mower almost cuts my feet and the space gets smaller and I dance faster & faster. . . .

One of the verses of my hamburger song talks about paying the rent and going and eating a hamburger. Another verse talks about being sick of sex and having a hamburger instead. Another verse talks all about if the bombs fall on your head then it's too late to go and eat a hamburger. . . . In 1964 I asked my Dad while we were waiting for a left-turn signal when we would be able to get a color TV. He said maybe in 1965. We never got a color TV. Not until I had left home.

This is me on the dinner table. This performance was about dinner-time. The audience sat all around me on this long thin table.

Some people I cooked hamburgers for. But there weren't enough to go around. This came after the lawnmower dance and before the lifelike recreation of the Hindenburg disaster. People liked being that close to me. . . .

It isn't unreasonable to just want a little order in your life. But sometimes that's too much to ask for and you just have to sweep everything into a pile and forget about things making sense or fitting together. Maybe this is where faith or something comes in. Or maybe you just get your brains blown out by a big gun. . . . You've got to be very careful. You've got to be very careful where you step. Or else something awful is gonna happen. I have this dream where I'm walking thru the desert kind of like the *Twilight Zone*. The air is very heavy. I get the feeling that if I make the wrong step the whole world is gonna blow up. So I'm trying to be very careful to not fuck up and ruin everything. Cause if you take the wrong step, that's it. You're out. There was this big white bowl shape in this dream. It reached up to the sky and all the power and danger of the dream was in it. I had this dream for about fifteen years. Then it stopped. I only realized recently that the big white bowl was probably Hoover Dam. I think my Mom held me over the edge too far and all I saw was a big white bowl and my five year old heart went faster faster than now.

Things are a mess. That's OK. I had this dream where I was responsible for the whole world and it was like on *Twilight Zone* and if I made the wrong move things were gonna blow up and break up and fall on top of everybody so I was very careful because I didn't want the dam to break. I just wanted to get from one side to the other. . . .

Floor It!

This lighthearted piece was performed at a 1986 benefit for a new floor at PS 122—the need for the floor deriving partly from Tim Miller's creative act of amateur arson described here. "Floor It!" conveys the heady early days at the performance venue founded by Miller and three colleagues. Written in the headlong lowercase style he affected in many early writings, its hectic pace anticipates humorous passages in his later performance works. The burning newspapers described here were an element of Paint Yrself Red/Me & Mayakovsky *(1980). The quoted inscription comes from a stained-glass window at PS 122, originally a school in the immigrant neighborhood of Manhattan's Lower East Side. The ketchup vandalism was aimed at the set of a feminist play about waitressing. Miller no longer recalls the "rolling rock" reference—perhaps beer, perhaps literal rocks in a performance, perhaps both.*

here we are on the floor. i'm going to tell you a few things about this floor for whose benefit we are gathered here tonight. i know a lot about this floor. a lot of my life has taken place on this floor. along these boards from one side to the other. tongue in groove. year after year.

there's a place on this floor over there by that person with the hat or whatever on where I burned a big hole in the floor when i was young or so it seemed in the fall of 1980. i was burning up russian newspapers just me and them crammed in a foot locker in a perform-ance I was doing. it was one of the first performances anyone had ever done here on this floor. i burnt off some of my hair and those burning papers snuck down and took a hunk out of this floor under-neath my feet. then two weeks later i burned another hole in the floor right over there by the pillar but that's another story. i don't mean to sound nostalgic. i mean, really, being the person who put the only big burns in this floor is no great shakes.

and then there was the morning in 1982 i walked in at 7 am and saw that someone had broken in here and had busted thirty-five ketchup bottles all over the floor and it looked like the sharon tate murders. i stepped in glass and saw long hand prints dragged along the floor and walls and the whole place stank like the dried dark red scummy stuff around the mouth of a ketchup bottle. it looked like some weird ritual death cult had been here and that something weirder yet was gonna happen. and in fact later that day a big dog fell out of a truck as it turned the corner and it broke its neck while I sat there eating my yogurt and later that week I got poison ivy. it looked like the end of the world but we cleaned it up. scraped it up. swept it up.

and there's a trillion other things i remember about this floor. like having sex over here and over there and by the pillar and gee can i borrow the keys to the space. the people changed over the years and that's how it goes. once doing it over there by the window we real-ized someone was watching us but that was all right it's a perform-ance space and the beat goes on and fights and food. and rehearsals and a million performances rolling rocks shin splints and these are the things that floors are made of. i can remember one boiling night in the summer of 1982 on tuesday night when people come here to dance around. there was a huge classic nyc summer thunderstorm and we turned out all the lights and opened all the windows and the lightning lit up the jumping and running and the wind blew sheets of rain clear thru the twenty-two windows you can't see right now but they're there. it felt like king lear or the flying dutchman except warm and it blew us around the space between 9th and 10th and the corner of 1st. and it seemed like the whole world or maybe the lower east side or at least right here was going to blow up and get carried away out over the east river and back to the old world of all the eastern european kids who sat here in 1894. everything going back to where it started. things poking out from below like all those corpses and gross stuff at the end of poltergeist till everything got wiped clean and everybody got blown home. back to where they came from wherever that is. maybe right here. like the inscription says: EVERY WAKING HOUR WE WEAVE / WHETHER WE WILL OR NO / EVERY TRIVIAL ACT OR DEED / INTO THE WARP MUST GO. but none of that happened and the floor just got wetter and wetter. and we realized the floor was getting warped and that we better shut the windows. so we squeezed out the clothes and got the mops. turned on the lights. slipping and sliding. year after year. tongue in groove.

Stories from Democracy in America

Democracy in America *began with a four-month journey across the United States during 1983–84, evoking the nineteenth-century travels that gave rise to the classic book by Alexis de Tocqueville from which Miller took his project's title. On his journey Miller conducted video interviews with a diversity of Americans and also recorded his own reactions. He was frequently accompanied by Dona Ann McAdams, who made her own photographic record of people and places. Back in New York, Miller created the epic multimedia ensemble performance that premiered at the Brooklyn Academy of Music's Next Wave Festival in October 1984.* Democracy in America *also generated two complementary works: a twenty-minute video (featuring clips from the movie* Mr. Smith Goes to Washington*) and a short book written in collaboration with McAdams. The* Democracy in America *book interplays "stories" by Miller with McAdams's photos on facing pages. Except for the gay rights demonstration and the Miller family's wishing well, the texts do not comment directly on the photographs but, rather, share with them the theme of looking for America. Miller's stories, of which fourteen are printed here, show how the project was grounded in direct observation and the personal history of Miller and his family. They also illustrate the naïf persona that Miller adopted in* *addressing political issues during these years before the AIDS crisis and ACT UP.*

Ever since I was a little kid I was always trying to figure out all this America stuff. How it all works. What it all means. How I fit in. What I'm supposed to do. I guess a lot of people think about this stuff. My mom says to me, "Tim, be proud. You come from good farmer stock." The other thing she says to me is, "Tim, just because you have a common last name you don't have to be common." This seems like good advice. But then I read the newspapers and read the books and it does seem like something has gotten fucked up somewhere. A little wrong turn. Half a shortcut. The middle of nowhere. And the strong feeling that I gotta figure it out. How it all works. What it all means. How I fit in. What I'm supposed to do. So I decided to really look into it all. Talk to some people. Ask questions. Go for a ride. A little ride. And when I was a little boy I really did want to be president. Which is no big deal. Which is nothing strange. Which is something you leave behind. With a pinch to grow on.

When I first moved to New York City I found a big American flag in the garage on Canal Street. It was all torn up and it made me kind of sad cause it was so screwed up. I took it home and washed it and hung it on my wall wherever I was living just to keep things in mind. I would look at that flag and really want to fix it up. Sew the stripes back together. The red. The white. The blue. Some people thought I was crazy having this fucked up flag over my bed. I guess I liked it there cause it made me remember where I was. It made me remember what I should be doing. And mainly it made me feel like there was something to be fixed up. This seemed like a good thing. I lost this flag a coupla years ago. I don't know where. It just disappeared from a box or fell off a truck or flew out a window. It went somewhere. I can really remember what it looked like though. The way I nailed it to my wall. I'd still like to fix it up.

For a while I really thought I wanted to be a normal person. What would that be? What do normal people do? Where do they gather? What are their customs? Can you join? Be chosen? I felt like a normal person recently at the beach: time with friends, eating and laughing. I felt like a normal person in a long line at the bank on Friday afternoon. Or when I went out with my honey on Saturday night—that's when I felt most like a normal person. If I got a dog I would feel almost completely like a normal person. I wonder if this isn't really stupid though. Does everybody want to be a normal person? Maybe it's foolish to even think that the world can be divided into the normal and the un- or the ab-. That me doing what I do is any more or less normal than that person doing what he/she does? Maybe I should move away from New York City. That sounds pretty normal. Then I can go live in Normal Heights near the Mexican border in Southern California. And live out my normal days in a normal manner. Away from all this.

When I was a kid I remember making a trip into downtown Los Angeles for the first time. I was maybe three or four years old. Me and my family were going to this big movie theater downtown to see this big movie *How the West Was Won*. I think it was about 1962. This was a movie with about a million actors in it and told the story of this family over lots of years as they moved west. It had buffalo and wars and river rapids and a train robbery and all kinds of exciting stuff. It was a Cinerama movie and they showed it on this monster screen and I remember hiding my eyes when this guy gets killed in the Civil War. My Mom and Dad got the record for the family at Christmas and I listened to it all the time, especially the big chorus part where they sing about the promised land and chant the names of the states where my great great grandparents started farms and lived and made it work. This kind of stuff always can make me cry, it's so fucking beautiful.

I grew up hating the Russians because I thought they were going to blow up my house and kill me and my dog. Later, when I became a

Democracy in America in performance, Brooklyn Academy of Music, 1984. Photo by Dona Ann McAdams.

communist for a while in seventh grade, I got real interested in this other experience and history that is such a big deal in our duplex century. Us. Them. The American way. The other way. Somehow these two big weird civilizations both excited me so much, full of gestures and ideals and the big time. And now everybody is supposed to sit tight and hope we don't destroy the world. Us or them. The big joke. Here living in mondo cosmo Nuevo York I have never even met a Russian, except for the guys in the cabs that drive like nuts. Do they count? Maybe someday we in the U.S. (that means us) will cool it with the big rip-off around the world and they'll get off the can, those Politburo insurance salesmen, and we can all have a big party on a wheat field in Nebraska, and I'll get to swap Thomas Wolfe for Vladimir Mayakovsky and make out with some Russian in a missile silo. Hurrah for Karamazov.

Recently I had a dream I was having lunch with Lyndon Baines Johnson at his ranch in Texas. We were eating like pigs by the B.B.Q., licking our fingers. He was talking to me like I was really one of the boys and was telling me all the tricks about how you shape a power base in America. This was a really clear dream, sort of like being in school. I think I might have been taking notes. He told me the secret is to make people think you are really one of them. And you make them believe this but really all the time you just keep pulling, wrapping and carving a position of power beyond them to be "revealed at some strategic point," he said to me. This dream really creeped me out. I was hearing this awful shit and my hands were covered with B.B.Q. sauce that you just couldn't lick off. I wondered why he was telling me this stuff. There's gotta be a reason why LBJ was in my dreams. I got really creeped out.

My best friend when I was a kid was named Dana Turman. I always sort of bossed Dana around. I was kind of a jerk then. It gave my friend Dana the moral superiority that is due to oppressed friends. He always seemed mysterious and subject to revelations in the way he could stoic-out on me when I'd start being pushy. Dana went on a trip with his family. They went to the Mesa Verde National Monument in New Mexico. I think he was about ten then. Me too. At Mesa Verde they have those great cliff cities that the Hopi Indians built. The Hopis of course are the spiritual guardians of the North American continent. Their most sacred place is called a kiva. It's a big hole in the ground where the wise men would sit and pray and stuff. The moment my friend Dana peeked over the edge of the kiva he blacked out and fell about fifteen feet to the bottom. He lay there sprawled in the most holy of holy places while the National Park Service rescued him. He even got to be carried out on a stretcher. I think Dana's going to be an environmental scientist, or maybe a Methodist minister.

On the Fourth of July during the Bicentennial I was still living in my parents' house in Whittier, California. I was sitting around with Bud and Betsy, my next-door neighbors. They are real nice people and had just had a baby boy. Bud worked for the telephone company and worked on telephone poles and had a red face from the sun. He had been in Vietnam and really didn't want to talk about it. I don't remember exactly what he said. It was clearly heavy and it was the Fourth of July. Somehow it came up and we spoke about it a little bit and then started talking about the baby again. I felt real grown up. I was seventeen and the big fat events of the world seemed like next door. I liked Bud and Betsy and was glad they had moved in next to my parents and had had a baby just when I was about to split. A new pair of feet to run up and down the driveway. I left their house and went up to my spot in the hills to watch the fireworks. I felt really old.

In 1965 or something, I was a little kid and I went shopping for the groceries with my Dad. We piled the cart high and paid for it all and I pushed the cart across the parking lot to the Rambler station wagon. Reaching up over my head to the handle and trying to maneuver as well as I could. My Dad was probably pulling it at the front and let me pretend I was doing it by myself. It was a really beautiful night, tons of stars and as cold as it ever gets in Southern California. We put all the stuff in the car and my Dad looked up at the sky and said to me something like: Wow it is so beautiful. He said, we all can believe different things but for me there is no better church than here under all these stars. This is what my Dad said to me. I remember getting all impressed and nervous that my Dad was talking to me about this big stuff. I think it made sense to me, but I didn't say anything and we got in the car and rode home.

My Grandpa homesteaded a ranch in the '20s in Arizona. You could get all this land as long as you'd build a house and try to grow stuff. I guess it never really worked too well because he and my Grandma had to go to Southern California and become housepainters. He really loved it out in Arizona. He kept looking for water on the land but he never did find a drop. It was probably there somewhere.

When I was a really little boy I was out in Arizona at Christmas time with about a million of my cousins. I was walking around with my Grandpa in one of the barns and he gave me something. There was this contest going on at this gas station chain in Arizona where you collected these plastic coins that had all the United States presidents on them. If you collected them all you got some kind of prize. I was saving them, so Grandpa gave me Teddy Roosevelt and Woodrow Wilson for my collection. I was really happy because I needed them and my Grandpa gave them to me.

I almost didn't put this picture of a NYC Gay Pride parade in here. I dunno—part of me wanted to keep everything tidy and friendly, and whose business is it anyway? But that's screwed up. I mean what is all this stuff with George Washington and responsibility and a brighter future and blab blab blab? How can I crank it out about all that stuff and not talk about back to basics? I'm not sure what my Grandma would think of this or me or that guy from Kansas marching onto her farm in Smith County in 1919. She might just shake her head for a long time, like she did about so many other things before she died. I dunno. I took my boyfriend home for Christmas last year. We had a great time. He's Jewish. My Dad kept making him bacon and saying it's kosher. We went on a double date with my parents and went out to dinner and saw a movie and had a lot of fun. I taught my Mom to play video games. I was very happy. We parted in the parking lot and my parents hugged us and said see you tomorrow. They got in their car and we got in ours. And my Mom and Dad honked as they drove off into the night, the promised land.

I was in Colorado last summer doing some stuff and I decided to go and see my great aunt who lived nearby. She and my Grandma and the other eight or nine children had been born and raised on a farm in Kansas in an area called "Twelve Mile Community," just because they had to call it something and it was twelve miles from the nearest place called anything. I went to her house and another of my

Photo by Dona Ann McAdams for *Democracy in America,* 1984.

great aunts came by too. I don't think I'd ever met them, since I'd never been there before. We had a great dinner and I ate like a maniac. I asked a lot of questions about the farm and Kansas. They were real happy that I was interested. I told them about this project I was doing about trying to understand America a little bit and I was so happy that they understood. It seemed really important to me that I could talk about stuff in a way that would make sense to my great aunts. I think about them all the time. That we were really able to talk together, that was really important.

My Dad built a wishing well in front of our house, my house, in Southern California. He designed it and built it himself. My Dad died a little while ago. He worked the whole week selling business machines for Pitney Bowes and then came home on Friday and died. My Dad worked very hard his whole life, doing all those things that lots of people do—getting married, having kids, being a neighbor, all that simple heroic stuff of day-to-day life. The wishing well that my Dad built has plants in it, so you couldn't toss coins in to make a wish. But you could jump off of it with an umbrella, thus discovering the fundamentals of flight. You could run a circle into the ground around and around, chasing or being chased. You could find your way home in the dark by the 25-watt bulb inside it, or stand on the very top and look into the future or down the block. My Dad built a wishing well in front of our house. My Dad died a little while ago. I liked my Dad, I loved my Dad. Make a wish.

The sun is really bright sometimes, so you have to squint up your eyes or wear a hat or hold your hand up over your head high enough to see a little bit—around the corner, a wrong turn, half a shortcut, the middle of nowhere. I thought I might run for president of the United States in 1984. Seemed like a good idea, seemed like a thing to do. But then I decided it was stupid for me to do that. I decided there was other stuff to do first. Like go for a little ride and figure it out—how it all works, what it all means, how I fit in, what I'm supposed to do. I read newspapers, I read books. I am proud of some stuff. I do have a common last name, and I did want to be president when I was a kid. But not now. And I could squint my eyes or wear a hat or hold my hand up over my head between me and the light. Or I can take off my dark glasses and see. . . . This land is your. . . . Oh beautiful for. . . .

Live Boys

TIM MILLER and JOHN BERND

Tim Miller's pioneering festival of gay men's performance inspired his first collaboration with John Bernd, We Had Tea We Ate Cashew Chicken, *performed at PS 122 in November 1980. True to the festival's title, "Men Together," Tim and John focused on the development of their relationship as lovers in a dance work with readings from Proust and Miller's own writings.* Live Boys, *which followed in March 1981, dealt with conflicts in the relationship, caused primarily by Tim's reluctance to accept commitment. The final episode,* Live Boys: I Hate Your Guts, *had one performance in August 1981, followed the next day by a ritual burning of the blue pajamas they had worn throughout the series.*

As David Gere points out in How to Make Dances in an Epidemic, Live Boys *has a historical significance that no one in 1981 realized, in that John's speech about his skin outbreaks is the first reference in theater to what eventually became known as AIDS. Tim's spray-painting of their bare chests with letters that, the two together, spell out FAGGOT, resonates through the subsequent health crisis (and John's death in 1988) to the activism that defined Tim Miller's generation of gay men.*

Live Boys *attracted critical and audience support, but in the years immediately following, Miller devoted most of his energy to the multimedia spectacles beginning with* Postwar. *He returned to* Live Boys *as a model in rethinking his art in the wake of* Democracy in America. Buddy Systems *(1985) mixed solo segments with significant collaboration by Douglas Sadownick near the beginning of their fourteen-year relationship. More important, the difficulty and necessity of commitment became one of Tim Miller's basic themes. Limited to personal relationships in* Live Boys *and* Buddy Systems, *the theme of commitment soon developed political urgency; but for Miller commitments of all sorts would always necessarily rise out of the struggle for self-understanding and self-acceptance.*

The script printed here is transcribed from a videotape of Live Boys *made at Hallwalls, Buffalo, New York, in June 1981. Movement and gesture were an essential part of* Live Boys, *interacting with spoken and recorded statements by Tim and John. The text, however, can stand on its own.*

[John and Tim enter and move slowly through the space. Tim lies on the floor and sleeps.]

JOHN: I'm not sure. I'm not sure what to do.

I don't know about it. I've been thinking about it, but I'm not sure—

I'm not sure what to do about it, and I don't know

And I want to do the right thing.

[John wrestles Tim's limp body to his feet.]

I don't know what to do.

MINGLED VOICES OF TIM AND JOHN, RECORDED: I started thinking—

I was drinking beer on the stoop—

I was sipping my tea—

Letting it all go by—
Today I was confused—
I was making the bed—
It was cold last night—
I want to suck his cock—
I fucked him in the ass—
Hi babe, hi—
I wasn't jealous—
I love New York—
I want to be a child—
I couldn't calm down—
He called last night—
If this were the summer, or even the spring or fall, just not this
cold cold month—
Going over to the park—
It's hardest for me now—
I started thinking—
I started thinking—
JOHN: I can't think about it.
I'm tired of thinking about it.
I don't want to think about it anymore.
I'm tired of thinking about it, talking about it.
I think about it constantly—

[Tim and John run rapidly around the space.]

TIM: John, John, hi.
hey! hey! wait up!
hey! slow down!
John, slow down!
JOHN: I can't. . . .
hey, slow down—

[Projected slide: an East Village pizza shop]

29

TIM: I'd like a slice please.

JOHN: What you do want?

TIM: I'd like a slice of pizza. Yeah, I'd like a slice.

JOHN: Yeah, well what is it you want?

TIM: Can I have a slice please? One slice. I'd like a slice of that. Yeah.

JOHN: What else?

TIM: I'd like a slice of that.

JOHN: Is that what you want? That? Is that what you want?

TIM: I'd like a slice of him.

JOHN: What?

TIM: I'd like a slice of him.

JOHN: Which one?

TIM: I'd like a slice of him.

JOHN: Well, what do you want? Do you know what you want? Are you sure what you want? Do you know?

TIM: And a coke please.

This is the corner of St. Marks Place and Second Avenue in the East Village of Manhattan.

JOHN: And that's where you can get anything you want. It's open twenty-four hours.

TIM: You walk out on First Avenue and the corner of First Avenue and Ninth Street. You walk south on First Avenue to the corner of St. Marks and First Avenue. You go east towards the Hudson, along St. Marks to the corner of Second Avenue and St. Marks. That's the corner right here.

JOHN: That's the corner where I met two old boyfriends. I met them on the corner, right there.

TIM: You walk down Second Avenue, down Second Avenue on the right side of the street because the right side of the street is better. You walk past the Gem Spa, past the Chinese restaurant, past the newsstand, past the mysterious store with no painting on the window, past—

JOHN: If you're really lonely you can go to that corner and you just

John Bernd and Tim Miller performing *Live Boys* at PS 122, March 1981. Photo © 2003 by Johan Elbers.

stand there for about five minutes and you always see someone you know.

TIM: past the Ukranian restaurant, past Seventh Street, past the Kiev Ukranian restaurant, past the kosher bakery, past the Immigrant Savings Bank, all on the right side of the street on Second Avenue. So you go

JOHN: down First Avenue to Eighth Street—

TIM: down First Avenue to St. Marks Place—

JOHN: Right where the pizza place is, and then you go west on St. Marks Place to Second Avenue—

TIM: Come back here. Come back here.

JOHN: Yeah?

TIM: OK. You go down First Avenue to St. Marks, this way. No John, St. Marks is this way. Second Avenue—north and south is like this. Come on.

JOHN: Where are we gonna go?

TIM: St. Marks Place and Second Avenue. OK, there's the Gem Spa.

JOHN: Stand right there! Come over, right here. Start over again.

TIM: Past the Gem Spa, past the Chinese restaurant, past

JOHN: Are we down Second?

TIM: past the Immigrant Savings Bank, past The Saint, past 103 Second Avenue, past Block Drugs, and then you're at—

I'd like two bialys, three pumpernickel bagels, a quarter-pound of cream cheese.

JOHN [in an accented voice]: What can I get you? Anything else? What do you want?

TIM: Let's see . . . quarter-pound of white herring. Cup of yogurt. And two bialys.

JOHN: Good morning gentlemen, how are you? Ah, you have pennies for me, I love you. ANYTHING ELSE?

TIM: And he rammed it into me.

JOHN: Anything else?

TIM: And he rammed it into me

JOHN: Is that it? Ah. Such nice boys. What do you want? What do you want?

TIM: And he rammed it into me. And he rammed it into me, rammed it into me, rammed it into me. . . .

JOHN: AND HE RAMMED IT INTO ME. And he rammed it, and he rammed, and he rammed, and he rammed. And he rammed it into me.

TIM: I'd like two bialys, three of the small challah rolls, and two pumpernickel bagels. Thanks.

JOHN: And you cross Second Avenue. You go out—

TIM: Second Avenue. Down Second Avenue. And then we're at Sixth Street. Sixth Street and Second Avenue in the East Village of Manhattan.

JOHN: We're almost there.

TIM: We're almost there. We're almost home. We're almost home. And now we're home.

Five flights.

[Tim does elaborate stair-climbing movements, with heavy recorded stomping sounds.]

JOHN: I'm really tired. Hey, I'm tired. I'm tired.

TIM: We're home. We should leave in ten minutes.

JOHN: I'm just tired. Oh but I'm tired.

TIM: I think before we go any further—I think we should lay down ten minutes before we go any further. Before we try to keep this up. I think we oughta lay down for a while.

JOHN: I want to lay down. It's just, I'm tired. For ten minutes. I can't think. I just can't think about it—

[Both lie on the floor.]

Babe?

TIM: Yeah? What?

JOHN: I can't think.

TIM: So we'll just rest a little bit.

JOHN: I just can't think about it. I'm tired.

TIM: I got very excited when I fell in love with John. Then we did all this performing together, and then I began to think, I'm going to fall in love with somebody else.

JOHN: I'm very tired.

TIM And then after a while I got bored or tired or somethin'.

JOHN: We just got tired.

TIM: I guess we just got tired or somethin'. I thought, I'm going to fall in love with somebody else. I guess we just got tired.

JOHN: It was too much. It was just too much to do.

TIM: At first when I fell in love with John—I always wanted to sleep with him, and everything was great. But then after a while I got tired.

JOHN: He wouldn't leave me alone.

TIM: And then I thought, I think I'll fall in love with somebody else.

JOHN: He wouldn't leave me alone. He just wouldn't.

Just when I met Tim, I had all these things wrong with my skin. About a week before I met him, I had a fungus on my skin, and I had psoriasis where the fungus was and I had psoriasis on my scalp and I got poison ivy and I was very depressed. The only place that the poison ivy stuck was just in this one place on my wrist. So I had to walk around—I was very depressed, and I had to walk around with bandages on my wrist.

TIM: "I had to walk around with bandages on my wrist. I was very depressed."

JOHN: I looked like shit.

TIM: "It looked like I tried to kill myself. It was just poison ivy."

JOHN: —on my wrist. I had thought about it, I really wasn't going to do it. Right here, I had to bandage my wrist, and I had a cream for the poison ivy, and a cream for the psoriasis on my skin and a cream for the psoriasis on my scalp. You should've seen me when I was in bed at night. Then he wouldn't leave me alone.

TIM: When John first met me, he had all these skin problems. Poison ivy. It looked like he tried to kill himself.

JOHN: It was very funny. No one would talk to me if they saw me at a concert or something. They were afraid to talk to me because they thought I'd slit my wrists or something. I really hadn't, I just had poison ivy. But they didn't come up to talk to me because they were afraid to talk to me. They didn't know what to think, so they kept a distance.

TIM: How's your skin now?

JOHN: It comes and goes—I mean the psoriasis. I need some sun. That'll do it. Just a little rest. Just a little rest. And some sun, that ought to do it. 'Cause I can't think about any of it now. I just can't think about it.

TIM: How's your skin today?

JOHN: Sort of a holding pattern. It's OK. It's not bad.

[Tim, who has been shaking a can of spray paint, raises his pajama top and sprays FAG on his torso. John raises his pajama and Tim sprays GOT on John's torso. During more interactive movement, they change from pajamas into street clothes.]

[In the following, John's monologue is on tape, with Tim's live monologue interacting.]

JOHN: So—I was walking home from First Avenue on the north side of St. Marks Place. It was early evening, it was dark, there were a lot of people on the street, and I was about to cross from the north side of St. Marks Place to the south side. And I saw this boy.

TIM: I was laying in the sun, I was laying in the sun by this reservoir—

JOHN: And the first thing that struck me, before I could think about it, was how much he reminded me of myself.

TIM: And I saw this boy, and I'm watching him.

35

JOHN: He was wearing a coat, an old coat, and a hat with a long tip on it—

TIM: He didn't have a shirt on. It was very sunny. I watched this boy.

JOHN: and he was bouncing in place. He was doing a little dance in place as he was waiting for the light to change. So instead of crossing St. Marks Place to go down Second Avenue home I decided to wait for the light and cross Second Avenue. I wanted to follow him.

TIM: He was laying in the sun. I was laying in the sun by this water.

JOHN: So I stood there in a crowd with him with the other people waiting, and the light changed and we crossed—

TIM: I watched this boy—

JOHN: and as we crossed I looked at him from the side—

TIM: and he was very pretty.

JOHN: and he was very pretty. So we crossed Second Avenue and then the crowd started crossing St. Marks Place to the Gem Spa—

TIM: So I watched him.

JOHN: and we were all in this crowd together. So I was hoping he was going the same way I was going, and we both walked down Second Avenue. I got a little bit ahead of him. And I started walking slower than I usually do.

TIM: And I thought, maybe we'll fall in love or fuck or something.

JOHN: Kept walking, I got to Seventh Street. I felt him behind me. And I crossed Seventh Street and between Sixth and Seventh Street—

TIM: I thought maybe, maybe. Maybe we'll fall in love or fuck or something.

JOHN: I looked behind me, looking at the clock, and he wasn't there. So I thought, oh well, that's that.

TIM: So I thought, maybe we'll fall in love or fuck or something.

JOHN: I thought, I wonder where he lives, I've never seen him before. So I got to Sixth Street, and crossed Sixth Street and waited for the light to change to cross Second Avenue, and I got a good look up Second Avenue and I couldn't see him on either side of the street. So I crossed Second Avenue.

TIM: We were laying in the sun. So I watched him. So I watched him.

JOHN: I started walking toward my doorway, which is just in from Second Avenue on the south side of the street. And started getting my keys out.

TIM: So I watched him.

JOHN: While I was trying to find my key, I looked around. Didn't see him.

TIM: I watched him.

JOHN: I was just about to enter my door and I looked once again, and when I looked he was standing right across the street looking at me.

TIM: Maybe we'll fall in love or fuck or something. Maybe.

JOHN: And we looked at each other and I didn't go in the doorway. And he was pacing in place across the street. . . .

TIM: Maybe. Maybe.

Buddy Systems

Two Excerpts

TIM MILLER with DOUGLAS SADOWNICK

Buddy Systems *was created during a period of transition, when Tim Miller was rethinking his art and, with the writer Douglas Sadownick and their black labrador mutt Buddy, planning a move from New York to Los Angeles. In form,* Buddy Systems *is a hybrid of the autobiographical solo works from Tim Miller's New York years and the relationship-based duet created in* Live Boys. *As in* Live Boys, *the theme is faithfulness in relationships, with the dog Buddy serving as a metaphor for commitment. The solo sections of the work contextualize these issues within questions of self-awareness and self-acceptance. Highly verbal and laden with metaphors, narrative, and humor,* Buddy Systems *is the first of Miller's works clearly to emphasize text over movement— though it remains highly kinetic. Surprisingly for a work created in 1985,* Buddy Systems *has no overt political content and only one indirect reference to AIDS. In retrospect, Miller's probing of the roots of ethics in self-acceptance was a crucial step toward his more overtly political and activist stance in performances of the later 1980s.*

The two excerpts printed here illustrate solo and collaborative segments of Buddy Systems. *The Hollywood Bowl fantasia is the earliest example of a distinctive Miller technique: a rhapsodic speech intertwined with recorded music in a unique kind of*

Singenspracht. *(The best-known example of this technique is the Bolero finale of* My Queer Body.*) In the second excerpt, Miller and Sadownick work out the ethics of a love relationship, using the metaphor of training the dog Buddy, who gave this piece his name.*

Liebestod *on Hollywood Boulevard*

I found myself on Hollywood Boulevard.

I found myself, an eighteen year old homo boy, on Hollywood Boulevard in search of True Love, Wisdom, and Worldly Experience!

[Pounding rhythmic punk music as Tim picks up microphone]

I met this guy and we did it. Well, he did it, to me. There on Hollywood Boulevard. I had just turned eighteen and I had just broken up with my first boyfriend, which had been a mondo passionate intense thing full of learning and more. But it hadn't worked out. No. He wanted to marry me and I wasn't ready for that. So he was working on Santa Monica Boulevard as a male prostitute. I was working at May Company department store selling wristwatches. Sometimes I think it's not the first time, it's the second time at bat—when you realize you're in it for the long run.

And I met this guy and we went back to his place and he knocked me down and stuck it in me and said, "BITCH PUSSY CUNT TAKE MY BIG DICK!" which was ridiculous—he had this little eeensy weeensy dick . . .

"BITCH PUSSY CUNT TAKE MY MAN PRICK SLAVE YOU LOVE IT!" And I thought, I just wanna get out of here . . . this isn't like Whittier!

So I got up and threw on my clothes and I ran from that crummy apartment on Hollywood Boulevard. I was breathing fast. This had all been a little too much for me. I had wanted some romance. A nice dinner, a stuffed bell pepper—maybe a blowjob. I followed some people up Highland Avenue . . . and that's when it happened.

[Tim begins monologue to the Liebestod *aria from Wagner's* Tristan und Isolde. *His monolog follows the music and builds with it. The German text in italics is to help the opera queen readers follow the bouncing ball!]*

"MILD UND LEISE . . ."

I found myself at the entrance to the Hollywood Bowl. A concert was about to start.

There were all these people . . . there were lots and lots of people. They were all wearing things, wingtips and brassieres, top hats and silk dresses. Some of them were by themselves, some with family or friends or lovers. They were carrying things like food and blankets. It looked like they were going on a journey to a new and a better place . . . like Mars or Australia.

"STERN-UMSTRAHLT . . . HOCH SICH HEBT? . . ."

And up up up up up up up up we went, to the cheapest seats, about two hundred miles from the stage.

There was this big lady singer and she was going to sing us a very big love song.
Big enough for a coupla centuries. Big enough to fit in my fat head. Big enough to fill in the gap I felt that night at the Hollywood Bowl.

40

"WIE DEN LIPPEN..."

This song came loud and clear across the smoggy air of the Hollywood Hills and went straight to that feeling of wipeout and disillusionment:

There's nothing worth living for. And nothing's like I expected it would be. And there's nothing to look forward to. And people are scum! And being a homo doesn't seem as fabulous as I thought it would be in eleventh grade.

And Love! HA! HA! Sex is just poking and pulling and something you put in your bank account!

A sadness bigger than my body. All the things I couldn't fit in my pocket of this fucked up world. That night at the Hollywood Bowl in my eighteenth year.

"HÖRE ICH NUR..."

But but but but but but but!

The big lady's song began to shake all of that up. It was like jumping in the ocean or standing on my head. And this thing started to happen—this inspirational art-changes-life thing. Which later, when you get older and become too smart for your own good, you start to think is some kind of big joke. But then it had form and craft and power. It had a role to play in the universe and it was gonna happen to *me!* And all the doom and gloom and weight of the world I felt got turned into something else. This little graceful wise glow at the back of my head—courtesy of Wagner, the Hollywood Bowl, and the big lady too.

"IN MICH DRINGET..."

And I began to rise from my one-dollar seat. I was floating up, pulled up towards the three stars you could see in the sky that night, pulled up by the big lady and her song. I looked down from that starry height, and I saw a great bowl full of . . . people like you! Full of people trying to do things. Who would have adventures. Who would make love. Who would design small cars. Who would get hit by cars. . . .

"*SIND ES WELLEN . . .*"

And then I went into warp factor zillion and began to WHOOOSH! WHOOOSH! all over the greater Los Angeles basin. From Mt. San Jacinto in the east to a lifeguard stand at Malibu in the west. Back out to Pasadena to the hospital where I was born, my first baby cry echoing in the halls. Then out to L.A. International Airport, disturbing the flight paths, grabbing on to a 747 racing down the runway! UP! UP! UP! UP! UP! UP!

"*SOLL ICH SCHLÜRFEN . . .*"

And then one more whoosh at last along that Boulevard with all those stupid stars where I walked, just like you're supposed to, looking for God and myself. And then up to the Hollywood sign . . . in and out of each letter. Feeling and smelling like a new car! Ready and willing to clean my plate, wash behind my ears, seek wisdom and worldly experience! I swear to God!

Hey God! That's right—YOU! I'm talking to you! You with the ugly hat. Come down here, I wanna talk to you! Hey! Hey! Hey!

"*ERTRINKEN . . . VERSINKEN . . . UNBEWUSST . . . HÖCHSTE LUST! . . .*"

I finally settled about one mile over the Hollywood Bowl. And then floated gently back into my seat without anybody noticing, just in time to hear the last graceful sigh of the big lady's song. And to go like this with everybody else, to thank her for her song. And then it was over. And we got up—changed some. We went out of the row, across the aisle, down the stairs through the gate, out of the Bowl, and into . . . into . . . into the night.

[The monologue ends precisely with the final orgasmic sigh of the Liebestod. *Tim collapses to the floor.]*

Dogfight

TIM: I just called to say. . . .

[Recorded actual telephone message with transcription projected. Doug plays haunting keyboard music onstage. Tim performs a movement sequence on the large sculptural doghouse set.]

DOUGLAS *[recorded]:* Tim, you wanna deal with this?—both of us were involved in it. If you wanna not deal with it—I don't know, you know? If you wanna work stuff out, if you don't wanna work it out. There are definite ego problems. Hello? And I think that the only way it's gonna work out is if there's a lessening of the ego, the desire to be omnipotent and always in the right, basically a power situation all the time. I don't know, but I'd like to know, how 'bout you? It's cold outside. Too cold outside. Bye.

[The phone message ends. Tim moves toward audience dragging the doghouse and speaks.]

TIM: With my new dog, with Buddy—when I was going through a crisis of love and confidence with Buddy my dog, my boyfriend Douglas said to me: Tim, give the dog a break, let him recover

43

from his kennel cough, let him get over his post-pound depression, make that offering of love, make the gesture of understanding to Buddy your dog, and maybe everything will get better.

Now this was good advice. This was advice I have almost never been able to take, but I was gonna try this time, I was gonna try. And so I asked Buddy to come over. I said, Buddy: I give, I offer, I make that gesture of love, I make that offering of understanding. I give. I know we can escape from this dreaded spiral of desire and disappointment. Buddy, I give—like this, like this. And after a few days things did get better. I stopped expecting so much from my relationship with my dog. And Buddy, he started doing all those dog things I'd hoped he would: acting joyful, jumping joyfully when I came home. . . .

[Doug can't take this dog business anymore, stops playing the keyboard, and interrupts Tim.]

DOUGLAS: OK, OK, I'm gonna have to do something—I don't know about you people, but as far as I'm concerned this dog metaphor has gone a little too far. Correct me if I'm wrong, but you don't have to be a semiotics professor to see that Tim is making some connection here between human love and animal love, and quite frankly I don't buy it.

I'm gonna let you in on a little dirt. A while back my boyfriend and I had this fight. I'm not talking about a little marital tiff here, I'm talking about atomic warfare—broken dishes, black eyes. The dog Buddy was having a nervous breakdown. . . . This fight was really bad—it was so bad that not only did we almost break up, but all these performances would've been cancelled too. I don't know what you people do at night—but whatever you do, you wouldn't be here.

So we're gonna reshuffle the performance cards a bit and we're gonna have a debate so you can hear the real story. It'll work like

Douglas Sadownick and Tim Miller performing *Buddy Systems,* 1985. Photo by John Warner.

this: Speaker #1 will have fifteen seconds, Speaker #2 will have fifteen seconds, and we will have a fifteen-second rebuttal.

OK, Speaker #1, get in your place. Are you ready?

QUESTION #1: How did the fight begin? Speaker #1—go!

[The doghouse is put on its end to create a kind of debate-cum-game show lectern. Tim speaks; Douglas holds stopwatch and airhorn.]

TIM: We'd been to a wedding. And as everybody knows, weddings intensify the inner life between two people. Plus, Foucault had just died so we were very stressed. Now Douglas, he goes to weddings and wants to forget he's a homosexual—so we came home and of course he got on the phone immediately with his mother

45

in the Bronx for a very long time, and we had things to talk about, things to do—this was clearly passive-aggressive behavior, and I—

[Douglas blows airhorn.]

DOUGLAS: Speaker #2! Speaker #2!

Everybody knows a Jewish boy has to talk with his mother after a wedding! Let's be serious: Tim's missing the point as usual. Let me give you the lowdown. We'd been boyfriends five years, the whole shmear, living together, having a dog, sharing money— mostly my money, but who's counting? At this wedding he comes up to me and says to me, Doug, I think I'm attracted to the new Brazilian bongo player in town. Brazilian bongo player! Whatsa matter—I'm not exotic enough for you?

[Tim blows airhorn.]

Speaker #1! Speaker #1! Fifteen seconds!

TIM: I was so confused. Here I was happily in love, basically, with Douglas, and I was gonna do this thing that was gonna hurt him terribly. I had been feeling too domestic, it had gotten so the most exciting thing in my life was having a peppermint patty on my way home at night. I was having my midlife crisis at the age of twenty-eight! I felt so guilty, I felt like Anna Karenina. I walked on the streets of the East Village, looking for a *New York Post* truck to throw myself under—

[Douglas blows airhorn.]

DOUGLAS: QUESTION #2: What happened during the fight? I go first.

Be reasonable, I told myself, be enlightened, be modern. Hey, what's a few kisses between friends? A little rub-a-dub-dub on

46

some Brazilian's butt—it's not gonna hurt anybody. I'm confident, I'm mature, I know how to handle these things. . . .

I'll get on the train to that guy's house in Brooklyn, and I'll stay real calm. . . .

Of course I'll find those two in bed together. I'll tear Tim from that guy's embrace, I'll hurl them both to the floor! I'll break bones!

I'm laid back. . . . You two-timing motherfucker!

[Tim blows airhorn.]

Speaker #2—Fifteen seconds, fifteen seconds!

TIM: So Douglas gave me an ultimatum. He told me I had to stop seeing this guy. You can't just stop these things, they have a power, a momentum, it's why they happen.

So we had this huge fight—yelling, screaming, punching, the whole thing. Now Douglas is from the South Bronx, and he is of lower middle-class origin. Don't laugh, it's important. His impulse in fighting is to immediately escalate to physical violence and psychological terror. It's cultural. But me, I'm from California: "Can't we just talk about this for the next twelve hours, please?"

[Douglas blows airhorn.]

DOUGLAS: Fifteen-second rebuttal!

When we fight, it's total war. Every carefully stored resentment about sex, money, personal hygiene, makes for great ammunition. I break outa this guy's half-nelson, I run screaming to the front door, I say, why don't you get a job? and why are you such a slob?

And sex sex sex sex. How can I be sure you guys are having scrupulously safe sex? You want safe sex? I'll give you safe sex, and it's gonna be totally safe—I'm moving out!

So then, FINAL QUESTION: How did the fight end? Tim, fifteen seconds!

TIM: So I came home, back to our apartment, and I saw Douglas had moved all his stuff out to a friend's apartment on the upper West Side. He had even taken the coffee filters. I thought, uh oh, this is getting serious. Better do something, better do something quick. What can I do? I know, I'll call him and beg him to come back. No, I can't do that, I'm too proud. But wait—my mom, my family, they all love Douglas, they'll kill me if we break up.

I'd better call. No, I can't. yes, no. yes no. yesno.

[Douglas blows airhorn.]

DOUGLAS: So in the three hours it took for this guy to crawl on his hands and knees up to the apartment on the upper West Side where I was staying . . . I really had to think about my options. Should I accept this guy with open arms? Should I call my lawyer? It was a difficult decision. I mean, could you finally depend on a guy like that? Next year it may be somebody even more exotic—who knows? It could be a Filipino. a Laplander. a Kuwaiti. an Eskimo. Then I heard the buzzer.

[Tim and Douglas face each other and pantomime reaching out. Tim pulls Douglas's hand. Douglas resists, then offers the hand.]

Tim, you have the floor.

TIM: I would return at this point to the dog metaphor, flawed though it is. Because just as it was in the case with the dog, it was like that with this fight. We were gonna have to do this—or we were gonna pack it up and throw it away. It's like training, it's training yourself not to be so quick to pack it up and throw it away.

Douglas Sadownick and Tim Miller with meat, *Buddy Systems,* 1985. Photo by Dona Ann McAdams.

[A funny piece of music begins to play, made from sampled rhythmic dog barks and the commands SIT! STAY! COME! Tim composed this on the Fairlight CMI (computer musical instrument—OK, it was the '80s!).]

Now, I've been telling you about the dog. Douglas and I have a dog, and every day I train him. I say to him, good morning Buddy, sit. SIT! And then he does, usually, because Buddy is a good dog. But for a much longer time I've been training myself. I say to myself, all right Tim, in this situation you're in right now, I want you to sit. OK, just sit. SIT!

And sometimes I do, because to sit can be a very useful skill. It's like my teacher said in second grade. She told me, Tim, you have a very short attention span. You ought to learn how to take stock, appreciate, pay attention to the things around you. Tim, she said to me, SIT! because to sit can be a very useful skill.

Because the modern world is a very complicated place, full of temptations, distractions, wrong turns. And if you don't want to always be chasing your own or somebody else's tail—because there are millions and millions and millions and millions of these in the world—to sit can be a very useful skill.

But I am the first to admit, and you here tonight are all quite ably demonstrating, that to sit is not the paramount achievement of western civilization. No. There is something final, there is something harder, but there is something better. STAY! SIT—sit was not so difficult. COME was no problem at all. But STAY!

DOUGLAS: STAY!

TIM: STAY takes some doing, STAY takes some learning, STAY takes some attention. STAY!

[Tim and Douglas unwrap slabs of supermarket beef and slap each other with the raw flesh.]

Because the modern world is not always up here like this, even though we think that in America everything should always be great—and as soon as you get one good thing you should immediately throw it away and get another even better. Like this new piece of meat! No, life is also down here like this.

TIM AND DOUGLAS *[chanting rhythmically in unison]:* I'm in my life, and it's not great all the time, but I am willing to keep working—

I love my boyfriend, I love my dog, I love my Mom too—

I'm willing to keep working, working on my life, because I know I'm in my life, I know I'm in my life and there's lots of things to learn—

I'm willing to keep working—

I love my boyfriend, he's a good guy. I'm good too. I'm willing to keep working—

I love my boyfriend, I love my doggie, I love my mother too. I'm willing to keep working. . . .

[The music goes crazy. Lots more slapping with raw meat. Tim walks to the side and returns with a wide roll of masking tape. They wrap themselves tightly together back to back with tape, struggle against each other, then cooperatively slide and dip across the space. Doug is at the keyboard again and plays the final melancholy music of the piece.]

TIM: There's no simple way of looking at it. Sorry. But I thought about it, I thought about it a lot, and this is what I thought. At first there are these impulses, and they come up from the earth.

[With a marker, Tim draws an up arrow on the tape over his abdomen.]

They come up, they mush up here with all these things like our ideas. Like: what will my life be like? what is expected of me? what do I hope for? what do I dream for? They come up, they mush, and then they go out like this. With experience, adventure, choice, they come up, they mush, and then they go out like this, all over the place, all through this life.

But at a certain point all that isn't enough, and this thing starts to happen, about here . . .

[Tim draws a heart over his chest.]

and it comes up, it's an instinct, it makes this heart thing happen. It's the heart thing everybody talks about, everybody reads about, makes movies about. It came up, it mushed, it went out, then from here it went like this . . .

I was at my swimming lesson at Swim Arts Swim Academy,

and I was drowning in the deep end—bubble one, bubble two, bubble three. And I remember hoping and praying that maybe somebody would come and help me get to the other side. But I couldn't count on it, I definitely couldn't count on it. So in the meantime . . .

[Tim makes swimming motions with his arms.]

I better go like this, like this, like this. It came up, it mushed, then it went out from here, like this, like this, like this. And that's what I would call a swimming lesson. And that's it, in a nutshell. OK?

DOUGLAS: OK.

TIM: OK?

DOUGLAS: OK.

[Slow fade to black.]

Coda

John in the dream realm

John Bernd died in August 1988. This entry from Jim Miller's journal comes from 1994, when he began performing Naked Breath, *in which John figures prominently.*

I dreamed I was performing at Hallwalls Performance Space in Buffalo. . . . I did *Live Boys* there with John in 1981. I went outside of the space and suddenly I was on the roof of John's building on East Sixth. John is alive. But it's almost like we're in the future. We are talking together like we can talk about anything. . . . I compliment him on the gorgeous sun deck he's built on the roof (John and I ever both sun lovers). He says, *"I'm more interested in your dick than this deck."* I was a little nervous at that. I ask John how sex stuff has been. John answers this like it is long ago. Like the whole subject has been drained of importance. John says, *"Oh, it was pretty rocky when I was sick. There was a time I was having tea with Brad. This was right after Howard had died. He is so pretty. All I can ever say in those situations is 'I like you!' Brad seemed to take this the wrong way and got hurt because he was confiding in me about his lover's death. I didn't want to be a stand-in for Howard. I wanted us to fuck."*

John Bernd at home, East Sixth Street, New York, fall 1980. Photo by Tim Miller.

Coda: John in the dream realm

John and I talk some more, like this is the first of many conversations that we're going to have in the dream realm. . . . Very much the conversations I wish we could have had had John lived and we had been able to be typical ex-boyfriends. I look forward to these dream discussions.

Part 2

Activism

Tim Miller performing at demonstrations demanding an AIDS ward at Los Angeles County Hospital, January 1989. Photo by Chuck Stallard.

Professional Autobiography, 1990

Although Jim Miller involved himself in political causes from his teenage years on, the later 1980s crystallized his sense of himself as an activist artist and of performance art as an ideal vehicle to promote social goals. Miller collaborated with editor Thomas Leabhart to produce this interview-essay, which was published in Mime Journal *in 1990. It contains Miller's most extended review of his career from an activist standpoint and details the factors that have been primary in directing his thinking and activity: his return to Los Angeles in 1986 and subsequent founding of Highways Performance Space with Linda Frye Burnham in 1989 and the AIDS crisis that led to his involvement in ACT UP. Particularly valuable in this selection is his discussion of politically aware, community-based performance traditions in Los Angeles, which he contrasts to the conceptual and spectacle-oriented scene in New York.*

Part of the reason I came back to L.A. is that performance here is work that is connected with social context, coming from cultural communities: Asian or Latino or lesbian or gay or whatever. Which is different from another idea: of visual spectacle, which is a calling card of the elegance and technical virtuosity of much highly visible, multimedia performance. This visually oriented work is not strong in L.A., where the artist is also a social creature, a social worker and a social activist. That's what attracted me to coming back to L.A.: to be able to have colleagues like Rachel Rosenthal, John Malpede, Los Angeles Poverty Department, John Fleck, Luis Alfaro, Keith Antar Mason, and Guillermo Gómez-Peña. What I love about their work is its connection to the world.

When I first began, after doing various theater-dance-music studies as a teenager, I went to New York when I was nineteen to seek my fortune as a performance artist. I was interested in post-Bob Wilson/Merce Cunningham visual theater, though on the other hand my own tribal drums in the heady days of post-punk America were much more expressionist-oriented, text-oriented, defined politically and artistically as a gay person. The work I did in New York was a reaction to the postmodern cool of the preceding generation of images without politics, gesture without social action. I was bratty, too: I criticized people, called Merce Cunningham and Bob Wilson lazy fags, in print, got myself in trouble. I had an expectation of what I wanted from the artists who were my elders, or what I thought an artist should be and what kind of job the artist had: to create work in a context of the world and of social events, especially for gay artists. I had just come from being in San Francisco right after the assassinations of Harvey Milk and George Moscone in 1978, the successful rightwing political coup of a major city, decapitating the progressive leadership of the city and getting away with it. And all of that has gone into my work, as I define it within the autobiographical, sifting through what happens in my life, the stories, the images.

Much of the world is an unfriendly place. Even as a white, middle-class kid, I've been launched into a world where people that I admire, like my political idols, have their brains blown out in San Francisco City Hall. Dozens of friends and artistic colleagues have died of AIDS. It's been a rocky road for the twelve or thirteen years that I've been making work. That was the climate as I went to New York and began creating works which were influenced by the feminist performance history in L.A., a dominant reason why my work is the way it is.

There was an explosion of feminist performance work here in the '70s and '80s. That amazing decade—there's a wonderful book about the era with that name—helped to spawn the autobiographical personal political return to story and text which went on in the late '70s in New York, as people started to talk again and to tell stories and put value on what happens to people. The power of the small: the Wooster Group in the late '70s with the trilogy building on Spalding Gray's autobiography. This high energy stuff had an enormous impact on me and was the single biggest influence on my work. Spalding's autobiography suddenly opened up the world to the incredible specificity of everyone's lives. What we can create from what happens to us can be done cheaply and simply; it's transportable, it's subversive, it's all kinds of things and can take all kinds of forms.

I started making pieces in 1980 about my twenty-one-year-old perspective and about being a gay kid coming from California to New York. The works were big, because I was interested in placing individual history, personal history, in social context and in social history. My first work was called *Paint Yrself Red/Me & Mayakovsky*, which I began performing on successive Monday nights at PS 122, the space I founded with some other people in 1979. I arrived in New York and there was all this energy and this post-punk gang of people who wanted to deal with texts and with more political material, with pushiness, with specificity, and with breaking out of the '70s quagmire. Those people helped in the founding of PS 122, which over the last ten years has been the most energized performance space in New York, and today is the most active center of performance art in that part of the country.

We were fueled and challenged by Reagan's election: suddenly people felt our country was in a crisis period for artists, a crisis that has not abated since. Our world changed when Ronald Reagan was elected president. We didn't think it could happen, and suddenly our country was not just this bumbling, benign Carteresque thing, but real scumbags had taken power. Artists as a community, at least the forward edge of our community, said "What's going on here? Our country has changed; we have a new job to do." We took it seriously—I certainly did; that was the climate. At PS 122, I started making pieces that were about our country, about what was going on at that time, but filtering it through my family, and through WWII. A piece called *Postwar* was about placing myself in the history of my family, and about my father who had fought in the war, and about the election of Reagan. This piece was eventually done in eight different languages, two hundred times all over Western Europe and North America at a time when the SS20 nuclear missiles were being deployed by Reagan. It's about the first term nuclear paranoia, about the fear that Ronald Reagan would blow up the world. That piece was also in some ways about my identity as a gay person.

I've played a role as an organizer, at the same time I've been making my own work. I've been creating context for other artists to work in and, in fact, have cofounded two spaces that are the most active in the country, PS 122 and Highways here in Santa Monica. The first thing I organized at PS 122 was the first festival of gay performance art in this country. It was a huge success and an event that helped articulate a new ethos. In New York, most gay men were creating performance art about issues we were dealing with, like sex and gay bashing; they were somewhat simpler issues than the ones we're dealing with now.

The intriguing thing was that these solos I was doing each week got too much attention in the press. I was twenty-one years old and I was getting all this newspaper attention, and what could have been a laboratory process became a real product. I was touted as a new golden boy of performance art and I began to get engagements all over Europe and all over this country. That was what I wanted: it was interesting and exciting, but in some ways it subverted a growth process. I was too young to be fixing my work for international consumption, and it also made me buy into the "bigger is better" idea that dominated New York performance. You had to have big

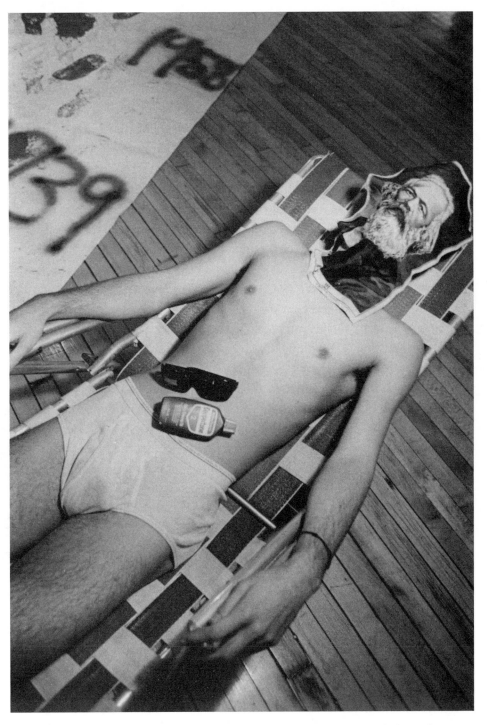

Tim Miller performing *Paint Yrself Red/Me & Mayakovsky* at PS 122, 1980. Photo © Kirk Winslow.

spectacle, you had to take personal material and make it Broadway scale. The next couple of pieces got bigger and more bloated until the piece I did at the Brooklyn Academy of Music [*Democracy in America*] was huge. The work was a disaster, a critical flop and a mess—an interesting and energetic mess. What is strong about my work, which is its specificity, is seen best in my solos. That's what I mostly do now. The thing I am interested in now, and which was the strong part of my work when I first started, is my point of view, my world view, my strange cosmology which begins to take life on stage, dynamically and passionately. As the pieces got bigger and bigger, they lost all that. That's why Spalding Gray eventually stripped everything back until he was just sitting there, just speaking the speech.

My next piece after *Democracy in America* was totally stripped down, a duet called *Buddy Systems* about my relationship with my boyfriend Douglas Sadownick, dogs, sex, and swimming. With it I began a return to honing my solo performance ventures, and made *Some Golden States,* which was about the apocalyptic world I'd been occupying in the late '80s; my home town of Whittier wiped out in the earthquake; friends dying from AIDS; the assassinations in San Francisco. It was a highly undependable world in which everything either gets its brains blown out or its foundation undermined. Then I created *Stretch Marks,* which I premiered in 1989. These works created since 1986 are what I am about now. They bring in, in as pointed and direct a way as possible, the experiences I am going through, especially those connected to my life as a gay person, my life as an American citizen, my political point of view, my social activism—all brought into performance-making. It is as queer, political and pushy as possible. Which is certainly why I am having troubles in Washington—that's a subsidiary effect of this direction.

Other than the solos, I spend time working on interesting and dynamic collaborations that have some cross-cultural magic. I work as an artist and an activist with ACT UP/LA, and the performance artist in me now is also able to design and execute civil disobedience spectacle in front of the Federal Building, whether it's around AIDS issues or censorship. This is a new artist's skill that I've had to learn. I collaborated with an Episcopal priest, Malcolm Boyd, on performance art sermons over the last two years, certainly something I never would have thought I would do during my ego-laden days in New York. We created a performance art piece for a morning mass, in a big Episcopal church for a dynamic community of people who had never seen the work I do. In it we explored the connecting and dual roles of performance artist-priest and found we share ground: the sermon is a building block of Western theatrical tradition, and the Eucharist is a performance art of its own.

In this interesting world which I now inhabit in L.A., performance artists are also defined as citizens and social activists. If your work is about homelessness, you'd better have worked extensively with homeless people, as John Malpede has, and if your work deals with the AIDS crisis you'd better also be functional in trying to end the crisis. This throws a challenge to high artism. Most of us in the West were raised with the idea that art was separate and sufficient and needed to be universal, and should stay out of the world. Many artists, myself included, are rejecting that, saying that what we do in performance spaces and galleries also had better be matched with some agenda that functions in the world and might create change. It's not enough to make artwork about the AIDS crisis: you also have to be working to end the AIDS crisis.

This is a dividing point, and it's partly why Latin American artists have provided an example. In Latin America it's not unusual, artists may also be political and are almost always involved in political activity. They may hold political office, may be killed by a death squad. The idea of an artist as citizen has been explored in Latin America in the twentieth century. The art world as we knew it in this country is dead, and certainly the direct federal government attacks on the art world are showing us that the world has changed. If we thought we weren't political, we know better now. Art is now deeply politically contexted, and they'll shut our performance spaces down or they'll shut artists up. That's what we've been interested in exploring. That's been the motto at Highways: to encourage artists in finding connections between our society and ourselves.

Part of the reason to choose to be an artist in L.A. is the presence of Hollywood—it is part of what makes the performance art world in L.A. so hard core. In New York I found the art world was trying to create its own star system, with its own Academy Awards, creating new personalities. The careerist mode in New York is strong, and I lived in it for nine years. There's great performance there, but there is a strong careerist impulse. When you live in Los Angeles, a city that has the strongest careerist impulse in the performing arts in the world, it makes it all seem stupid and tawdry. The idea of replicating that in the art world becomes absurd beyond belief, and ugly and crass. In New York you feel separate; you never go to Broadway, but you're aware of Hollywood. I know we function outside of that and it's part of what makes the community in L.A. interesting. People are good to each other and want to make sure they don't fall into the Hollywood thing, because you are aware of it and you know what it is

Our proximity to the Mexican border is also about L.A.'s defining itself as the most culturally diverse city, perhaps of all time, certainly in this country in the late twentieth century. L.A. is obviously part of two borders, the Pacific border and the Mexican-American border, and that has a large effect. L.A. is in many ways the northernmost of Latin American cities; Broadway in downtown L.A. is like Mexico City, it has enormous vitality. What you want to do as an artist, the audiences you want to encourage, the structure you create to show performance, all change when you have the city of L.A. prioritizing it: AIDS and homelessness are two issues the city of L.A. wants its artist-citizens to be dealing with. You're getting a signal from Al Nodal, head of cultural affairs at City Hall, from Peter Sellars at the L.A. Festival, and from Cal Arts. Our major institutions are encouraging a culturally diverse future. If this were coming from Lincoln Center, N.Y.U., and the Brooklyn Academy of Music, New York would feel like a different place too.

Tim Miller with Buddy on the roof of PS 122, 1985. Photo by Dona Ann McAdams.

The grass roots organizations and artists are already doing work that connects to their communities, and their social identities are being encouraged by the biggest institutions—the City, the Festival, the schools. This has created an extremely exciting place for dialogue. The L.A. Festival, which is influenced by the multicultural dialogue that's been going on here for a long time, is coming to a flowering. It's full of struggle and conflict and people getting angry at each other, as it should be—but there's the desire to make the effort. That's why I live here, why I left New York to come back here. It's extremely rich, and it has influenced me greatly; it's helped hone my work much more precisely, more intelligently; my work has to be smarter and stronger because I live here.

In *Stretch Marks* I use a section of a piece I made for a demonstration in front of County Hospital in East L.A., and I explain to the audience that I'm doing it. A demonstration is every bit as good a reason to make a performance as creating it for opening night. I was deeply involved in work to pressure the County of Los Angeles to provide an AIDS ward in the biggest hospital in the world; my political work for a year and a half or two years was primarily around that issue. The AIDS ward now exists; I was arrested twice, and beaten up once by the police—but now in this county of nine million people, there is an AIDS ward. That doesn't mean the world has changed, but there was a specific goal in my work and in my social life: improved health care in the County of Los Angeles, where I was born and where I live. The struggle continues, but the results are tangible. This would not exist without thousands of hours of protest people put forward to embarrass one of the most corrupt bodies in the country, the L.A. County Board of Supervisors, to get off their butts and shell out.

The ACT UP model has had a huge impact on artists in the last five years. Many performance artists spend great effort as part of ACT UP, either here or in New York or Chicago or someplace else. It's training a whole generation how to take over the streets, how to shift public policy, how to get millions of public dollars released, how to get buildings built, to learn if there's a certain kind of social practice you can put into play to change the world. And it's more practical than trying to dismantle the nuclear stockpile, which is an extremely tall order. We also have international examples of artists overthrowing their governments in Eastern Europe in the last year. It's a charged time.

Part of the reason the first performance I made was about Mayakovsky, a theater artist and poet who interests me enormously, is because of his transformation from a member of the bourgeois avant-garde into the most influential artist of the first five years of the Soviet Union, both in theater and writing. He was also obliged by Stalin to put a bullet in his head in 1931. The artist and the avant-garde are not there just to diddle the middle class; they're there to restructure societies.

In the postwar period we have a number of examples, one in the effort of the artists and intellectuals in Mexico finally supporting Cardenas and, hopefully, the eventual takeover of power from the P.R.I. It's been going on for ten years. Look at what's happened in Nicaragua and the ways artists there continue to organize themselves now in a pluralistic society. The most dynamic are events in the theater community in Czechoslovakia, overthrowing their government, and an artist becoming president of a republic. We're hard pressed to come up with a better example than that. Imagine someone like Edward Albee or Sam Shepard becoming president of the U.S.! In Czechoslovakia, many of the leadership in the Civic Forum were theater people. Not just Havel; theater people were in the forefront of the Charter 77 signers. That contrasts with the feelings artists have in this country, that the federal government will directly attack us. My friend who is a producer of the TV show *thirtysomething* was commiserating with me a month ago: "oh, it's terrible what the federal government is doing to you." And two weeks later, rightwing pressure on his advertisers had him censored. The gay episode of *thirtysomething* won't go into syndication; it'll never been seen again. And these are hardly the most intense forms of trying to make a community invisible: artists' studios have been invaded by the FBI, which makes the NEA stuff seem bureaucratic and silly.

I see it in the artists' community in L.A. If five years ago someone had told me two hundred artists would be gathered in front of the Federal Building downtown, and thirty of them would blockade the building and be arrested and taken into custody, I would've said you're crazy. It was referred to in Congress, that artists were taking to the streets and ready to shut down the federal government in L.A. for an hour or two. That's the real change. It's also extremely exciting because artists are getting rid of a lot of the bullshit and the smallness of the idea of what it is to be an artist, especially a performance artist, which is by nature a social act. It's a public act, people performing outdoors or in churches or on skid row.

The NEA controversy has re-energized theater in this country—suddenly theater matters again. What people write or perform on stage is considered volatile and challenging and maybe threatening to the status quo. It suddenly makes what we do in our theaters and performance spaces matter a great deal. It's under the closest scrutiny. I travel all over the country every year performing, and a lot of the strength that I bring is because I'm bringing into the performing arena my identity as a gay person and an AIDS activist. Performance art becomes a useful and simple tool to create public identity in a society that is trying to bland everyone out and make everyone seem the same. It's easy to talk about multiculturalism or diversity, but when it comes down to it, it's different kinds of people. The identity issue is beginning to seem more interesting as a way of understanding this, because diversity is such a big idea. You have to like getting to know other people. You have to get to know an African American who was raised in a West African spiritual tradition, as Keith Antar Mason was. I see him every day: it's part of our dialogue, part of what it is to know someone, and it's messy. Identity creates conflict or creates dialogue, and it's rough sometimes. We've had intense struggles at Highways because we have a culturally diverse community of artists, all of whom are working from points of identity. Diversity is being explored in L.A., and now being taken to other parts of the country because of the mix that's happening here.

As I travel this country and abroad, I go as a politicized gay activist, gay cultural person, AIDS activist, American citizen. That often means that when I arrive in a city, I go first to a demonstration, not to a theater. There's no time to go to the hotel. It would be much nicer to have dinner, unpack, then have the tech the next day. It takes work and communicating with people. My work is my identity connecting with the audience, finding a window for diverse audiences. There are almost always discussions after the performances; you have to stick around and talk to the people afterwards. It's all performance. Performance art is important because of its flexibility, its economy. There's something about getting things just hot off the griddle, maybe within a day or two of the events that are being talked about in the piece. That's also part of the reason why performance is becoming the focus of censorship. I refer often to the Federal Theater Project and the WPA from the '30s; that history is fresh and exciting. And the *Living Newspaper* was fascinating. Most performance is in that tradition whether the creators know it or not; they're probably using those influences in some way. Each performance has some topical life because it may be only marginally scripted to begin with, and especially if it's a one-person performance you can change it each night.

Thanks to Jesse Helms and gang, more people know about performance art than ever before. It's always been growing, but now there's unparalleled interest. Right before my difficulties with the NEA, I finished a seventeen-city tour of the country. It's happening in performance because we're performing in big theaters, we're in the media with lots of press attention, and we're all opinionated. I get on TV or talking to the *Washington Post;* we get enormous opportunities to hold court, often about political, cultural material, and it's happening because we're sticking our faces out there. We're getting into trouble with the federal government because we're getting attention from the media. Performance art is a lively form and seems to be getting stronger all the time. Maybe at some point it will become a particularly energized part of the performing arts, as modern dance is separate from classical ballet. We're in a crisis time, and performance art is peculiarly suited for crisis because of quickness of response, directness, and the possibility of cutting to the bone. Even though we've been learning our jobs for years and I've been a working performance artist for fifteen years, we're just beginning to see the dynamic and challenging role this work plays in our culture.

$\mathcal{ACT}\ \mathcal{UP}$

As Jim Miller notes in his interview with Steven Durland that appears in Part 3, ACT UP has been "the single most influential thing in my life, . . . as a model, as a worldview, as a kind of cultural practice." The journal entries printed here recount his initial contact with ACT UP as well as several demonstrations between 1988 and 1993. These passages set the stage for later selections in this and the next section, which exhibit the impact of ACT UP on Miller's life and work. Two ACT UP actions are specifically treated in Jim Miller's performance works: the 1989 Los Angeles County General Hospital demonstrations in Stretch Marks *and the "Art Attack" of 1990 in "Civil Disobedience Weekend."*

November 20, 1987

[In New York for performances of *Some Golden States.*] Went to the ACT UP meeting (AIDS Coalition to Unleash Power) on Monday night. Very energized. It was good to be there. Hundreds of people. Lotsa cute boys—which ones of them are sick? Everybody in their pink triangle buttons which say "Silence=Death." So strange, fucking heroic and inspiring. A healthy contentious discussion process has been arrived at. A civil disobedience action was being planned for the steps of

Tim Miller in Minneapolis, 1992. Photo © Thomas Strand.

City Hall to protest city money for AIDS stuff being held up. The
various issues—chalk vs. spray-paint to be used to make the
outlines of bodies on the pavement, timing the action in terms
of TV coverage, and general focus of the demands—were rolled
around the group in a pretty healthy manner. A good balance
between group process and the inevitable slowness of same.
In a way this is what I've always wanted: politicized gay people,

cute boys with agendas, a world view, and ready to storm the barricades. It sucks it took all this death for this to happen.

Early 1988

I was in a demonstration a few weeks ago at the Federal Building here in L.A., an ACT UP action protesting the F.D.A. and Reagan's limpdicked response to AIDS. We fell down in the streets and someone would trace our outline with chalk, and then the name of someone who had died would be written inside the form. There were thousands of these left all over that part of town by the time the hundreds of us were through. It was pure spectacle: drums were beating ... complete action ... hands and bodies covered with chalk ... The big picture, the only one that matters. I feel ready to continue storming the proverbial and actual barricades ... and to keep witnessing my pals, only some of whom are artists, and myself trying to make some sense of this mess. Or at the very least make a mess, in some sense, of this strange time we find ourselves in.

October 12, 1989

I had wanted to be part of the ACT UP action to shut down the Federal Building [October 6, 1989]. To put pressure on the government to get with the program and start dealing with this crisis that has killed so many people I know. It was part of a nationwide action. . . . I guess I wanted the experience of putting my body on the line, a ritual act maybe to show that I mean business. Along with the hundred other people who were ready to be arrested. I raise money for ACT UP, I go to demonstrations, I am a cultural organizer, I make work dealing with this time. But am I ready, even for a day, to put my body in the hands of the state, the authorities—go to the slammer, the joint, the big house?

I did my civil disobedience training in the rec room of an ugly apartment building in West Hollywood, this good bunch

74

of people in a basement. . . . It's so exciting to me that one hundred people would be arrested at 6 A.M. at the Federal Building as part of an ACT UP demo, and it would be almost half women—tons of them from the anti–Operation Rescue project—lotsa Latino activists, the publisher of [the gay newspaper] *Frontiers*, Troy Perry [founder of Metropolitan Community Churches], Torie Osborn [who runs the gay center], much of the community leadership, all ready to be arrested.

It was an intense thing for me to have gone through, this for the first time. It humbled me about my own limits and fears, about what it must be like to be a political and cultural activist somewhere that has death squads, or what it is to be in this legal system when there aren't lotsa cameras and other people around. I know this kind of thing is going to happen more and more. That it is an essential American experience, and not just because of Thoreau or MLK or whoever. That soon it may be necessary for the commitment to deepen far beyond this ritual spectacle of civil disobedience. I feel energized, humbled and charged up.

August 23, 1992

Just back from the Republican Convention in Houston with ACT UP. This was a very heavy time. These are scary people who run our country. Being in Houston and seeing their hate in action for those days has filled me with the most intense desire to get these creeps out of Washington. I want Bush to fall so bad that I can taste it.

I got to Houston the day the convention opened. Went to the ACT UP hotel, the Days Inn at the Airport. 150 ACT UP people, 150 Republican delegates—this made for interesting encounters in the coffee shop. We had a big march towards the Astrodome of people protesting the AIDS genocide of Reagan/ Bush. We finally got to a line of five bezillion police and were stopped. This march had been very badly planned and there

75

were no tactical plans of what to do when we hit the inevitable police line. The women had a clear action: they laid down in front of the police. I joined them. But then, the lack of focus or support led to the usual flags and effigies of Bush being burned some forty feet behind us, which led to a police stampede over us and into the crowd. People fled, being beaten and chased by cops on horseback. A number of people got hurt pretty bad. This did not have to happen. If we had clearly taken the space in front of the Houston Police, they could not have done this. We were forced to slink off into the night on buses through the police cordon.

Back to the hotel where ACT UPers watched [Pat] Buchanan's nasty culture war speech on the TV in the lobby. This was one of the more depressing things I have ever seen. My image of this country at this point is sitting around a hot tub in Houston with a bunch of fags while Republican delegates shout pro-KKK slogans at us from across the pool.

The next day was a big Freedom of Expression rally at the Menil Collection (The Big Museum). This went better. A huge turnout, lotsa energy. I performed the "Queer Birth" section from *My Queer Body*. It is very easy to get people excited after they have sat through forty-five minutes of speeches. This cheered me up considerably from the night before.

There was a big national ACT UP meeting where people were moping around about the disaster of the night before. Then a momentum got going for another national action. I proposed we do a roll call of the people who have died from each state, while the nominating roll call for Bush went on. This happened the next day and it came off pretty OK. It was in the sanctioned "Free Speech Zone." It was very haunting and powerful to hear the number of dead from each state while we lay in a field next to the Astrodome as they nominated Bush again. A PBS crew had wanted me to come onto the floor of the convention on their credentials and do a performance

76

Tim Miller protesting with ACT UP during the Republican National Convention, Houston, August 1992. The sign behind him reads "DON'T GAG." Photo courtesy Tim Miller.

while Bush was talking, but I thought I would probably get arrested and not make my plane to Atlanta the next morning.

I left pretty down. I felt like ACT UP had not gotten a clear message out. That the leadership that had made other national actions so strong was absent here. A lot of adolescent giving the finger to the cops and losing focus of why we were there. A complete absence of organization that you need to have to confront the danger of these situations. I know, it is easy to Monday-morning quarterback. I should get more involved in the organization of these things from the beginning and not just criticize. In spite of all of this, and the generally negative media it generated (at least in Houston), it did show that people do not believe the Republicans' lies. That there *is* dissent. That while the GOP was celebrating people were being beaten in the streets.

May 3, 1993

Back from the March on Washington. It was so intense to feel my strange capital city be taken over by a million queer people. It started from the beginning. The plane from L.A. to D.C. was mostly queers—a very festive flight. The airport was jammed with gay people. *Everywhere you looked!* In front of Congress, the Washington Monument, each street.

On Saturday there was a huge ACT UP demo. Thousands of people surrounding the Capitol. Hands held. Larry Kramer railing at these times—at his best. The next day, the March itself. So clumsy a million people are. It took many hours for everybody to walk down Pennsylvania Avenue. I marched with ACT UP and we were up towards the front. Got to the rally site as Mike Callen (on the big video screen) was beginning to sing. Later that night, I performed a little tribute to him at the Flirtations concert. His farewell concert.

This from my notes: "We're lucky to be here tonight, here with the Flirtations honoring Mike Callen. Mike is many things: teacher, friend, warrior, slut, guide & mapmaker. Mike is very wise about sex and these bodies we are in. He helped make up safe sex. Helped guide our hearts and heads and bodies thru these last twelve years." Then I did "My Skin is a Map" from *My Queer Body*. I left the stage and kissed Mike. Left thru the stage entrance. Hopped on the Metro. Walked through Dupont Circle. Thousands of people hanging out, making out, making history this day.

Civil Disobedience Weekend

"*Civil Disobedience Weekend*" *is an "artfag fantasy" based on the March 1, 1990, "Art Attack" protest in Los Angeles, when five hundred artists "arrested" the U.S. Federal Building for crimes against art. Tim Miller and others organized the protest in response to mounting pressure on the arts by the radical Right and their allies within Congress and the Bush administration. Twenty-four protesters were arrested and held for a few hours within the Federal Building, which provides the setting for Tim Miller's imagining of a fantastical orgy with magical consequences. In reality the protest had a different consequence for Tim Miller, since it is likely that publicity resulting from the Los Angeles action contributed to the decision to target him in the NEA Four affair that began three months later.*

The orgy scene in "Civil Disobedience Weekend" may have been suggested by an experience recorded in Miller's journal for 1988, printed as a coda to this section. The utopian climax, performed to the "Ode to Joy" from Beethoven's Ninth Symphony, employs the sung-speech technique used earlier in the Liebestod *from* Buddy Systems *and anticipates the* Bolero *finale of* My Queer Body. *"Civil Disobedience Weekend" was incorporated in the anthology show* Sex/Love/Stories *(1990), from which this text is transcribed, and also performed separately.*

Although Miller regards it as a Disney-style fantasia, the piece's sexual explicitness occasionally polarized audiences, as exemplified by a 1991 performance at Sadlers Wells Theatre in London. As Miller recorded in his journal, the "well-heeled audience reacted like I had just spiked the punch with plutonium. People avoided me at the gala reception afterwards. . . . 'Too queer for comfort!' But then, like the happy tapdancing ending in some bad musical, a gaggle of spunky and energized queerboy performance art and dancer types came up to me and told me how great my performance was."

"You're all about to be placed under arrest. You are here in violation of federal law. National Endowment for Censorship Penal Code—yes, Penal Code—S-Q-143-W. If you do not disperse immediately you will be placed under arrest. . . . You are now under arrest! The charge is blocking a Federal orifice—I mean office! You are now under arrest!"

We linked arms and chanted furiously: "ACT UP! Fight back! Save art!" And for our bilingual number, "Alto a la censura! Art is not a crime!" (Which would, the next day, be reported in the newspapers as "Hola a la censura." Oops.) We doffed our art criminal chain gang outfits and blockaded the Federal Building. Shutting that building down in protest of our government's attacks on the First Amendment and Freedom of Expression. This was the big moment, the time where all our careful training, our split-second organization, our carefully-honed message, no more rehearsing or nursing a part, we were about to enter—CIVIL DISOBEDIENCE WEEKEND!

We stood there: bicep to bicep, ego to ego. One by one, the cops took us away: Les and Adrian and Tom and Guillermo and Jordan and Kathy. . . . Finally it was my turn, and I felt the cold steel of those federal handcuffs so tight, so very tight around my wrists, so deliciously tight. And they lined us up underneath a picture of George Bush, our hands handcuffed behind us, in the perfect position to

The Art Attack protest (Tim Miller is holding Oscar Wilde), Los Angeles Federal Building, March 1, 1990. Photo by Chuck Stallard.

grab the crotch of the person behind. And then they marched us off and put the guys in one holding tank and the women in another.

It was a largish sort of smallish room. Square, with a bench around the edge and two forlorn open toilets in one corner. The Federal Cop came in and said, "Well, I see we got twenty-four real *artfags* in here. Well, boys, since you got arrested so late on this Friday, we're gonna keep you here all weekend!" We protested: "But our dogs! our jobs! our boyfriends!" The Federal Cop just gave us a cold stare and said: "Tough luck, boys! Welcome to *civil disobedience weekend!*"

I was sitting next to the cute semiotics instructor from Cal Arts who started rubbing something in his pants. It was not a book by Michel Foucault. It was not chopped liver. It was the beginning of *civil disobedience weekend!*

He said, "Boy, these ACT UP civil disobedience anti-censorship actions sure get me all hot."

I said, "Yeah. Me too."

He said, "Hey, I'm really stiff. How about a back rub?"

I said, "Sure, dude."

All eyes were on us. Hands began to move underneath *Action Equals Life* t-shirts, and that message took on a whole new meaning. One of the boys from Highways reached into the pants of one of the boys from the L.A. County Museum of Art and they began to kiss. Big wet sloppy larger-than-life tongue kissing, like the kind you see on late-night TV. Like the kind I practiced on a towel the night before I took my girlfriend to Disneyland in eighth grade and we made out on the "Journey into Inner Space" ride. Those kinds of kisses.

The semiotics instructor from Cal Arts has now pulled his dick out and is demonstrating the Theory of Signification to the graduate student from the Inland Empire. The pants are dropping . . . shirts are pulled over heads in a practical arabesque . . . generally stroking and soothing and generally fulfilling our foray.

Though the state may chain us, our crazed and juicy bodies and imaginations will not be imprisoned!

With love's light wings did I o'erperch these walls,
For stony limits cannot hold love out:
And what love can do, that dares love attempt.

And this is our revolt, our disobedience most uncivil, here in the bowels of George Bush's Federal Building. We will whip 'em out and cum on his Brooks Brothers lapel, wipe it on his CIA dossier, naked together on a burning flag in North Carolina, raising high the roof-beam, the standard, and anything else that's handy, including the sleeveless t-shirt stretched so tastefully behind the neck of the blonde boy with the lovely butt who comes from the Simi Valley Anti-Censorship and Homophile Auxiliary and is being tended to by the ACT UP outreach coordinator—who is, in fact, reaching out, from behind, pinching his nipples.

I remain distant, observant. My job is to stay aware of what is going on, so it can be written down. It must be saved—this part of ourselves, the jump-off point, ready to speak truth to Caesar *and* jerk off on his best toga.

Everyone is in the act now. It is a flurry of safer activist sex! Skin is slapping. Thighs are clenching. Breath is racing. One after another we cum on the face of Jesse Helms, on a banner with the word *Guilty* burned across his forehead. He is now awash in the semen of twenty-four pissed-off artist fags, deviant even in the slammer, saying *NO* to anti-sex, anti-life, anti-art nazis.

We fall on each other, spent. But then we hear footsteps. . . . We are being released! What has happened?

Out on the streets, there is a strange music in the air. Thousands of people are dancing in the streets, carrying garlands of flowers and speaking dozens of languages. People of every cultural and community background. They have taken the street in front of the Federal Building. I look up to the sky and see the stars winking as Beethoven's Ninth Symphony is played impromptu by the L.A. Philharmonic who have gathered on the Civic Center Mall.

Seid umschlungen, Millionen . . . Diesen Kuss der ganzen Welt! Be embraced, you millions . . . this kiss for all the world!

We begin to hear snippets of what has happened. George Bush has been defeated and is in exile in Baghdad? Mmm. The Federal Police have given up and joined ACT UP? Mmmm. President Clinton has appointed Holly Hughes to be Chairwoman of the National Endowment for the Arts? Hmmmm. Jesse Helms has given up smoking and come out as a gay person? Yeeechh! Oh please god, anything but that.

There is dancing and music, fireworks in the air. We hear more. A fax from Washington tells us that a special session of Congress has elevated the AIDS crisis to the top national priority. A telegram arrives from Yeltsin. He wants to meet with us immediately to form a world artists' government to address nuclear disarmament, economic restructuring, global warming. The world has been moved by our deeds! We have triumphed! The day is ours!

I think of the work left to be done and I glance up at the top of the Federal Building, which has now sprouted strange and beautiful vines, tendrilling into the night, testament to the seeds we planted there on this civil disobedience weekend . . . reaching up and rooting deep, growing toward something new.

Toward something that, if we all put in a lot of vision, a lot of imagination, and tons of work. . . .

They're growing toward what just might . . . what just might be our future.

"The artist becomes really woven into the community as a worker"
Interview with Linda Frye Burnham

Linda Frye Burnham, founder of High Performance *magazine and co-founder with Tim Miller of Highways Performance Space, conducted this interview in 1990. The excerpt printed here contains Miller's fullest discussion of how the ethos of ACT UP affected his work.*

LINDA FRYE BURNHAM: I'd like to get to the particular character of ACT UP/L.A. What attracts you to the combative style?—for instance, the incidents of heckling politicians who take a friendly stance but are too soft in general, the constant exposure of how little politicians are doing, and the statements against working inside the system?

TIM MILLER: All those things . . . are so consistent with the history of the avant-garde, of shocking the bourgeoisie. Except now you actually do it, you don't pretend to do it by being in coffeehouses. You actually go to the halls of justice and law and power and confront them on their turf. So that idea of "oh, you're just a crazy artist critical of everything" becomes a really outgoing and directed kind of response. It's all pure performance—challenging, exposing dishonesty, lies, and contradictions.

What happened in L.A. at the Federal Building has not happened in any other city in this country, where the major organizations line up with ACT UP on civil disobedience—the head of AIDS project L.A., Being Alive, the Gay Community Center, Minority AIDS Project, Cara a Cara. Also, that was a very mixed-race, straight/gay, male/female, worker bee/executive director kind of event. It's what was most important about it. Very important things are going to come out of that for this community.

BURNHAM: What has been the most interesting action you've taken part in?

MILLER: The real departure point for [ACT UP/]L.A., and in another sense for me as an artist, was the Los Angeles County Hospital vigil, the most important thing that's happened so far because it was about the creation of an alternative space. The vigil was also a performance space; it was happening every day—music, poetry, dance, performance art—and that's a very useful model. The artist becomes really woven into the community as a worker. Everybody talks about being a "cultural worker," but I think people are really starting to realize what that means, people are living it.

And most of it is work, not writing sonnets. The work also happens to be highly creative and really interesting. When the art finally happens it comes forward intimately woven into life and community, in a way that changes the image you have of yourself in the world and what you do and your sense of service and being connected. The other thing is that the vigil had tangible success: the AIDS ward still exists. It was the beginning of a more culturally diverse movement that has really come to fruition, because people have been ready to go into conflict with each other and are ready to not write each other off on both sides.

BURNHAM: One of the things we brought up when we did our AIDS panel at Highways was the impulse toward activism that's come out of the AIDS situation. I mean you get an idea and you do it, instead of letting it sit there on the table, because you might not be here tomorrow. I think we can link this with ACT

UP's "zap" philosophy—you know, do it now, do it quick, strike while the iron is hot.

MILLER: Right, which is also ideally connected to the whole reason for being an artist in this particular performance realm—to respond quickly, effectively, and surgically to what you want to do. I really see this with Guillermo Gómez-Peña. It's like a ray gun: he's going zzzz-t. It's very specific. There's no other art form or cultural way he could use to get at that. He couldn't make a movie about something that specific, he couldn't write a novel about it; but he could prepare a text, something he wrote that morning, and present it for public absorption that evening.

My first impulse with performance, the reason I liked it, was because it was quick. It's still the reason I like it. You just do it. And that's probably why ACT UP and those strategies appeal so much to a certain kind of artist. This artist is intuitive, wants to move quickly, doesn't want to be bogged down in bureaucracy or over-discussing, just wants to do things that are grounded in process, as every artist's quick decisions are. And ACT UP is most successful in its ability to respond quickly.

BURNHAM: Can we come to a thesis that activism is speeding up because of AIDS activism now?

MILLER: It's been the front line for two or three years. It helped re-fuel and prepare people for women's health clinic defense actions. And I know in all these cities ACT UP and its troops have been crucial for those actions. For whatever reason, more and more middle-class people are well versed in activism—and not in a romantic way, not for this month or for one event, but as an ongoing daily practice, almost a meditation. . . . We're doing something really interesting that's not bullshit. It's going to provide us with the tools to do everything else that's useful.

BURNHAM: But we're so overextended.

MILLER: Yes, and it's not going to get easier. You don't finish it, you don't acquire wealth and retire, you just keep working. That idea is very strong in ACT UP, that it is a great privilege to continue to work when people are dying. The great luxury of exhaustion, being able to work till you're tired is a great gift of life, because you get to go to sleep and wake up again and work some more. That keeps people from burning out. You see very little burnout in AIDS activism. You do not have the luxury of burnout because the stakes are too high. I will not be offered a choice because my friends will keep dying. Hopefully I will not die because it's more fun to be doing this!

BURNHAM: What about your own work?

MILLER: Artists like me can't think that they're just working citizens who also happen to be making art. We have to keep refining the dialogue about what it means to be doing your own work but also contributing significant parts of your art energy to other activities, to keep refining that idea and do more within your communities. For me it's to keep on being one of many weird poet laureates of gay male sensibility in Southern California in the late twentieth century. You don't have to create the uncreated consciousness of your race. You have to be a little bit helpful in articulating a small corner of your time and community. And figure out what it is to parcel out your energy to your many activities and keep them all energized and alive. Say I got some fabulous career opportunity like an HBO special where they want to do the trilogy of my solos as a "masterpiece of late-twentieth-century performance art around gay themes" or something [laughs]—it would be a tragedy and a betrayal for me to leave other things I'm doing. It would be an equal tragedy for me to become only an administrator or a bureaucrat or an activist and not keep the work going. So those have to play off each other. That's two very useful angels on your shoulder.

AIDS Test

Tim Miller's account of awaiting the results of a test for HIV, a nearly universal experience for gay men of his generation, comes from his journal for 1990. Though he is always aware of the complex effects his HIV status can have on his art and his career, this account also provides a glimpse behind the assertive persona of his activist writings. The psychological and ethical impact of being HIV-negative became a principal focus of Naked Breath, *the performance work of 1994 that is Miller's most extended treatment of the impact of AIDS on gay men's sexuality and relationships.*

OK, here in the countdown. I get my results tomorrow. Finally went and got an HIV test with Doug, almost two weeks ago. This has been a roller coaster of weird emotions and logics and reasons. I'm not sure why we're doing this now. For years I always felt like there was a pretty good chance that I would test positive, so why find out? It was as if I enjoyed the intensity of feeling vulnerable to this time, but also feeling the escape hatch of not knowing what my status was so I could go about my business without the worry. Hmmm. This is sort of like having your activist edge but avoiding it too. I think I felt like the not knowing made it easier and stronger for me to do my work as an activist and artist without getting spooked by my own health concerns. I know this would rate fairly big on the Denial-O-Meter, but it seemed to work. There was a funny thing about sex too. I wanted to feel like I could have safer sex with my boys on the road without having to deal with my own HIV status (my version of which is to assume that everyone, including me, is HIV positive). Dwell in the land of the unknown.

My biggest worry about testing positive, if I do, is that I will have crossed a border that you can't ever go back over. I will be in the very particular fraternity of seropositive folks. This is, of course, scary. But it's also wanting to keep having a few more years of my young life there on the field as it were. Not that testing positive means I won't be able to have sex with other people. It just will never ever be simple again. There will always be the discussion. I guess I am focusing on sex stuff as a kind of life force that keeps me connected to the world. I worry about getting cut off from that. Of beginning to worry about every cough and cold. I know that if I test positive I am in good shape to take the information in and to activate even more my life and creative work. This is a comfort. And if I do test positive, it will probably mean that I have been positive since 1980 or 1981. So that means I will have already functioned most of my adult life as someone who is HIV positive—so no big deal. You know now.

The existential playing field of knowing you gotta die at some distant future to knowing that you'll probably die at a somewhat less distant future is a pretty big jump. I know if I test positive that I am already pretty lucky in the scheme of things. I could have gotten sick eight years ago. The incredible fear of that time, before there was some kind of coherent community, political, and cultural response to the plague. To deal with AIDS before ACT UP was probably really different. At least it would have been for somebody like me. I guess also, that if I am positive I have a responsibility to deal with it and look after my health more and charge up my work and not waste any time. I would probably pull back from some of the administrative stuff at Highways. I would probably be pretty out about testing positive. That opens up whole cans of worms. Doug and I have been communicating real well about all this stuff. This two weeks has brought us closer. We've been sharing our feelings and thoughts about what we're going through. I am not alone. I am in good health. I know what my work is in this life. These are all powerful things that can help me deal with this situation. I am just afraid to get the information; I am not so concerned after that. My WASP survival mechanism will probably kick in. I just don't wanna go to the testing place and have some stranger tell me this news. It's so fucking intimate. That intimacy scares me.

And what if I test negative? It is possible. Though my ex-boyfriend did die from AIDS and he and I did have a considerable amount of unprotected sex in 1980 and '81, I guess it is possible that I would test negative. Not real likely, but possible. And that will have its own set of crazy responses. How did I escape? Will it make me afraid to ride my scooter? To fly? To have sex with new people? Will it make me lose my "edge"? I know that sounds dumb but it is a real fear. What if Doug tests negative and I test positive? The reverse isn't so likely, but I guess it could happen. I think our relationship is strong enough to weather that stuff, but it would be a challenge. All kinds of angers and resentments come up. God! This is like being thrown into a pot of boiling water. Well, this time tomorrow something will be different.

Next day. Tested negative. I can't really believe it, but there it is. Doug and I were so nervous on our way there. I felt like we were about to face a firing squad. We were both a little in shock I guess. We got there and we seemed to be parked in wet cement, so we moved the car and then went for a little walk. I looked at the plants. We went inside. We didn't have long to wait. We sat there for a coupla minutes, and then they called Doug's number. He went inside and I slipped over towards the door to see if I could hear anything that would give it away. I didn't hear any big emotional thing, but I wasn't sure if that meant anything. The weird counselor with the moustache glared at me for eavesdropping and I sat down. The painter Andre Mirapolsky came in and asked how I was doing. I said, "Well, right now, I am in a bit of an existential situation." He said he hadn't quite thought about it in those terms. Doug came out and looked at me almost sheepishly and said "I'm negative." He sat down beside me and we hugged and I felt so much. I said, "We've won already." I felt that the worst was past. That at least I hadn't infected Doug, which had been a weird subtext to our relationship all along.

Then I went in and sort of collapsed into a chair. The nice woman looked at me and said, "Well, your test results came back negative." I felt a rush and said "God, I can hardly believe it." We talked a little bit and I told her why I always assumed I would test positive. She didn't seem overly interested. I went outside and told Dougie "negative," and we hugged standing up there. Andre Mirapolsky was looking at us and I felt a little bit on display, but fuck it. We went outside and Dougie started blessing everyone—the lab technician that had taken our blood, the reception person. We walked a little dazed to the car, trying to believe what we had heard. Doug wanted me to drive very carefully. We had been least prepared for this result, so we hardly knew how to respond. I didn't feel a huge relief, just a huge feeling of not knowing how to respond. But I also felt so fucking lucky to be feeling that confusion.

And where does this leave me? A little confused. A lot grateful. And totally humbled and ready to become even more committed to ending this crisis. I thought of John. I thought of Jackson. I thought, why them? And why not me? There is no order to it, certainly no fairness. No describable criterion, just a big dice roll that has nothing to do with anything. This is also no dispensation, no permanent freebie, no bought indulgence. It just means that probably my blood didn't get infected so far. Will this make me afraid to fly again? It can't. If it does I'm a wimp that doesn't deserve the luck of this particular draw. I gotta jazz up the total involvement with my time and my community. The world is HIV-positive in some weird way. I gotta keep doing my works in the world. Heat it up, make it stronger. I already felt so blessed to have gotten through so long, now I gotta turn up the heat. Feel the blessing that this body probably isn't gonna be going down one particular path, but there are plenty more where that came from. Keep bringing my spirit and energy to the world and my community. Be good to Douglas. Keep loving sex as I always have. Write articles. Make pieces. Start another performance space if I fucking have to. Honor the memory of friends and lovers who are gone and oh Jesus, every day is so good that I am here to remember them and make the day matter. I have not eluded death. Fat chance. Just maybe one particular version of it that might have cut things short in a certain way. Keep alive, knowing that it is all frosting at this point. I very easily could have died in 1986 or 1987, or 1984 for that matter. That I did not *is* a good thing because these years have been strong and as full of good works, good sex, and good friends as I could possibly make them. Keep it up, dude.

Coda

A circle headed towards the future

This journal entry from 1988 describes a party following an Art Around L. A. performance. The account anticipates the central scene of "Civil Disobedience Weekend."

A strange thing happened. It was a big party, a hundred or so folks. Some energy was humming among the boys, and the strong energies and attractions that exist among this art performance gang came to the surface. The physicality and genuine love I feel for my friends found a funny form. I had been talking to Steve . . . flirting, and then Jackson came over— Jackson, who looks so much like John Bernd it makes me cry. Eventually we were all in the kitchen and I was rubbing Matt's neck, and then Dougie was being rubbed by Jackson, and then a woman was touching him and then Gavin squeezed in, and then Alan was beside me and we were arms around shoulders. Meanwhile a man and woman were really going at it out in the doorway. Finally, David Schweizer came in carrying his Orson Welles beaker of booze. . . . and he came into the middle and the circle closed and lots of stroking and touching and neck kissing and kindly joking ensued until there was a crowd of fifteen fellows and one lovely woman . . . doing an Age of Aquarius routine. It was lovely and I was glad to be in the middle of it. Everything was completely safe and childlike. This went on for an hour or so, with people commenting as they came in for ice, with more joining in, with some choosing not to take part. It stayed very nice and inexplicable how this kind of thing could happen among a bunch of accomplished fellows here in the Reagan-AIDS '80s. Clothes didn't come off. Nobody came. I suppose on some level it was bad manners. I'm trying to decide what made it possible. The series of parties? The Santa Ana wind? The fear of death and the love this circle feels for each other, that may not have time to find a path towards expression? The relative ecology of comparable cuteness that existed in this cramped kitchen? The hope for a future that still holds the possibility of intimacy and love among the gay tribe— especially us artists here who are moving towards something. I can only think of it as a circle headed towards the future.

Part 3

Culture War

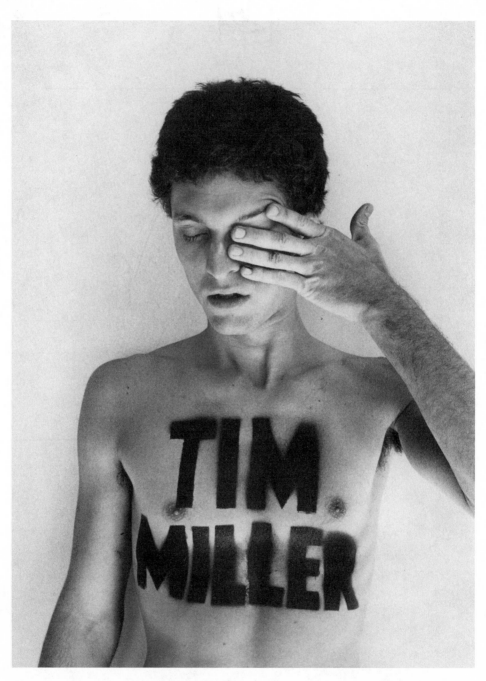

Tim Miller performing *Paint Yrself Red/Me & Mayakovsky* at PS 122, 1980. Photo © Kirk Winslow.

The NEA Four Case

Along with the photographers Robert Mapplethorpe (who was dead and beyond direct reach) and Andres Serrano, the "NEA Four" performance artists (Karen Finley, John Fleck, Holly Hughes, and Tim Miller) became poster children for the "culture war" of the early 1990s. The episode played out in two acts: the 1990 rejection under Bush administration pressure of the four performers' grants by a weak-willed chair of the National Endowment for the Arts, and their subsequent lawsuit against the NEA, which yielded an ambivalent result, since the artists received their grant money in a 1992 settlement, but the "decency" standard used to rationalize the NEA's action was upheld by the U. S. Supreme Court in 1998.

As the materials that follow indicate, Tim Miller was a vigorous if reluctant participant in the episode, making use of polemical opportunities that came with the publicity. At the same time, he quickly realized how notoriety oversimplifies an artist's work—to say nothing of the drain on his time and his creative and emotional energy. The documents collected here begin with Tim Miller's pointed "Artist's Statement" submitted as part of his grant application. The statement set off alarms within the NEA, which tried to convince him to suppress it. Immediately following the defunding, Miller used the Fourth *of July holiday to release his own "Artist's Declaration of Independence," which, like its 1776 predecessor, contained a list of grievances against "King George." His deposition in the lawsuit (ironically taken one week after the 1992 election defeat of George H. W. Bush) provides some little-known details about the episode and describes the harsh personal and professional effects of being targeted by right-wing zealots. The end of the case is told in Miller's accounts from 1998 of hearing oral arguments as the U. S. Supreme Court considered the "decency" clause of the NEA's funding criteria and of learning the Court's decision.*

Artist's Statement, 1989

FROM TIM MILLER'S NEA GRANT APPLICATION

I am a mutant performance artist from Alta California . . . third generation . . . I am here to collaborate with Baja California . . . the pissed off . . . this hemisphere . . . cool priests . . . the Pacific Ocean where I live . . . the ocean air I breathe . . . the ocean air where my father is buried . . .

I am a mutant performance artist from Alta California . . . I believe my social activism . . . my sex juicy life . . . my provocateur organizing . . . my space building . . . and my family Sunday dinners in Whittier are as much a part of my creative work as my performances . . . and look here Senator Jesse Helms, keep your Porky Pig face out of the NEA and out of my asshole . . . because I got work to do . . .

I am a mutant performance artist from Alta California . . . a fag thru and thru . . . who has seen friends and boyfriends wither and die, and I don't know very much but I know a little bit of death now . . . and this is part of what makes me a mutant . . . and impatient . . . and ready to get to work . . . with my community . . . connecting to other communities . . .

I am a mutant performance artist from Alta California . . . I believe our cultures can and should be wildly specific . . . fuck so-called universality and neutrality . . . leave it to television . . . and our challenge is to connect the dots . . . learn from each other . . . find the intercultural . . . inter-genderal . . . inter-disciplinary common ground future for our city.

An Artist's Declaration of Independence, July 4, 1990

When, in the course of cultural events, it becomes necessary for this artist to get pissed off and dissolve the political bonds which have connected me with the censorship of the state and the dishonesty of my government, ya gotta explain why you're stomping mad.

I hold these truisms to be self-evident: that all women and men should be created equal; that they should be endowed with certain inalienable rights; that among these should be life, liberty of expression, and the pursuit of happiness. This pursuit is not easy, especially for the homeless, lesbian and gay people, Latinos, women and African-Americans. . . . who this society screws over and would like to make invisible. That to secure these rights, an artist has a big responsibility in these troubled times, and when a government gets too big for its own wingtips and tries to tell its citizens what to think and feel, it is the job of the artist to speak truth to King George Bush in a challenging and angry way. To prove this let facts be submitted to a candid world.

He has allowed artists that confront their society to be censored, distorted, and used by right-wing demagogues to advance their political careers.

He has allowed his sleazeball appointee to cowardly undermine the cultural freedoms that are the root of our life as a nation.

He has allowed a cynical politicization of the First Amendment's freedoms to distract attention from his dishonest tax increases and his own son's billion dollar Savings and Loan bailout.

He has constrained our fellow citizens with the ugly revival of a

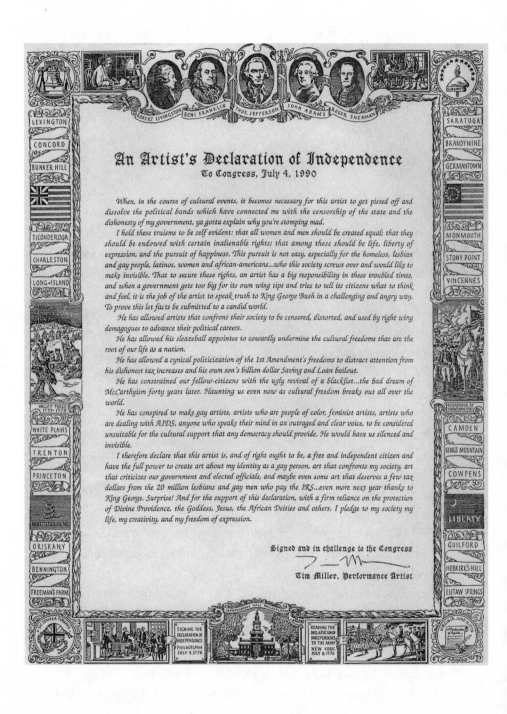

An Artist's Declaration of Independence
To Congress, July 4, 1990

When, in the course of cultural events, it becomes necessary for this artist to get pissed off and dissolve the political bands which have connected me with the censorship of the state and the dishonesty of my government, ya gotta explain why you're stomping mad.

I hold these truisms to be self evident: that all women and men should be created equal; that they should be endowed with certain inalienable rights; that among these should be life, liberty of expression, and the pursuit of happiness. This pursuit is not easy, especially for the homeless, lesbian and gay people, latinos, women and african-americans...who this society screws over and would like to make invisible. That to secure these rights, an artist has a big responsibility in these troubled times, and when a government gets too big for its own wing tips and tries to tell its citizens what to think and feel, it is the job of the artist to speak truth to King George Bush in a challenging and angry way. To prove this let facts be submitted to a candid world.

He has allowed artists that confront their society to be censored, distorted, and used by right wing demagogues to advance their political careers.

He has allowed his sleazeball appointee to cowardly undermine the cultural freedoms that are the root of our life as a nation.

He has allowed a cynical politicization of the 1st Amendment's freedoms to distract attention from his dishonest tax increases and his own son's billion dollar Saving and Loan bailout.

He has constrained our fellow-citizens with the ugly revival of a blacklist...the bad dream of McCarthyism forty years later. Haunting us even now as cultural freedom breaks out all over the world.

He has conspired to make gay artists, artists who are people of color, feminist artists, artists who are dealing with AIDS, anyone who speaks their mind in an outraged and clear voice, to be considered unsuitable for the cultural support that any democracy should provide. He would have us silenced and invisible.

I therefore declare that this artist is, and of right ought to be, a free and independent citizen and have the full power to create art about my identity as a gay person, art that confronts my society, art that criticizes our government and elected officials, and maybe even some art that deserves a few tax dollars from the 20 million lesbians and gay men who pay the IRS...even more next year thanks to King George. Surprise! And for the support of this declaration, with a firm reliance on the protection of Divine Providence, the Goddess, Jesus, the African Deities and others, I pledge to my society my life, my creativity, and my freedom of expression.

Signed and in challenge to the Congress

Tim Miller, Performance Artist

blacklist—the bad dream of McCarthyism, forty years later. Haunting us even now as cultural freedom breaks out all over the world.

He has conspired to make gay artists, artists who are people of color, feminist artists, artists who are dealing with AIDS, anyone who speaks their mind in an outraged and clear voice, to be considered unsuitable for the cultural support that any democracy should provide. He would have us silenced and invisible.

I therefore declare that this artist is, and of right ought to be, a free and independent citizen and have the full power to create art about my identity as a gay person, art that confronts my society, art that criticizes our government and elected officials, and maybe even some art that deserves a few tax dollars from the twenty million lesbian and gay men who pay the IRS—even more next year thanks to King George. Surprise! And for the support of this declaration, with a firm reliance on the protection of Divine Providence, the Goddess, Jesus, the African Deities and others, I pledge to my society my life, my creativity, and my freedom of expression.

Signed and in challenge to the Congress,

Tim Miller, Performance Artist

Excerpts from Jim Miller's Deposition in Finley et al. vs. the National Endowment for the Arts et al., *1992*

PRE-CENSORSHIP

My understanding of the artistic statement was that it should include what I think I am doing, who I think I am as an artist, what my work is about. And actually I think this is probably the best artist's statement I have ever written, really what I am interested in doing as an artist. Plus it is easy to read. And short. What I hoped it would indicate is my seriousness, aggressiveness, that I am very contextualized with where I come from as a third-generation Angelino. . . . That I see being an artist as drawing on many parts of my life: my role I play as an AIDS activist, as a gay rights activist, my role I play in my family. That I am deeply defined as a gay man. . . .

Somebody from the NEA called me. . . . It was very clear to me they did not want to receive, they did not want to acknowledge this as an artist's statement. . . . I felt like they were trying somehow to maneuver me to send in something else. . . . They wanted to pre-censor me by getting something blander . . . they hoped I would submit a new statement. And I categorically refused.

It was a very unusual Kafka-esque encounter. . . . They were somehow trying to finagle me into submitting something else that was, quote, more appropriate. I took it to mean less politicized, less specific, more veiled, more highfalutin, less queer. Those signals I have been hearing since I was two years old. I am very tuned in to when people are trying to tell you, "would you please just shut up," or "don't be a loud obnoxious fag artist."

"HIS WORK IS ALWAYS POLITICAL"

QUESTION [reading from a *Washington Times* article]: "His work is always political." Do you believe that is an accurate statement?

TIM MILLER: I only believe that is accurate [because] unfortunately in this culture anything that an out lesbian-gay artist does is perceived as always political.

THE STRESS OF SYMBOLHOOD

QUESTION: Can you tell me how emotional trauma and mental distress manifests itself?

TIM MILLER: Not having time to do anything but deal with this crisis. . . . The total emotional drain of both being sought after for comment and talking about nothing that has anything to do with your work other than its potential controversy—that really knocked the hell out of being able to create any work. It threw me out of sync for probably a year. And the tremendous stress it created at the organization I run: the controversy dominated the life of that organization because of its association with me. . . .

The extreme disorientation that comes from having your work held up for ridicule and for mischaracterization, and that wherever you perform people were seeing you differently. My image at that point was that people were trying to find what would be potentially shocking or homoerotic or politically transgressive—and that ruined general audience response to the work for a period of six months or a year. . . .

I do a lot of things, many of them for free, including running Highways. But suddenly the enormous time it took up, as well as the time it took to process the emotional battering—whether it's seeing your performances mutilated on TV, or made to look absurd, or debating neo-nazis in Huntington Beach—all of which I could have filtered myself from more if I had been ready to just not talk about it, not engage, not go to public forums. But I am so concerned about the assaults on freedom of speech in this country, to not do that would be to me an ultimate wimp. And so that wasn't really an option. These were things I felt like I had to do then, that the crisis situation demanded that I do, but it took lots and lots of time and energy.

THERE IS SUCH A THING AS BAD PUBLICITY

Negative press creates negative events for presenters, as it did in Dallas where they had to not use the money they had been initially awarded for their season. In a conservative city like Dallas it became almost a crippling blow to this organization who, to their credit, did not cancel their contract with us, which would have been much easier for them. . . .

I have not been presented by another lesbian-gay theater since that time. It inhibits before people even begin to think about it, because these people talk to other people who say, "oh, we presented Tim and Holly, but we had huge problems. We couldn't use our grant money. We ended up losing money on that event." Some gigs don't even begin to be discussed because of this.

In San Diego I was performing at Sushi Performance Gallery, the only space that has presented all four of the NEA Four, and because of that has come under a constant right-wing attack, to the point that they're on the verge of closing. Whenever I performed there, this becomes a major trauma topic, because they're committed to presenting us, but their association with us has also added to their troubles and burdens.

Two Supreme Court Reports, 1998

ORAL ARGUMENT: TIM MILLER'S
SUPREME COURT REPORT

April 1, 1998

I am back from my day in court, the Supreme Court that is. It was a crazy journey to go to D.C. for two days to be at the oral argument for the last driblets of the NEA Four case, but I am glad that I made the effort and schlepped to see the spectacle of the Supremes finally taking on the Culture War. I took a late flight to D.C., spent the night at my brother's house in McLean, Virginia, around the corner from Ken Starr's house, and was woken up at 6:30 A.M. by my two fabulous nephews bouncing up and down on my bed saying "Uncle Tim! Uncle Tim!" Interesting to have my adventure in court as a queer artist begin in the lap of the heterosexual family unit.

I managed to coffee up and make the morning commute with my brother Greg to Arlington where I hopped on the Metro. For once in my life I am early for something! I meet my great friend photographer Dona McAdams at Union Station and we stroll to the Court. The camera piranhas are already gathered, waiting for fresh meat. Skirting the long line—I know we are on a list with the U.S. Marshal—I walk up the long steep marble stairs of the Supreme Court and all at once it feels like a sword and sandals epic from the '50s. Dona and I go through many layers of security as we run into Karen Finley and Holly Hughes and Esther Newton also waiting in line. Other familiar faces from the last years of this controversy: ACLU lawyers, journalists, Willem Dafoe and other

Press conference at the U.S. Supreme Court, 1988: (from left) Holly Hughes, Roberto Bedoya (executive director, National Association of Artists' Organizations), Karen Finley, lead attorney David Cole (Center for Constitutional Rights), Tim Miller. Photo by Dona Ann McAdams.

Wooster Group folk. For a moment it feels strangely like a high school reunion.

Finally we get in and take our seats. I am sitting next to a woman from the NEA who seems to think we should be buddies, even though we are on opposite sides in this case and I believe it is shameful that not a single one of the NEA bureaucrats ever resigned in protest. Dona is on my right and Karen next to her, Holly and Esther further down. The room is high and pillared with big faggy swags of bordello-red fabric between. The tall ceiling is covered with the usual marble bas reliefs of humpy workers and wise men passing judgment. Directly above where the Justices sit is a marble carving of two men with excellent abdominals sitting on thrones side by side. One is bearded (Steve Reeves as Hercules), the other smooth shaven, boyish but built. These carvings will be the perfect backdrop for the day in that not too distant future (I hope) when this court will finally pass judgment on lesbian and gay marriage.

Oyez! Oyez! Oyez! The judges come in—the Big Daddies, even though two of them are women. Every disciplinary visit to the principal's office in elementary school comes back to me as the Justices take their seats. Once in fourth grade, Principal Lambas made me fill a dixie cup with my own spit in his office after I had spit on another boy in my class. This was Principal Lambas's idea of a just punishment. It takes a very long time to fill a big dixie cup with your own saliva. This was what I remembered as the Supreme Court took their seats.

The oral—was this why I remembered that afternoon in Principal Lambas's office?—arguments begin. They earlier had distributed a pamphlet which instructs us "How to Behave at an Oral Argument." The Justices, who rock a lot in their comfy recliner chairs, seem to me to be quite surly with the Solicitor General, Seth Waxman, presenting the government's case. I start to think the Court is leaning our way. The Solicitor General tries to pitch that the "standards of decency" language is not really censoring speech. "We don't think there is any constitutional problem here." Justice Kennedy seems to reject this and sensibly responds that all art inevitably carries with it "viewpoint" and is by nature vulnerable to curtailment by vague notions of "decency." Clarence Thomas, as usual, says nothing throughout the proceedings. Our lawyer David Cole gets up and I think does very well, though the Justices are on his butt too and will hardly let him finish a sentence. The Court seems annoyed that they are having to deal with this matter. David boldly spins the argument that the speech of artists needs to be protected even when the government has supported it with a grant. The decency rule "singles out art which has a nonconforming or disrespectful viewpoint. Government can't impose an ideological screen" without abridging the First Amendment. The Justices seem skeptical of this notion, or that any "chilling effect" had really happened on account of this language.

Time's up! Suddenly the oral argument is argumentative no more and is done!

It had taken an hour. After eight years of drama and hate mail and blabbing and death threats and demonstrations, it all ended up with the Supreme Court spending an hour on this subject. I felt quite dazed. We were ushered out and the next case was already on. Walking back down the marble stairs, which now felt more like I was leaving Principal Lambas's office than the Forum in Rome, Holly, Karen, and I made our way to a garden of microphones for the press conference. I was dreading having to say something. The part of me that is Mr. Sound Bite was nowhere to be found. It all felt too overwhelming and on the spot. We lined up. Lawyer David Cole was articulate and upbeat. Karen said she felt like she had been in an abusive relationship with Jesse Helms and that he had been sexually harassing her at her workplace. Holly made the crucial point that the reason we even were at the Supreme Court was yet another betrayal by Clinton, who could have let stand the lower court decision that "standards of decency" were an unconstitutional criterion for the funding of the arts. I tried to make the point that younger artists all over the country have received the signal loud and clear that work about sexuality, politics or gender gets in a mess of trouble. I brought up my students at Cal State who struggle through all the censoring shit to try to claim their expression. I wanted to remember that it is the emerging artists that are really getting fucked with this "chilling" limiting of creative speech. That felt like a sensible message to speak to the cameras in front of the Court. It was the best I could manage amid my jet lag in any case.

We walked across the street for a little reception and post-game huddle. I felt really tired. My usual excitement about Democracy in Action (civics class had been one of my favorites) was pretty depleted at this point. Fittingly, as the reception wound down, a bunch of us went and had lunch at the restaurant "America" in Union Station to debrief the day. I think the Court will probably kick the case out and not make a decision. I am pissed off that Clinton challenged the Ninth Circuit decision. I am convinced that though this business with the Supreme Court is a big battle, there are a zillion little struggles that are really where my work needs to be done. Like continuing to dismantle that censor in my head that got put in there through a thousand experiences in my life—including that time when Principal Lambas made me fill up a dixie cup with my own spit. Like making sure we keep Highways open and thriving and training new and fierce artists. Like encouraging my students at Cal State and everywhere else to do our wildest and most truthful work. Like continuing to dig deep into my life as a queer citizen and figure out what the stories are that I need to bring forward for myself and my community.

Your court reporter signing off.

THE DECISION: A SUPREME DRAG

June 25, 1998

While I was performing *Shirts & Skin* at Theater Lab Houston, in the Steers and Queers State, I had to pause as the naked, clothespins-on-nipples climax of my show moved through me. I realized that at that exact moment industrious little District of Columbia elves were probably proofing, collating, and stapling copies of the Supreme Court decision on whether "general standards of decency" were a constitutional criterion as applied to federal funding of the arts. This was going to be the last roundup of the NEA Four case.

What could be indecent about me anyhow? Is the fact that I am outspokenly a gay man indecent? Is the fact that my performance work lovingly details my experiences growing up queer in this fucked-up society indecent? Is the fact that I explore the rich terrain of sexuality, so full of feeling and discovery, indecent? Is the fact that I take off my clothes in my shows and try to acknowledge that our bodies actually exist under our clothes indecent?

As I finished my show, full of all the complexity, memory and metaphor that naked queer flesh is heir to, I knew that it was just a matter of days before I would find out whether my indecent ass was

Los Angeles protest against politicization of the National Endowment for the Arts, 1990: (from left) Alan Pulner, Tim Miller, and Jordan Peimer. Photo by Chuck Stallard.

grass. Let's face it, there in the Lone Star state, as in one third of these United States, it is still against the law to have queer sex! How much could I rationally expect from any governmental body in our troubled country?

Well, the Supremes decided that it was okey-dokey not to fund "indecent art." The law "neither inherently interferes with First Amendment rights nor violates constitutional vagueness principles," Justice Sandra Day O'Connor wrote in her majority opinion. In a disappointing 8–1 decision the high court hitched up with Helms and his ilk and said the National Endowment for the Arts can consider "decency" in deciding who gets public money for the arts. I was grateful that at least Justice David H. Souter showed he was sensible to the reality of how much artists have been under assault in this country for the last ten years. He was the lone Justice who dissented, saying the law should be struck down as unconstitutional because it is "substantially overbroad and carries with it a significant power to chill artistic production and display."

I wasn't surprised when I heard the decision early in the morning of June 25. This was, after all, the same Supreme Court, if not the same white men in black robes, that had ruled in the 1857 Dred Scott decision that African-Americans could not come before the high court because they were not citizens. This was also the same court that decided in *Bowers v. Hardwick* in 1986 that it was constitutionally cool for the State of Georgia to have laws that make it illegal for gay people to have sex with one another in the privacy of their bedrooms. Understandably, I had low expectations all along that queer artists would be allowed our fair share at the Federal feedbag. (That's the last cowboy reference, I promise!)

But part of me was still shocked. Can the justices not understand how censorious this language is? How often seemingly bland words like "decency" or "normal" or "natural" have been used to discriminate against lesbians and gay men and as weapons against us?

I spent the day of the announcement doing dozens of interviews, spinning away the sound bites like the good gay artist/activist that I am supposed to be. I was available to whoever called—the *New York Times*, the *Los Angeles Times*, the *Philadelphia Inquirer*, the Australian Broadcasting Corporation, and my Mom! But late in the day it started to really hit me. The Supreme Court, the Big Daddy court in the land, thinks it's okay not to support artists whose voice and vision is outside the middle-of-the-suburban-mall sensibility of some fantasy America. I became so depressed that I had to resort to two pints of Ben & Jerry's Cherry Garcia and a half-hour with an Eastern European gay porn movie. Then I became very pissed-off.

Okay, Mr. & Ms. Supreme Court, the gloves are off. It's no more Mr. Nice Gay Guy! I am not going to be satisfied with small potatoes anymore. You could have gotten off easy by tossing a tidbit my way and allowing this queer artist the illusion that I am an equal citizen and worthy of support from the NEA should it be awarded. The truth is I didn't have a snowball's chance in a Houston heatwave to ever get support from the NEA again regardless of what decision the Supreme Court made. So I am going to up the ante of what I expect from the U.S. government. I now want the *whole* ball of wax, the cart *and* the horses, my cake *and* the eating too!

I've got a little list.

I'm not going to be content anymore with the odd NEA grant that used to get tossed to gay film festivals and queer performance artists. I want the *full* measure of my rights as a gay American citizen. I want it now!

I want the Employee Non-Discrimination Act passed by Congress *yesterday*. I'm sick of this shit that lesbians and gay men can be fired without recourse from their jobs, fired just because of who they are!

And while we're at it, repeal all the damned sodomy laws in those medieval states that still have them on the books. These bigoted statutes make the U.S. an outlaw nation that could not participate in the economic community of European nations without striking them all down. Not only does this country censor our queer art, but they also make laws against our queer bodies! Cut it out, now!

I want the government to put at its highest priority the creation of safe streets for lesbians and gay men. Why is it that I can't find it surprising that two men I have been in relationships with have almost been killed in gay-bashing incidents? Fix it quick or I'm going to get cranky!

I want the anti-gay military shit to stop right now! Hey, you generals, don't ask me, don't tell me anything! Get off your five-star dildo and make the military safe for the dykes and fags that want to be there and are not bothering anybody. (You won't find me in uniform, but that doesn't matter.) Instead, why don't you pick on the white supremacists the military seems to breed, who end up exploding buildings and killing black folks!

I want immigration rights for lesbian and gay men pronto! This is real personal because my boyfriend Alistair is from Australia. Our relationship is denied the rights that every heterosexual person has in this country, to be able to turn their lover into a U.S. citizen. Not long ago, I was speaking to the Diversity Council of the University of Arizona. Suddenly I found myself weeping crazily at this big public meeting. All at once I actually felt the deep hurt of the fact that my relationship, this deepest personal place of who I love, is completely unseen and unvalued by my culture. I felt the terror in my guts that Alistair will have to leave this country. Well, U.S. government, give me immigration rights for our lovers or I am going to get *really* unpleasant!

While I'm on a roll, I want the whole kit-n-caboodle of full marriage rights too! Now that you've annoyed me, I'm not going to settle for any second class domestic partnership benefits. I want full church-sanctioned marriages. Any denomination that denies gay people our civil right/rite of marriage will lose their tax-deductible status. How 'bout that? One more thing, I want the government to guarantee us the man or woman of our dreams to marry! . . . This last point is negotiable. I don't want to be unreasonable.

That is a good start. Lovely readers, feel free to add a couple of dozen of your own demands too! I don't want this outrage from the Supreme Court to depress me any more than it already has. I can't afford too many pints of Ben & Jerry's—I need to stay on the naked performance artist diet! I would rather get pissed-off and feisty and look forward to the day when this particular decision will seem as absurd and embarrassing as *Plessy v. Ferguson* does to us today.

I will look forward to the time (in the not too distant future, I hope), when a teacher will step before a community college class exploring late twentieth century social movements and say, "Now, students, I know it is shocking to believe this, but there was once a time as recent as the late 1990s when lesbian and gay men were actually denied certain civil rights within our democratic society. The Supreme Court even upheld a series of laws that constitutionally discriminated against them!"

Until that day in school, I'm in it for the long haul.

An Anarchic, Subversive, Erotic Soul

Interview with Steven Durland

In 1991, in the immediate aftermath of the NEA Four defunding, The Drama Review *published this interview along with the full text of Jim Miller's* Stretch Marks *as part of a special segment labeled "Offensive Plays." Durland, editor-in-chief of* High Performance, *focused the interview on questions of how newfound notoriety might affect both external and internal aspects of Jim Miller's performance work. The excerpts here are adapted from* The Drama Review.

STEVEN DURLAND: What was your view of the NEA before the initial [Andres] Serrano controversy?

TIM MILLER: Over the years, people have been involved in discussions about the relative cleanliness or dirtiness of various kinds of money. I got my first grant during the Reagan administration with a piece that directly criticized the government, so I felt good about the Peer Panel system. It was free of a certain kind of political influence and patronage. These recent incidents were concocted. They're coming from direct outside agitation—requesting files and utilizing people's congressional abilities to call out the Government Accounting Office or the IRS to attack individuals and organizations. The heart of it touches on so many things—First Amendment, sex, politics—it's pretty juicy terrain. There's a whole other political agenda that's going on here, to undermine diverse cultural voices and political artwork.

DURLAND: In the midst of all the scrutiny from the media and the government, what aspects of your work have undergone change?

MILLER: For the last two-and-a-half months I've mostly been focused on responding. I made one attempt to begin this new piece. The work that I've been doing feels different since all this mess. Every review in Seattle referred to my work as "pornographic," a word that I don't think had ever been used in a review before. What Holly [Hughes] calls "the people" are in there with a clicker noticing what might be problematic or objectionable.

DURLAND: Were they saying "pornographic" pejoratively or just picking up on the rhetoric in the media?

MILLER: The criticism mostly referred to "Civil Disobedience Weekend," which admittedly does describe a homosexual orgy that brings down the Bush administration. But that's been reviewed seven or eight times, and no one has ever drawn those conclusions. It's sort of a general, Jimmy Stewart–type queer persona I project, and it has always been received as that. Suddenly it feels more threatening. They don't see the humor in it as much. The frame this is providing brings up a whole set of interesting choices. Do I do "Civil Disobedience Weekend," so that it fulfills everyone's expectations of this anarchic, subversive, erotic universe? Or something like the "Maw of Death" section from *Some Golden States,* which frustrates people's expectations? Or do a reading of *Spoon River Anthology?*

DURLAND: [Groups] of people you might characterize as anarchist, nihilist, or maybe violent revolutionaries probably identify strongly with your situation. How closely do you identify with them?

MILLER: I share lots of things with my anarchist friends in San Francisco. My strongest identity is as a part of ACT UP—one of *the* genuine, authentic social movements of our time that's restructuring things within the lineage of civil rights—something at least resembling a mass fringe movement. When I go to perform somewhere, ACT UP is a larger community I'm part of. I always tune in to the local chapter, and they tend to be everywhere I go. On the other hand, hopefully, except in weak moments, I'm not telling other people that they can or can't think something. I'm definitely more of a reformer. Living in California, the state that provides Republican presidents and the money that elects them, it's harder to disconnect from the forces that govern our country and most of the world. You're less apt to totally disassociate or think you can create structures without addressing them.

DURLAND: When you were writing *Stretch Marks,* which parts of it challenged you the most personally? Where were the edges where you had to debate whether to keep lines or scenes, or take them out? Not the kinds of lines and scenes you take out because they're not working, but the kind you take out because you're approaching your own limits?

MILLER: I've definitely tempered the manifesto section. That bit of text has created a lot of trouble for me—people feel it's too art-in-the-social-realm-mandate kind of thing. Which maybe it was, but at the time I wrote it, it was very genuine, and maybe the dialog has developed too, since all the NEA stuff. It's a text that I modified because of the harsh discord around it and people feeling attacked by it. In terms of sex stuff—like talking about being fucked by Richard Nixon while hanging over the audience—I've done that text in fairly different situations. I did it standing in a baptismal font above the audience in Miami.

DURLAND: One of the things you said, if I'm not mistaken, in your manifesto was that you didn't want to see another piece deconstructing print advertising. Why such hostility toward the form and what would you like artists tackling?

MILLER: There is a whole style of performance that was primarily concerned with the insignificant or the arcane that at a certain point just made me want to throw hand grenades onstage. I would sit in the theater or art gallery literally pretending I had a grenade in my hand. The monolithic idea around at the time I started making work in the late '70s was that political art was bad, that art that was connected to the world was feeble. That art coming out of communities was like folk art. People would bad-mouth work connected to issues. Especially work that even sniffed of social work. . . . What I want to see and what we're seeing all over is—in our own fumbling fucked-up way—people trying to take art out of the academic environment. And mostly failing, but trying to place it in different situations, trying to tackle stuff and connect with different kinds of audiences. The NEA stuff puts a big, big challenge to us to create some kind of new social contract about what an artist does.

DURLAND: Suddenly the cutting-edge artists are in bed with the indigenous artists, with the political artists, with the socially concerned artists—people who were at opposite ends of the spectrum ten or fifteen years ago. What do you think has brought all that about?

MILLER: Reagan and AIDS, I think. I'm not sure in which order. My work really started after Reagan's inauguration; a lot of us were forged by this unbelievable event. I sort of burst onto New York with all that post-punk expressiveness. Work should be about things. It should be talking. It should be pushy. Away from the formal clarity, line, design, or minimalism. Away from the cooler visual theater that characterized a certain kind of performance in New York in the mid-'70s. I think things began to change at that point. Shortly after that, Artists Call, all the Youth Movement stuff, the Performing Artists for Nuclear Disarmament started happening.

DURLAND: You have been heavily involved in very activist work for the last few months—almost exclusively. Do you see this as a temporary necessity or is this becoming a preferred mode?

MILLER: In the early '80s I was sporadically involved with neighborhood issues in the Lower East Side—gentrification, antinuke stuff, gay political stuff. After '83 or '84, as people began to create a political-culture response to AIDS, several things happened. The '86 *High Performance* issue documented a whole set of responses pre–ACT UP. ACT UP is the single most influential thing in my life, as a model, as a worldview, as a kind of cultural practice. Especially since artists have played such a big role all over the country in forming this kind of political response, giving it spectacle.

DURLAND: The early kinds of participation you were talking about, I would tend to characterize as an artist behaving as a citizen. At what point did those two things merge inextricably for you?

MILLER: I think it paralleled a lot of people's growing involvement or merging of their identities—from going to a few meetings to becoming more involved. It's given us one of the few models of artist activism. In the last year, it's become more and more of my life, between my involvement with ACT UP and with the various anticensorship actions I've helped coordinate. I don't imagine I would be as involved with ACT UP if I were married with two kids. It's because there's a personal stake within my community and whatever the future holds for myself that creates this rationale. It's deeply personal.

DURLAND: Is it becoming problematic to think in terms of a stage and an audience and the more traditional forms you've worked in?

MILLER: Right now it's hard because I don't have time to make new work. On the other hand, I can hardly wait to go to Austin next week. I'm heading into a really juicy situation. I mean this is not just a gig: I go to Austin and I'm there as a provocateur. There's a huge crisis going on at UT. There was a big kiss-in and then all this right-wing reaction and violence. They're in the middle of an election and our performances are somehow seen as a weird political football. It'd be a relief, once in a while, to have just a gig. Every gig I've gone to in the last three months has meant going right to something happening—a protest because [NEA chair John] Frohnmayer thinks he can go to the Seattle Opera without being hassled or whatever. That's a very recent state of affairs. You don't get to go to the theater at all.

DURLAND: What do you consider the relationship between what is personally dangerous in your work—that you might choose to self-censor—and what has been deemed publicly offensive and potentially censorable by the government?

MILLER: My manifesto file in my personal archive gets fatter all the time. The manifesto section in *Stretch Marks* stretches people. Audiences get nervous. They think it's a leftist diatribe or anti-formalist or accusatory. "Civil Disobedience Weekend," because of its anarchic sexuality, is challenging to people. They both make audiences uncomfortable. At certain times I've performed the little nudity section in *Buddy Systems* or *Some Golden States* where there are lots of teenage girls in the audience. Maybe it doesn't seem like the best idea, but I don't think I've ever cut it out or kept my underwear on.

DURLAND: How has the situation affected the evolution of your work?

MILLER: It gives me more confidence and the belief that it matters to be doing it and that you need to speak louder and clearer. I'm very careful about seeing the silver lining in any of this because I think there's very little silver lining. Especially for younger artists. I think this really inhibits younger artists: you won't get money, you won't get support, people will be afraid to present you. And you don't want to do it to fulfill people's prurient interests. Karen Finley's always had these people. I remember at The Kitchen, sometimes it'd seem there'd be four or five men making strange motions underneath their overcoats. Weird kinds of people coming for the scandal and all that.

DURLAND: Even more so at her late-night club performances, when the whole male, black-leather crowd would show up and treat her more like a stripper than an artist. You've evolved from work that was more dance-oriented to more text-oriented. Do you think gestures are safer than text? Given, for instance, that text can be quoted out of context, although certainly gestures can too, given Karen's trouble.

MILLER: Well, for a long time I had a certain theory that performance, because of its ephemeral nature, was safe from this because you couldn't really plop it down on Congress people's desks. Obviously that was false, because the descriptions or mis-descriptions seem quite enough to get people worked up. With or without the more confrontational Mapplethorpe photos that [Senator Jesse] Helms would invite people into his office to look at. I'm just more interested in texts now because they're more specific. And it seems we're in a very specific time when words matter a lot. And you probably can't translate your piece for, say, France—and you wouldn't want to. They can import or create their own visions.

DURLAND: Do you have a sense of gesture informing the verbal aspects of your work?

MILLER: I think of it more as actions. In *Stretch Marks* the visual things that delight me create fun performance actions. Like an airplane that you can be. It takes the light. It's funny. It creates shtick. It creates movements that connect back to the text. Those are the kinds of things—a toilet coming from the ceiling—that refer to all kinds of things: slapstick, Dada. That weird gene of human delight informs all kinds of things we enjoy.

DURLAND: You seem to provide the audience with a certain level of entertainment, perhaps as a way of making the pill easier to swallow.

MILLER: We are part of a movement toward a theatricalized performance. All these are scripted performances. For the most part— allowing for energy and momentum and shamanic possession— the form has become more comic, autobiographical, text-heavy, transformational. Bowing to the conventional Western theatrical time of an hour and a half, maybe you buy a whole bill of goods. Does that mean you also have conventional Western notions of "entertainment"? I hated theater because it was boring as shit. All these people being characters. I'd lost what I liked about theater or the theatrical, which was ritual, humor, body—stuff realistic theater had left at baggage claim. Performance is ready to draw on anything, from vaudeville to ritual suicide.

DURLAND: What's untouchable for you right now as an artist? Where do you draw the line?

MILLER: I think I would shy away from direct anal penetration onstage, for example. Or some kind of direct, live sex act. I would definitely not kill an animal onstage. I disrupt performances where that happens, or where the carcass of a dead animal is abused and its being is not respected. I would not do that kind of performance just because I live with animals. I've seen people kill animals onstage in a way that I think had integrity. Performance artist Elia Arce as part of the Cinco de Mayo celebration at Highways killed a fish onstage. But since she cooked the fish and everyone ate it by the end of the night, I think a certain kind of cultural respect for killing animals for *food* was respected and transformed.

DURLAND: Do your limits as an artist coincide with your limits as a programmer or administrator?

MILLER: We allow a lot more stuff to happen at Highways. The only thing I think we would really discourage is something that physically endangers the audience.

DURLAND: This climate has produced a whole rash of work that is much more "out there" than the work that was happening pre-controversy. Is it censorship to not deal with that work? If the artists become more aggressive, are you forced to become more liberal in your curating? Can you maintain standards that might mean excluding some of the new work that's coming out and still escape charges of censorship?

MILLER: I think it's really vital for people to react to their time. Especially young artists. People have to find their boundaries. I'm sure there will now be a whole school of work that is purely about confrontation, as opposed to it being part of what you're doing.

If you want to hit your head against a wall, you need a wall. We're flexible enough at Highways—it hasn't felt like it has come up so much yet.

DURLAND: At the base of this whole censorship issue is a notion of respect. Is being subversive necessarily disrespectful?

MILLER: I think the whole idea that everyone can get along and that everybody is the same is an idea we have to abandon. This right-wing idea that everyone should do the same thing, think the same thing, is not true. And it's a lot of what this is about. "Subversive" is a real value-laden word to suggest that actually giving voice to your point of view is only for confrontational purposes when in fact it's happening for representation, for community building. That question assumes that subversion is the agenda or the purpose. And in some texts it is. Most of my experiences as a performer have very little to do with subversion and more to do with entertaining the troops or cheerleading.

DURLAND: Well, in terms of that idea and the idea of respect, you've suggested—even though the NEA isn't willing to admit it—that the reason you were refused a grant was because you said (and correct this quote if it's off a little), "Jesse Helms should keep his Porky Pig face out of my asshole." Is that right?

MILLER: I think, "out of the NEA and my asshole."

DURLAND: OK, "the NEA and my asshole." Now, I would suggest that those are fighting words in just about any context. Would you consider it inconsistent on your part to expect the system you've just confronted to entitle you to a measure of respect?

MILLER: Making fun of political figures is a deep, rich tradition in this country. In political cartoons, in essays, in films. It's very much part of our cultural life. It's part of a democratic society to be ready to shake it up. It's part of not taking your hat off to the king. And Jesse Helms is not the king to begin with. This is an attempt to muzzle people. There's absolutely no reason you can't criticize the senator from North Carolina. In fact, the only way you could face yourself in the mirror the next morning, or continue to think you'd want to get any money from the federal government, is if they're real clear that you're going to make work that's queer and critical of right-wing radicals like Senator Helms. And if that's suddenly no longer possible in this country, then it means this country has shifted. The reason I say this is that the first NEA grant that I ever got was for *Postwar.* There's an extended section where someone dressed as Ronald Reagan is beating the shit out of me while I'm trying to order the world with the *World Book Encyclopedia.* That was the work sample I sent for the first NEA grant I ever got. At that time I made a deal with myself to only show the most challenging work. That was a piece I was performing all over Europe when we were deploying a new generation of short-range nuclear missiles. There were riots in the streets in all the Western European capitals. If suddenly we are now considered state artists and are signing away our ability to criticize our social structures, then the rules of the game have changed.

The Battle of Chattanooga

A pernicious effect of the "culture war" has been the media-stoked "controversies" that result when performances by Tim Miller are scheduled, particularly in smaller cities. "The Battle of Chattanooga" recounts a 1999 episode in Tennessee—hardly unique, as discussed in his lawsuit deposition and shown by similar events in Dallas, Durham, Seattle, and elsewhere. As Miller notes, these episodes are typically initiated by self-characterized concerned supporters of the arts who seek to cancel controversial presentations in order not to jeopardize funding for sponsoring institutions—the arts equivalent of destroying a village in order to save it.

This account situates Miller's post-NEA troubles within the context of his knowledge of American history, suggesting how intricately Miller weaves his defense of his rights and responsibilities as an artist activist with his belief in the rights that have been guaranteed to—yet all too frequently denied— various groups of American citizens.

As a wandering queer performer who travels to up to forty cities a year, I have a front row seat to witness the lively diversity of audiences and artists who gather in hundreds of gay theaters, arts centers, bookstores, choruses, and film festivals. On the other hand, almost as often I am witness to the homophobic fights that seep out of the septic tank whenever a lesbian or gay man dares to raise their voice in much of troubled America. The much-touted "culture war" has been more a fight over whose voices get heard—whose memories and life story matter—than over whose money is being spent.

Recently I performed in Chattanooga at Barking Legs Theater, sponsored by the Chattanooga Performing Arts Center. I had imagined that this might be a garden-variety gig. I would fly in on a small commuter airplane from Atlanta or Memphis or Raleigh/Durham, meet the local queer and artist energies, teach a workshop, do my shows, get on the plane, hope my check wouldn't bounce, and go home to snuggle with my boyfriend Alistair.

But I soon realized that this was going to be "one of those gigs." One of those gigs where a local art bureaucrat, or a Baptist minister or the local KKK, decides to politicize my generally good-natured gay presence in a city and try to get the feathers flying. In this case a woman named Molly Casse, the head of Allied Arts, the local consortium of arts organizations, sent up the Jolly Roger by imagining that I was going to bring wrack and ruin to the arts infrastructure of Greater Chattanooga. It's interesting to me how frequently the opening shots of these battles are fired not by the local fundamentalists, who are happily unaware of the alternative arts community in their own backyard, but by supposedly well-meaning local arts funders. Funders or fundees, it doesn't make much of a difference—you're in a pickle either way. Without the hue and cry raised by these arts "advocate" types, the local right-wing minister would be no more hip to my presence in Chattanooga than I am to his church's pancake breakfast fund-raiser. But once these panic-meister municipal funding agencies get on the ball—look out! Artists' heads are sure to roll. They project their own homophobia and hallucinatory fear of having to explain things, and turn what is not even a blip on the right wing's radar screen into a full-scale front-page-of-the-newspaper war.

Ms. Casse got on the phone and began sending out panic-filled signals about how my arrival in Chattanooga would lower the water table! corrupt the children! poison the Tennessee River! God knows what else. As she said to the *Chattanooga Times Free Press,* "We are very concerned that his appearance here will be offensive and could jeopardize the funding all our agencies get from Allied Arts. We don't want to be the arts police, but we feel strongly about community standards." Her generous sharing of her homophobia and artphobia with whoever would listen quickly resulted in raising the awareness of the local press, who started to report on a story that existed only because Molly Casse made sure that it showed up on their radar screens. A journalist began making calls to conservative churches, and we had a full scale civil (culture) war brewing, complete with nightly protest demonstrations on the streets of Chattanooga. The *Chattanooga Times* eventually ran a piece on the front page of the Sunday paper, to let everyone know who didn't already that a big gay performance artist was coming to town to frighten the horses. Just in time for Sunday sermons, the article got more folks worked up. Suddenly the congregations were roiling, the First Amendment arts supporters were sending solidarity checks, and the audience was making lots of reservations.

A worried e-mail from Barking Legs Theater raised a red flag for me, that maybe they were getting ready to cut their losses, play it safe and cancel my engagement in Chattanooga. Had I been better acquainted with these arts folks in Tennessee, I would have known they were not made of such cautious fiber. Oh Courageous Spirit of the Daughters and Sons of the Volunteer State! I needn't have worried about it for a second! Nonetheless, since at that time I had no solid information on the backbone-content of the organizers, I didn't want to make it easy on them to cancel. As a tonic spine-stiffener, I quickly bought my plane ticket and sent them the flight information to make the whole thing feel non-refundable.

To tell the truth, I was feeling a little spooked about what kind of nuts had been unleashed in Tennessee. I have had more than my share of death threats and hate mail over the years, but for some reason this situation in Chattanooga had hit me hard. Maybe because it's the smallest city in the South that I will have ever performed in! The pressure that was being put on the theater in 1999 seemed so retro, so early culture war: obviously we are still fighting that war. The Artistic Director of Barking Legs Theater, Ann Law, kept me updated on the dramas surrounding the gig and the clumsy threats of what might happen if I did indeed perform. Happily the shows had sold out—what a front-page story in the daily newspaper will do!—and Ann let me know that people were sending in donation checks of support. In fact, certain prominent people were coming to the show who had never bothered to come to Barking Legs before. I had also been invited by Professor Peter Smith to be a Tennessee Williams Fellow in the Theater Department at the University of the South in Sewanee, Tennessee, as part of my Chattanooga residency. Barking Legs has shifted the financial sponsorship of my shows to them, so the credit (or blame) can be diffused by the cool episcopal halls of academe. No Allied Arts of Chattanooga moneys here!

I must pause now to praise our culture warriors around the U.S., like Ann Law and Prof. Peter Smith, who brave these all-too-frequent dramas. As I dip my spoon into the delicious lesbian and gay culture soup, I find myself in awe of the feisty courage of these people and the messy, human immediacy of our homegrown national queer culture that manages to thrive under the hostile conditions I am describing here. Where would we be without the homo-friendly theaters, alternative art spaces, sleazy drag bars, and independent coffeehouses that enable us to have a unique, non-globalized experience of the edgiest, purest, trashiest, most amazingly fabulous queer expression that money or love can buy? As happy as I am that here in the new millennium we have saucy mainstream representations like *Will & Grace,* it can also be said that the more prime time these images get, the more likely it is they will be sanitized of any juicy sexuality or confrontational politics. I would bet you a round of Cosmopolitans that if we ever get *Will & Grace* action figure dolls, we'll find asexual flat plastic where Jack's & Will's meat and potatoes ought to be! That's why we can be proud of our thriving grassroots lesbian and gay culture that encourages us to be as raunchy, spiritual, or pissed-off as we are in real life. We need to remember the bold arts organizers, straight and gay, that make sure there's a place for this work to happen.

Our community is blessed with heroic lesbian and gay arts organizers all over the country, not just in the big cities, who are making festivals happen on a dream, a song, and frequently *out of their own checkbooks.* If we were to take a tour we might find ourselves in the steamy basement of a St. Louis church where Joan Lipkin, LGBT culture queen of the Show-Me State, is having another packed night of dyke performance. We head north where Howie Baggadonutz has single-handedly made Portland, Oregon, a must stop for every gay touring artist. Cut over a few states east on Interstate 94 to Patrick Scully's eponymous Patrick's Cabaret in the Twin Cities, where for years he has nurtured a sex-positive and provocative music, performance and spoken word scene. Then we can scurry down to CSPS arts center in Cedar Rapids, heart of the queer arts in rural Iowa. Dive below the Mason-Dixon Line to the feisty theater Man Bites Dog in Durham, North Carolina, which consistently offers everything from Holly Hughes' *Preaching to the Preverted* to Durham's own St. John's MCC Gay Gospel Choir. Each of these venues, and there are hundreds more, is gathering the artists and energies and audiences in their communities to make the fiercest lesbian and gay culture on the planet. These journeys through Gay Culture USA fill me with optimism for our tribe's community-based arts, the people who make it happen and the diverse audiences that gather to be challenged, emboldened and mirrored. It serves as a poignant reminder how our lives, our politics and our community can be transformed as we raise a ruckus through your own local, neighborhood queer culture. As Chairman Mao—or maybe it was Paul Lynde—said, let a thousand queer flowers bloom!

Here now in Chattanooga, I try to remember that my presence, facilitated by these lively arts organizers, can in some small way really challenge the local brew of homophobia and make it publicly reveal itself. The performances can also be a gathering place for the local forces of diverse (queer & otherwise) progressive hipness to come forward and embolden one another. This realization certainly helps make me understand why I have sat on a noisy tiny turboprop heading from Memphis—I didn't even get to see Graceland!—to Chattanooga!

Though I didn't see the home of the King, I will visit the Civil War battlefields around Chattanooga. For a Civil War buff like me, this is a great opportunity. Get me started on the events of 1863 and I can bore a table full of people quicker than you can say Gettysburg. In the days before flying to Tennessee, I have been reading about the bloody battles at Lookout Mountain, Missionary Ridge, and Chickamauga, just south of town.

I get to Chattanooga late and we go right to the theater to negotiate the grunt work of technical preparations for the show. Other than death threats, technical rehearsals are my least favorite part of this solo-performing racket. But this also gives me a chance to meet the fierce folk who keep the Barking Legs Theater yapping loudly. Ann has pulled this place out of her hat with equal parts chutzpah and her own version of southern charm. She is like an orchestra conductor who has waved her hands over Chattanooga and said, "Presto chango, an alternative performance space on Dodds Avenue!" Her contributions of energy, artistry, and hard work have made a great dance and performance space thrive there on the Tennessee River. Her husband Bruce and fellow workers Charles and Julia have been rafting the white water of the political situation for the last three weeks. Their daughter, the lovely nineteen-month-old Leah, sleeps angelically nearby as we hang the lights. This is my version of American family values: the whole family helps with the technical preparations for the visiting queer performer!

When I arrive at the theater the next day for my performance, there is a palpable cloud of uncertainty. We assume that there will be protesters, but will someone try to get into the sold-out show and heckle the homo? Ann, Charles and I have a tense conversation about how we would handle that. Ann has sensibly engaged an off-duty Chattanooga police officer as a security guard. A physically impressive African-American man in full police uniform including gun, he makes us all let a little exhale happen. As the audience begins to arrive, so do the protesters. They set up shop across the street, a motley bunch of seven or eight men. They have stashed their wives and children at the corner. People arriving for the show are forced to walk past the protesters across the street, who wave their confederate flag (the black cops we hired for security don't seem too thrilled) as they shout the usual charming greetings: *Faggots! God made Adam and Eve, not Adam and Steve! Sodomites burn in hell!* The children down the street join in these cries. This seems to demonstrate this particular church's version of family values: The Family That Mates Together, Hates Together. There is both the rambunctious spirit of a carnival and the fever of a public hanging full of blood lust. The situation is simultaneously absurd and terrifying.

As I warm up for the show, stretching my body and waking up my voice, I take a break and sneak to where I can get a peek at the demonstrators. I see their faces snarling in a bizarre mad-dog hate. What a strange way to spend their weekend evenings! One man in a cowboy hat is working himself into a froth of hate as he screams at the diverse audience of gay people, sensitive straight folk, and college students. An audience member shouts back to the protesters: *Jesus loves you!* At that, the most vicious of them lunges across the street with his confederate flag to slaver more inexplicable hate at his fellow citizens of Chattanooga.

I can hear the protesters shouting the whole time as I perform my show *Shirts & Skin* inside the theater. It adds an edge to the show, that's for sure. I never learned how to handle this in the Stanislavsky exercises in high school drama class. It's odd how *their* symbol of memory, the confederate flag, is being used as a weapon outside a place where *my* most deeply held memories and life-narratives as a gay man are being given a small venue for a couple of nights in Chattanooga. I often think that the culture wars come down to a civil war

Protest against Tim Miller's appearance at Barking Legs Theater, Chattanooga, September 4, 1999. Photo by Chad McClure © 1999 *Chattanooga Times Free Press.*

over memory—whose stories are going to be seen as worthy. With those garrulous shouts and waving flags outside Barking Legs Theater as background for my show, I am led to think about this whole strange terrain of autobiographical performance. I am puzzled by the contrary energies that get unleashed when lesbians and gay men speak up about what we have lived and what we remember.

With the fights and curses from the protest outside the theater still echoing inside my head, I spent the afternoon before my last show at Barking Legs going to the local Civil War battle sites. Many major fights happened here during the Fall of 1863: Missionary Ridge! Lookout Mountain! Chickamauga! At long last I get to prowl the battle site at Chickamauga. In my book *Shirts & Skin* I describe my first impression of Alistair, when we met in London, as "the look of

a scared Scots-Irish boy about to be slaughtered at Chickamauga" —
so of course I have to go see what ghosts dwell there.

I wanted to walk these battlefields — to savor the narratives echoing there — even as I continue finding myself in the middle of my
own mini Civil War. Allow me a moment of drama-queenism: the
images of the protesters waving the rebel flag, so fresh in my mind,
made me realize how much the war is still going on. As I look over
battle maps in the Civil War book from my childhood, I see so
clearly a connection between then and what I am doing now. Another piece of the ongoing struggle to make this fucked up country
less fucked up, to make more airspace for more different kinds of
people. The front lines have changed and the *dramatis personae* have
shifted somewhat. The flags are pretty similar, though we might add
a few more colors for a rainbow flag. All our nation's civil wars surround us everyday. I hope that this week in Chattanooga I have
managed to make a little more breathing room for queer people and
their friends.

I drove the few miles into North Georgia to Chickamauga. After
a depressingly ugly series of chicken stands and used car lots, the battlefield has the prim tidiness typical of the National Park Service. It
was a relief to leave the grim storefronts *(Battlefield Muffler and Ra-
diator)* and tawdry billboards *(Good Cars for Good Christian People)*
of the highway and pull into green Chickamauga.

As I walked the vast, lush landscape looking for Snodgrass Hill
where Union General George Thomas, "the Rock of Chickamauga,"
saved the Federal troops from a total rout (I know this stuff, I can't
help it!), I thought about my own little corner of history, my own
performance-art Snodgrass Hill as it were. I know have a big story to
tell right now. It fills my memory. It's a story of how I met a man
from another land and how I want to be with him, but my country,
which I both love and hate, doesn't allow such things. I need to tell
this story or I will go crazy. When I tell my story I can howl out the
rage I feel both at our medieval government and my own shortcomings as a man and a lover. I can draw attention to the injustice. This

telling becomes a completely necessary act, an act of looking at the past as a means of negotiating a more empowered and grounded relationship to an uncertain future. Each in our own way, Alistair and I are tending our memory as a way of creating a future together.

I wandered back to the car and drove back toward Chattanooga. My last stop on my war tour was Orchard Knob, at the foot of Missionary Ridge. There's a big monument there in the midst of greater Chattanooga. On the ground surrounding the marble cupola dedicated to Illinois or Iowa was debris from contemporary battles: a quart bottle of King Cobra Malt Liquor, a Big Burger Bag, and three red used Hygeia condoms, still moist from their recent action. How blurry the edges between what happened once and what breathes and struggles, triumphs and fails now! I recognize the swirl of this debris there at the battlefield monument. How familiar these struggles seem to me when I consider my own life: the slaughter of so many of my comrades-in-love by AIDS, the posturing of Carolina senators, the human frailty of all of us, the sex and love moist under the pocked and gray marble of our history.

Later that night after the final show, I went outside on Dodds Avenue after all the protesters had gone home. After I thanked the African-American cop for looking after us, he said to me, "Oh, it's no problem. Those folks started waving that damn flag in my face and I went and put tickets on all their cars. They got no business here. These gay folks are good neighbors. Live and let live, that's what I say." I felt buoyed by this expression of native good sense. I felt hopeful enough to go enjoy real Chattanooga barbecue with Ann, Bruce, and baby Leah.

On the plane back to Los Angeles, I was hypnotized by the rolling green beneath me. I realized again my completely unsubstantiated faith that if I tell my story to my country, I may be able to affect how the narrative will end. The hypocritical senator will be exposed, the lovers reunited, fairness will triumph—okay, I watched too many Capra movies as a kid! I perform stories of who I have been in order to imagine who I might become—who we might become.

It's my own flag that I furl from theater marquees all across the land. In some ways the protesters in Chattanooga are right to try to silence these stories. Our narratives throw down an enormous challenge for our country to drag itself kicking and screaming into a new century and to finally create space for all of our voices.

Coda

Notorious me

From Jim Miller's journal, 1992.

I dreamed a coupla nights ago that I was having sex with Bill Clinton. It was very sweet and romantic. I kept trying to tell him that we shouldn't be doing this, that it might keep him from being elected. He quieted my words of self-oppression with kisses (WOW!). I think this means that he will be elected president. (My sex dreams decide the fate of nations!) I have had a string of these dreams with presidents. It was very sexy and comforting. A protector and good lover. I think this got sparked a little bit because I am going to Fire Island on Labor Day to do a fundraiser for the Clinton campaign with all the rich fags. That Kennedy-esque banker I had sex with on the cruise ship is setting it up. It is all a vortex—.

I just got a call. Some people talked to him and said the campaign would find this problematic. Notorious me doing a Clinton benefit at Fire Island. Oh well. I got a wet dream out of it.

Part 4

The Teacher

this man will teach you stuff you already know.

presenting a faculty well schooled IN THE SCHOOL OF REAL LIFE

LIKE HOW TO BE YOURSELF.

Presenting *Tim Miller*, performance artist and adjunct professor at the UCLA School of Theater, Film and Television. Not one to sit still, Tim considers himself an activist as much as he considers himself an artist. Each year, his works raise eyebrows and consciousness across as many as fifty North American and European cities. Which is precisely why you'll find him in the role of instructor at the UCLA School of Theater, Film and Television.

Like every professor in the program, Tim is well schooled in the school of real life. Which means you get more than theory. You get firsthand experience from a highly respected professional. You see, it's Tim's belief that we all have a story to tell. "I help actors see themselves as empowered creators who, through each life experience, have material to make work from. It's a natural way to provide meaning to one's career and to conjure fierce new theater."

To give your career a hand, phone the UCLA School of Theater, Film and Television at 310-825-5761 and teach yourself a thing or two.

MFA degree programs: Acting; Design and Production; Directing; Playwriting. BA degree program in Theater.

U C L A
SCHOOL OF THEATER
FILM AND TELEVISION

Advertisement for UCLA School of Theater, Film and Television, early 1990s.

Embodied Pedagogy

Tim Miller wrote "Embodied Pedagogy" in 1998, after more than a decade of teaching and reflection on the value of performance for groups ranging from graduate acting students to gay men who summon courage to appear for a workshop. Though rooted in the practical workshop techniques Miller has developed, the essay also offers a rationale for performance as a means of moving individuals and groups toward self-awareness, self-acceptance, and creativity. As in "Suck, Spit, Chew, Swallow," which follows in this section, Tim Miller shows his full involvement in the workshop process, as participant as well as guide, and offers his own "body story."

Much of my work as a teacher and a performer is an exploration of the body as a site of memory, self and creativity. I am particularly drawn to a discourse of the body as the primary battleground on which our identities are marked by race, gender, ability, age, sexual orientation, class, and the commodity of "looks." The awareness of this struggle leads us to new possibilities for the creation of original performance work. The basis of my pedagogy is the exploration of our embodied experience as a prime avenue for learning, narrative and transformation. I am especially interested in the wounds, pleasure places and stories that mark our bodies. This skin, meat and bones within which we live are mysterious satellite dishes receiving signals from our past as well as the subtle stirred imaginings of the future. I believe that growing up in this society we are all veterans of non-stop assaults on our wholeness and sense of physical self. This war has left scars all over our skin, muscles and meat, hearts and brains. The first time I work with a group of people I frequently seek to draw some of these body-narratives forward.

I work with all different kinds of people, from my MFA actors at UCLA to more community-based settings with my gay men's performance workshops all over the world. I find the different sites where I teach surprisingly similar. All are struggling with the same material: the challenge to claim body and self amid a culture that has other plans.

I walk into the room with a head stuffed with questions. How to begin this work? What can I hope to achieve? Who are these people? These actors and artists. These humans. How can I start to get their juices to flow? Their risk-taking nature to come forward? Their courage to let their hearts be more open? What nerve I have to ask them to look into the abyss! Teaching people to perform is asking them to enter a series of embodied experiences of light, body, feeling and breath. Who am I to think that I can do anything?

Through my work, I try to share a variety of strategies to create performance from the tremendous energies that are present in our lives as we live them. I believe the journeys through our lives offer us tremendous opportunities to know ourselves more truly and to create a culture of witness that is crucial to becoming a human being. I will ask the group to look under their big rocks and find the hot and wet places of their stories, dreams and myths. I ask them to own their fierce living and bring that forward to be witnessed.

This culture, as we live and breathe in it, conspires to erase our uniqueness and our individual creative wholeness. We receive a million signals that tell us our lives do not matter, our bodies are not worthy, our stories are no good. This can be as true of people who understand themselves as artists as for those who do not. If I am working with actors, I attempt to encourage them to see themselves as whole, integrated primary creators. They do not always have to wait for the casting person to cast them, the playwright to write, or the director to direct. I ask them to see beyond the training tradition that sometimes encourages actors to see themselves as purely interpretive artists at the service of the understood modes of theatrical production.

These people I am about to work with carry the materials to create charged and vital performance all on their own. They have the body and the voice and the vision to do it.

First meeting. It is important to acknowledge that these people exist, to honor the fact that they got their butts into the room. I greet them as each person arrives. Ask them their names. I know that every time we enter a room full of strangers we are daring something extraordinary. I try to keep that in mind as I meet the people who have arrived to work together. I assume that most of us are coming to this work wounded and scared and tempted to bolt for the door. This includes me. I gather them into a circle and ask them to close their eyes. I ask them to notice the thoughts and feelings that are zooming through them. I ask them to notice those thoughts and feelings, but also to allow the mind and heart to quiet. I ask them to allow their breath to move in and out. I ask them to open their eyes and slowly walk among each other in silence. Notice the floorboards, the chips of paint, the shadows from the light outdoors. I ask them to allow themselves to be looked at and to begin to see these other people as if they have never seen a human body before. Eventually we settle onto the floor for a few minutes of simple leg and back stretches. As I warm up their bodies, I also try to warm up their feelings and inner life. This needs to be a slow process. As they gently hold one knee to their heart, I ask them to think of one thing from their lives that they would like to get rid of. Something that is stopping them, fucking with them, hurting them. I ask them to give that thing a word, then to write that word in the air with a big toe. I ask them to really look at that word dangling over them like a dark cloud, then to speak those words into the space:

FEAR. INSECURITY. JUDGMENT. SHAME. FEAR.

It's important to name your demons, to start a conversation with them. This is a crucial step toward self-knowledge. I ask the group to fill their body with a breath and to disperse that word to the four corners of the earth so that all that is left is the creative and integrated part of that fear or judgment. In hundreds of workshops in many parts of the world, perhaps half the people say the word *FEAR* as the thing they would like to get rid of. This simple exercise, as part of a warm up, allows the group to acknowledge from the very beginning that they feel fear. This can be enormously freeing.

As crucial as it is to name the demons, it is equally important to call forward the desires. After some more physical work, a gentle stretching sequence for the opposite leg. I ask the participants to locate something they want more of in their life at this point. What is the thing that they would desire in greater abundance to surround their living and their creative work? Draw that in the sky above your head. Draw it in big letters. Call those words out loud into the room:

COURAGE. CLARITY. LOVE. INTIMACY. WHOLENESS.

They breathe and, as one, shout those words to the sky. What a beautiful sound that makes! I let it hang in the air. Somehow, in that simple exercise cradled within a set of stretches on our backs on the floor, the whole arc of this work is sketched out. We know our fears and call forward our strengths. Everything else comes from this.

I lead them through a few more simple stretches and then get the group onto their feet and playing with the physical possibilities of their bodies. They have quick physical conversations, then I ask them to pass these movements to each other. Begin the play. Don't judge the movements, don't let your brain get in the way with its judgmental voice. As much as we need to be worried about the hideous social forces that would silence artistic expression, I am always much more concerned with that censoring voice *inside our heads* that

Gay men's performance workshop, Highways Performance Space, 1992: Tim Miller, Chris Doggett, and Richard Harrison. Photo by Chuck Stallard.

this society has installed to tell us what to do. That censor is with us twenty-four hours a day; that is the censor we really need to tame.

I get our bodies moving together improvisationally, enjoying the ability to play and converse with each other through our embodied selves. I develop this into a circle dance, where two people continue this movement conversation while we surround them and let their dance lead the rest of us around the circle. A new person goes into the middle. The duet is new and the dance has changed. I ask the people around the circle to find in their bodies the breath and the movement that the inner duet is leading us through, to really get it into their own flesh. This circle dance can go on for some time. Our hearts will beat fast and our breath will deepen. Slowly I bring this to a quieter place and make a circle with our arms over each other's shoulders.

I invite them to sniff the armpit to the right. Now sniff the armpit to the left. Roll it around your nose like a fine wine. Yes, we all smell. This is the first of many simple exercises to begin to dismantle some of the body-phobias that are the legacy of our messed-up culture. Throughout the work I continue to introduce gentle techniques that allow us to look at how we see our body-selves and to notice our boundaries.

I ask the group to say a phrase or a word of a feeling or thought they had as they took part in the circle dance. *Crazy animal play. Sex. Fingers talking. Competitive. I felt nervous. Self-conscious.* In just a few moments, this almost poetic response takes the temperature of the group. This is an efficient way to tune in to what is going on inside the group without stopping the energy of the work and clumping down into a gab-fest. It is crucial to find ways for us to talk about what is going on in the work, without always diving into the brainy self that detaches from our bodily experience. This taking the temperature is a very good way to get at that.

I invite each participant to do a short physical and vocal solo in the middle of the circle, an improvisation that plays with the sounds and actions they might find in their first name. This simple exercise is a sure way to get to know the names of the entire group. It burns an image and action of the body performing that name. Knowing the names of who I am working with is the first step to being able to actually see them and the work they are doing. They reveal their name through the physical and vocal performance and the circle that surrounds them repeats it.

I then ask them to do something very difficult. A very alchemical moment can happen when a group is gathered into a circle and asked to do a very simple thing. I ask them to say their name and tell something "important" about themselves. The room usually gets very quiet and focused. That is my favorite sound. The group shares these parts of themselves and the work begins. It is a powerful moment when a person is asked to stand before other humans and say something that matters.

What is there in that quiet as the room begins to buzz with focus and honesty?

It is the sound of humans agreeing to be honest in the face of one another.

It is the sound of artists allowed to dig deep without the fear of being judged.

It is the sound of humans looking within and finding their treasure.

I look for this sound. I try to create the conditions for that tender attention to occur. Once that sound is in the room we are ready to dive into an exploration of the stories that live within our bodies. I ask the group to close their eyes and I lead them into this exploration.

BODY STORY MEDITATION

"I want you to see imagine you are traveling over your body. Really see the contours and canyons. I would like you to begin to open yourself to the stories that each part of your body holds. What is the story of your elbow? What happened to make that scar? The story of your teeth? The story of your genitals?

"What part of your body has a story that really *needs* to be told? It's a story so important that if it doesn't get told you might burst. That's a story that is important for a person to tell. I want you to allow yourself to see the metaphors of your body as fully as possible. I believe that hearts actually do break. I believe our heads actually can be in the clouds. I believe our feet can actually turn to clay. I believe that each of those things has probably happened to all of you here. As you open to your story, really let those associations leap forward. What might you have lost when your crooked teeth were braced and straightened, even though you now have a movie star smile? Where are your jagged places? These might be the places where we can let some light in. I want you to see what kind of transformations this story brought you. As you tell this story, really find what is the legacy of this place on your body, it might be either a positive or a negative legacy. The straightened teeth may have taken away a part of a jagged tooth song that your wild aunt in Kentucky still sings. The violation of your body may now give you the power to transform shit into gold. The baseball that hit you in the head might have knocked you into your artist self. The metaphors of our body may well be the keys to understanding ourselves in a deep way. They might be powerful ways of knowing ourselves. Really find that metaphor and that story of transformation that comes from this place on your body. I want us now, one at a time, to go into the circle and tell the group these stories. Take your time. Find your focus in the body. Let's begin."

I'm in a crummy hotel in Pittsburgh. There are snow flurries outside. It is cold. But at least in this crummy hotel room in Pittsburgh it is warm inside as I run my hair along a man's naked body. Along his feet, the spot on the calf with the muscles, past that golden rod and up to his heart. I plant my hair in his heart. My hair is my roots, planted long ago in north central Kansas. My hair is how I communicate with other planets and perceptions. I spread my antennae wide and start to receive signals. My hair saves me from being blinded by the light of a thousand nuclear blasts. My hair has been blond & black & brown, & some gray here now. My hair reminds me that (as the Italians say) in a hundred years we'll all be bald. My hair reminds me to live in this time, with my powers now, knowing that it will all pass. My hair challenges me to feel the wind moving through it on Venice Beach and to carry small flowers fallen from my olive tree as it blooms this April. My hair reminds me of my fragileness & my strength. I bury the hair cut from my head in my garden. I grow new life from it. See what flowers from the hair on my head! I grew and grew and pulled my head out of the ground. . . .

I was fourteen and I had a girlfriend. She looked like Marcia Brady. Her name was Janet and she was cool. We would kiss in the pool with our slick bodies pressed up to each other. My hair was straight and fine and lighter than now. I was glad to have a girlfriend who sang a song dedicated to me at junior high graduation. Then, one day, I was sitting combing my hair and one hair sprang up and became very curly. Like a piano wire breaking. Then another. Then another. Soon my head was a frenzy of tight curls. . . . and suddenly my friend Ralph Higgs was looking pretty good to me. I tried everything to make my hair straight. Great goops of Dippity-Do. I had my hair straightened. I even went to a barber in uptown Whittier, Big Al Stumpo, to see what he could do. Finally, he gave up and said "Basta! A curl's gotta do what a curl's gotta do!" And presented me with my very first afro pick. I went to the phone and called up Ralph Higgs.

One by one the participants tell, chant, sing these stories of the body. This exercise brings up very good stuff. The vulnerability of our bodies (self-judgment, shaming, wounds), which everybody is subject to but for performers is especially acute because of the physicality of the act. These stories that come from the body are especially rich with metaphor and urgency. We begin to really see each other. Not as our 8x10's. But as fully alive and complicated body-selves with stories to tell. The movie-star beautiful woman becomes a snaggle-toothed Kentucky girl howling at the moon—just like her jagged tooth aunt. That makes her wildly interesting and complicated. We can escape from this culture of sameness that wants all of our bodies to be tamed of their uniqueness. The moment we begin to let these stories come forward, we start to let loose the energy that is held captive in these places. I have often seen this exercise be a path for extraordinary revelations of humanness. The triumph and the challenges of being embodied people engaged with a highly physical art form of performing. The last line of these pieces is often the most important one, the one that opens up the vulnerability.

The moment of mourning for those stuck-forward canine teeth that might have allowed her to sing through the night—the naming of which allows her to see what work she may need to do.

The body enlivened by its stories becomes a much more articulate vehicle for expression. Human beings conscious of the narratives within are more ready to claim power over their embodied experience. The broken places on the body can also let a little light in. They are the setting for major revelations about self. Knowing the warfare that has surrounded your body prepares you for this raw activity of being a human being.

Suck, Spit, Chew, Swallow
A Performative Exploration of Men's Bodies

*The 1999 Birmingham, England, performance project recounted
in this essay was atypical of Jim Miller's workshops. Whereas
one-day or short-term workshops sometimes involved as many
as forty-eight participants, the* Suck, Spit, Chew, Swallow *project
engaged a small group of five gay men, most without performing
experience, who worked daily for two weeks, eventuating in
a public performance. Its model was* Queer Glow *in Glasgow,
Scotland, five years earlier, a similar group undertaking within
the context of an arts festival. Precisely because of the unusual
circumstances, the Glasgow and Birmingham experiences
provided Jim Miller an intensive, focused laboratory for
community-based pedagogical techniques, as well as opportunity
to reflect at length on the needs and creative potential of gay men
gathered together.*

I was invited to the United Kingdom in 1999 to work with a group of
gay men toward the creation of an original ensemble performance.
Mark Ball, the director of Birmingham's Queerfest, an internation-
ally significant festival of lesbian and gay culture, wanted me to work
intensively with a group of men toward the creation of a performance. We hoped that this process would culminate in an ensemble-
generated performance work culturally specific to Birmingham that

would also enliven and encourage local artists. I arrived in London full of ideas for an exploration into gay men's embodiment, the place where our dreams and disappointments, desires and dreads really seem to constellate.

All right, I admit it: I had hoped that my work there would offer the participants the opportunity to discover a new corporeal "discourse" of what it is to be men. Unfortunately for my highfalutin' plans, the truth is that our bodies are much more layered and complex and messy than a nice tidy word like "discourse" could ever suggest. The flesh that men occupy stinks, fucks, shits, is written on, is blown apart, is fetishized, triumphs, fails and eventually dies. It is so complex and multileveled that the more I approach this exploration the more humbled and silenced I feel in trying to talk about it.

On the plane ride from Chicago to London I devoured a *New York Times* article on the research of Prof. Harrison Pope, a Harvard psychiatrist who has monitored the inexorable growth of G.I. Joe's biceps throughout the last thirty-five years. As I child I was much more interested (and then powerfully disappointed) by the bulge in G.I Joe's pants than I ever was in his upper arms. Imagine my profound deflation, if not gender confusion, when I slipped his army fatigue pants down and saw no pillar of iron at his crotch but instead a gentle sloping mound of plastic. But that's another story. Since G.I Joe was missing this standard male equipment, his biceps will have to serve as a measurement of society's representations of the male body.

Harrison Pope reports that in 1964 Joe begins with a svelte, normally proportioned man's body with a biceps circumference (when scaled to a life-size male) that measured 12.2 inches around. He has that long, shapeless look typical of late '50s TV sitcom fathers like Ward Cleaver, father of Beaver. That was a simpler time when the only iron that an adult male was supposed to pump was a 9-iron out on the golf course. Ten years later G.I. Joe's bulges start to show. They come in at 15.2 inches: Joe looks like the tightly muscled kung fu fighter that I aspired to be in 1974. The next twenty years, Joe gained only a little more than an inch. However, between 1994 and

Tim Miller with Robbie Allen during workshop for "Queer Glow," Glasgow, 1994. Photo by Alan Crumlish.

1998, "GI Joe Extreme" hysterically added another ten inches to his biceps, attaining the cartoonish proportions of a 26.8-inch upper arm. These dolls—excuse me, I mean action figures, "display the physiques of advanced body builders and some display levels of muscularity far exceeding the outer limits of actual human attainment," as Pope's study dryly notes. Just as young girls and women have had to toil for decades under unrealistic and idealized physical images, now young boys also get to grow up feeling woefully inadequate when comparing their delicate carrot-stick arms to GI Joe's hefty honey-baked ham biceps. There is a certain gleeful revenge fantasy that I am prone to indulge here as a properly trained feminist-identified queer boy. Part of me wants to gloat that at last men's bodies are as colonized and marketed as are women's, but I also know the enormous damage this is doing to men in general and to gay men in particular.

The giddy proliferation of homoerotic, idealized male images in advertising, TV and film is triumphant in the complete objectification of all men's bodies, straight or gay, as something to be bought, taken home, eaten, and fucked. I acknowledge that straight men and boys are also subject to the slings and arrows of not making the grade of the perfected male body. However, they ultimately have the option of retiring to the nuclear bomb-proof cement bunker of straight male privilege if they are confronted with too much belly or not enough biceps. Gay men, on the other hand, whose bodies are endlessly contested and feminized by culture (and each other!) are in a real pickle. Gay men are forced to dodge a ricocheting male gaze that has created a marketplace where only the most perfect bodies get rewarded. If only these idealized male images stopped with G.I. Joe! Beyond the general trend of using hyper-idealized male bodies to sell everything from dish soap to personal computers, gay men must also move in a sea of utopian physical representations advertising bars, treatment programs, and AIDS medications. Michelangelo Signorile is on target in his critique of this trend in his occasionally annoying but always provocative book, *Life Outside:*

> Every major American city has one—or sometimes three or four— "bar rags" filled with images of "perfect" gay men, the ideals that set the standard. Most of these images are being used to sell us something: gym memberships to the trendy gyms of choice; all night parties at nightclubs filled with near-naked, young-and-buff men; phone sex; and even actual sex in the guise of "escorts." These same images are played back to us again and again in gay porn, on safer sex posters, and in dozens of gay newspapers and several glossy national magazines that often sport pumped up cover-boys and fetching ads selling products and events, from underwear to hot parties.

These images relentlessly discipline the narrowly defined ideal gay man's body: buffed and bronzed, stripped of humanizing body hair, extra flesh, and wrinkles. There are no boundaries too crass in this endless use of ideal male representations as currency in the exchange of goods and services. One particularly disturbing advertisement for a suicide prevention program boasts a handsome young man being zipped into a body bag, his eyes softly and seductively closed as if he were Sleeping Beauty waiting for a wake-up call from some handy Prince. Even corpses have to be beautiful in postmodern disembodied America!

Suck, Spit, Chew, Swallow

The project I was going to create with a group of gay men in Birmingham was festively called *Suck, Spit, Chew, Swallow*. I walk into the studio at the DanceXchange for the first meeting. The studios are perched over the Hippodrome Theatre whose marquee boasts larger-than-life billboards of almost naked men for the coming attractions: the gyrating men of Hen Party, a male strip show, joust with the Matthew Bourne *Swan Lake* and its sinewy butch satyr-like swans. There's no escaping! I'm surrounded by the homo-eroticized capitalist male body even at my work place! Leaving the mix of beefcake and fowl-muffin festooning the marquee, I trudge up the steep steps to the DanceXchange. I am always struck with a panic attack at the start of these projects. Who am I to gather men to dig deep into their hearts and memories and bodies? It helps that I know the men coming to these workshops are also frying in a griddle of panic and doubt. This evens the odds.

I watch the men one by one trudge up to the landing, their panic painfully obvious on their bodies. Later one of the men in the group, Carl, will say that as he walked up the steps, the four men waiting there seemed to be horrible beasts ready to devour him. It took all his self-control, not to mention my bounding down three steps to capture him in an overeager American handshake, to keep him from bolting. Carl's intuitive image of other men as monsters is pretty much on the mark. Men are socialized to see one another as strange creatures, potential adversaries to vanquish or die trying. For gay men this encounter with other men is a double danger zone, since every other man is also a potential site of complex erotics. Each man encountered is either an object that you desire who may well rebuff you, thus wreaking havoc on your self-esteem, or he is a predator who wants you even though you would rather eat fire than kiss him. These are the stakes that gay men dare to weather when they walk up those stairs. It's not surprising that such a gathering would be fraught with body terror and issues for days!

I have found that these workshops almost inevitably revolve around the men's experiences of their bodies sharing space with one another. There is something about gathering with a group of gay men for this purpose that brings up both the terrors of PE and the pleasures of bodily play as boys, the lost hell and the lost Eden. Regardless of what exercises I choose to lead, this raw physical proximity almost always leads the men to an exploration of what it is like to be in their bodies, and how they imagine the world judges, grades, disciplines their bodies.

These men from Birmingham are a small but interesting group. Gathered at random, they are ready to work together every day for two weeks to create a project that already boasts a provocative title. What enormous courage and commitment it takes to jump in feet first!

Kuli is a young South Asian man, twenty years old, who is studying science at Warwick University. It will become clear over the first meetings that he is not "out," and this in fact is the first time he has spent time in a self-identified group of gay men. His friends' nickname for him is "the atom bomb." His barely suppressed rage will be both a terror and an inspiration for this group.

Ken, a man of color and at fifty the oldest in the group, arrives with an enormous flourish of confidence. He has lived his life as a performer, toured the world in productions of *Hair* and dozens of other shows. His bravado covers a very wounded and tender heart. His honesty and risk-taking will pull the work deeper.

There's Carl, the man with the vision of the monsters at the head of the stairs. He's a teacher of five-year-olds at a local primary school. Twenty-three years old and just out of college, he presents himself very slickly and middle-class, but is lucky to have a lot boiling inside. The look of panic is always darting around the corners of his eyes.

Robert Shaw has a lean hungry look and is also my musical collaborator. In the mid-80s he had quite some success with his new wave band Swann's Way and is now entering his forties with his eyes open to what surprising new forms his creativity may take. His quiet, grounded quality is a tonic dose of a man who is capable of watching and listening. He has an ear for what is going on in the community of men and will bring that to his music and soundscapes for the piece.

My other collaborator is Joseph Potts, a talented young filmmaker and video artist who will work with us to create a rich décor of video images that will be projected at the DanceXchange during our performance. He and I have already plotted images of men's bodies detailed and examined under the relentless eye and bright light of a live feed video camera that will be used for the performance. Joseph is the only non-gay man involved with the project at this point, though everyone assumes he is queer since he doesn't indulge the usual straight-man maneuver of broadcasting his heterosexuality. This gives Joseph the unusual experience of getting to "pass" as a gay man for the first few days of our work. His extraordinary intuition and sensitivity is a great wild card in the process.

Then there's me. I'm in my fortieth year and feeling the miles. The odometer has been turned back more than once, believe me! As someone who has spent his life drawing from and marking on my body as a place for inspiration and narrative, I come to this work with a pocketful of agendas but also a healthy respect for the chaos that is likely to ensue. Like most men with more than a spoonful of Peter Pan, I have within me a ticking time bomb of having to confront getting older.

Remapping Men's Bodies

I usually begin my work with groups of men by asking them to do some imagination work and visualize a new way of "mapping" their bodies. I invite them to put away for a time the received hegemonic maps of the male body: big dick, big muscles, hard flesh, hard heart, etc. Instead I want them to see what metaphors their intuitive mind conjures of their embodied selves. Then they get the crayons and pens and I ask them to draw these new and improved maps of the body.

Here in Birmingham I begin our work with this basic exercise. Suddenly the visual imagination goes wild and through the group's work we see dense and complex representations of how men actually experience being inside their bodies. The drawings explode into images of men with locks over their hearts, with wings sprouting from their backs, with hooks holding their flesh in equilibrium, with feet balancing precariously on a house of cards.

In each of the drawings, the penis, the most over-determined body part known to humankind, surprises us with new potential. In various maps the phallus is covered with clouds, or propped up on a house of cards, or sending out roots to be more grounded to the earth. The exquisite caught-in-the-flashbulb vulnerability in these community-generated images touched me and reminded me how fragile and susceptible men's bodies really are. It struck me that all the fuss about men's rigid strength (the phallus as weapon and so on) crashes against the sweet reality of the melancholic, almost Chekhovian, recumbent cock. The penis can be so accessible in its quiet moments, its occasional tumescent shenanigans far in the distance. The softness of a man's dick can be tender and available, full of possibilities too. The flesh reminds me of Clark Kent just before he dashed into a phone booth to do his makeover. One must gently stroke and coax his penis to see if this is indeed a job for Superman.

I find it very poignant how urgent it is for men, gay men in particular, to get the chance to re-map their bodies. My agenda is clear in the exercises I do in the workshops. To some extent this structure I have proposed to the performers disciplines them to explore this more vulnerable and metaphoric potential body—but I actually find that men want to do this regardless of what kind of exercise focus I suggest. The menu of potential representations offered to (imposed on) men is so oppressive that the guys in the workshops grab the opportunity to re-imagine their embodiment. I am also re-assured that plain folks want to do this—not just performance art-ists and those inclined to theorize! It's amazing how much the shar-ing of these very personal representations helps men relate better to one another. Once we knew that Kuli saw himself as an atom bomb, or that Carl saw his feet chained to the earth, there was a more honest place for the men to connect from. Claiming the power, the specificity and the vulnerability of your most private metaphorized physical self-image really unleashes a lot of psychic and creative juice.

Body Stories

The next day, as I waited for the group to arrive for our second meet-ing, I kept my fingers crossed that I hadn't scared anyone off. One by one they arrived at the DanceXchange, more grounded and confi-dent than the night before. I could see how the participants had begun to claim this space and this process we were occupying.

I asked the men in Birmingham to look at the newly imagined maps of their bodies and to locate a story that lives somewhere on that map. I gathered the men in a circle holding hands (I am a Cali-fornian, never forget!) and told them to close their eyes and imagine they were traveling over the maps of their bodies. I asked them to really see the contours and canyons of the worlds they had imagined, to follow their noses, as it were, to the stories that each part of their body holds. What is the story of the elbow? What happened to make that scar? The story of the teeth? The eyes? The story of your geni-tals? What part of our body has a story that really *needs* to be told? Is there a place on our bodies that carries a story so important that if it doesn't get told a person might burst?

I invite the group to allow themselves to see their most idiosyncratic body metaphors as fully as possible. Our daily language is full of expressions like *He has feet of clay. I was caught red handed. He broke my heart. My head is in the clouds.* I believe that each of those things has probably happened to the men that I work with. As they open themselves to their stories, I ask them to let those image associations leap forward, uncensored by the practical mind. I want them to discover what kind of transformations the telling of this story might offer them. I want them to really find the legacy of this place on their body that has a story that needs to be told. The legacy could be either positive or negative. In my experience with this exercise I have seen how these metaphors of our body are often the keys to knowing ourselves in a deep way. I ask the group to dig deep and find that embodied metaphor and that story of transformation that comes from this place. Then I give the men the challenge of finding a physical action that expresses this story and then, one at a time, to go into the circle, perform that physical gesture as they tell the group these stories.

The stories that came forward in Birmingham were revelatory. Where twenty-four hours before they had been a group of men socialized to fear and mistrust each other, suddenly there was a huge offering of intensely intimate spaces within:

Carl told the story of his eyes, which loomed very large on his body map. When he was a small boy, Carl's father had become ill and died. No one would really tell Carl what had happened; the usual comforting platitudes were shoveled forth. He was not allowed to go to the funeral. This young boy kept looking around the house hoping that he might find his father hidden somewhere. Carl told a story about his eyes that have looked for his father ever since.

The map that Robert had created showed a man's figure with hooks attached to his belly and lower back. It was unclear whether these hooks were holding him up or tearing him apart. Robert told the story of his guts and how troubled they have been in his life. When he was coming out as an adolescent, he couldn't control his bowels. In his performance he told how the shit he felt inside him as a queer boy was literally exploding out of him during his sixteenth year.

The next man began with his hands dancing in front of him. Ken told how his parents never touched him as a child. In fact, they barely noticed him at all and shipped him off to boarding school as soon as possible. He was saved by a special aunt who came from Jamaica, scooped him up and held him, gave him the touch he needed, and let him know that he had healing power in his hands.

Kuli, the youngest of the group, did a piece about the time bombs inside him. Being in the closet, he was filled with rage that made him want to explode. As he talked about the things he was sick of being fucked-over by, he was slowly reaching his arm back as if to strike something. With a powerful integrated act, he made an explosive gesture as though slamming the door on all the voices trying to stifle the explosion he needed to make.

I told a story about getting hit in the hand by a bottle thrown at me two years ago when I was performing at Montana Pride in Bozeman. This was during a time when my boyfriend Alistair, who was born in Australia, had been refused a student visa by the U.S. government. I was feeling the absence of his hand in mine as well as the rage I have for the homophobic laws of my own country. I remember all the times my hand has been slapped: reaching for the cookie jar, touching myself as a child, and now struck by a bottle for wanting to hold the hand of another man.

One by one we told, chanted, sang these stories of the body. The room filled with images of eyes looking for fathers, of children denied touch and affection, of bombs inside, of the shit in our guts, and of the ways we get caught red-handed by an oppressive culture. These narratives that spring from our embodiment can lead a person to a deeper, more honest place within. Amid the distractions of making a living and keeping up appearances, men are encouraged to be stoically alienated from the unpredictable heat of the narratives inside their bodies. As the group spelunked inside, looking for the narratives of the body, it was a crucial beginning to a more intimate way of knowing our selves. Our vulnerabilities came forward and encouraged a tender empathy for our own embodied selves and the others gathered in the room. Telling these stories, performing them and having them witnessed, adds to their resonance. Since performing is always an embodied act, it is particularly suited that this body narrative be physically enacted as a means of owning the terrain of your own body, and that it be witnessed by the community of gay men.

The vulnerability of our bodies—self-judgment, shaming, childhood wounding—which everybody is subject to, can be especially acute for gay men because the physical body is such a persistent locus of where gay men's identity is constructed. These stories that come from the body are especially rich with metaphor and urgency. The group begins to really see each other, not as tidy 8x10s with resumes on the back, but as fully alive and complicated body-selves that have *such* stories to tell. We start to see the way to escape a culture of sameness that wants our bodies to be tamed of their uniqueness, fixed in the caste system of the beauty myth, and disciplined to productivity and consumption. The moment we let these stories come forward, we start to unleash the anarchic energy in the meat and blood of a more integrated physical self. These stories, which carry both our pleasures and our pain, locate how our bodies occupy space and move in society. This is a crucial step to seeing how our narratives are shaped by how the world sees us, as collections of data concerning race, age, size, and sexuality. Performing our narratives creates and shares potential models of resistance as we walk around in each other's shoes, see a dead father through a young boy's eyes, and carry each other's memory of unloving parents.

The creative re-imagining and re-imaging that came out of the workshop sessions in Birmingham was characteristic of many of the groups of men that I have worked with. The same issues come up again and again: the feeling of not quite making the grade, of not being properly parented, of some kind of residual trauma that ends up haunting men as adults. The themes are similar regardless of whether the men are straight or gay. The performances that came from this exercise in Birmingham were full of the challenge of being men. Often in these pieces, the last spoken words were the most important ones, the words that opened up the vulnerability and the potential space for empowerment and change. The last sentence of Carl's performance allowed him to mourn for his eyes forever looking for his dead father. The naming of a personal mythos like this just might allow a man to see what further work can be done humanly and creatively.

A Night in a Soho Gay Bar

The group had been brought together by the disarming intimacy of our several nights' work. Playfulness and hugs now marked their arrival in the space. You could see the transformation in their bodies as the men bounded up the stairs or walked into the rehearsal room and began to warm-up. Each person, including me, seemed to enter each night's work with a greater sense of empowerment and belonging. With the deepened sense of the vulnerability of our individual bodies, I now wanted to place these gay men's bodies in the complex vortex of how our bodies are seen and disciplined by outside social forces. With my highly developed sadistic impulses as a teacher, I knew it was time to invite the participants to make a little visit into hell.

In the weeks before my arrival in England, a right-wing nut had been setting bombs all over London. There were horrific explosions in Brixton, a predominately black neighborhood in South London, as well as in the lively district of Indian and Pakistani shops in Brick Lane in the East End. Most deadly of all had been a bomb that exploded in a gay bar in Soho called the Admiral Duncan. A number of people had been killed and dozens horribly injured. This event had profoundly shocked the gay community in the United Kingdom and fractured a feeling of safety and belonging that many gay people had experienced heretofore.

As we began our work this night in Birmingham, I gathered the men into a close circle with our heads touching. I asked them to list all the things they want from other men, the things they want from themselves as well. *I want to be seen. I want to trust him. I want his touch on my body. I want his respect. I want him to open his heart to me.* This list of wants echoed in the new studio we were working in (a flood had forced us to evacuate DanceXchange, and we were now in a rehearsal space at the Birmingham Ballet!). Then, from that place of desire and personal agency, I asked the men to imagine they had taken all those wants out on the town and had been there at the Admiral Duncan when the bomb went off. I asked each man to detail an imaginary story of what his experience was that night. What was he wearing? Who was he going to meet there? How did he feel as he sipped his pint of lager? Then I wanted them to describe what it was like as the bomb went off. One by one we told each other these ground-zero imagined stories while Robert's minidisk recorded our voices.

The most terrifying thing about this exercise was how *easy* it was for these men to imagine that they had been there. It took no effort at all to place themselves in a site where their bodies would be subject to the most extreme violation. The stark revelation here was that gay men so often have the feeling of being physically endangered that it takes no remarkable imagination at all for us to place ourselves in such a horrific moment.

Ken improvised a story of such disarming specificity that it was almost impossible not to believe he had been at the Admiral Duncan that terrible night. He vividly described the observations, feelings, and desires that moved through him until the countdown to the explosion. His imagination got right to how he felt he was looking, what cologne he was wearing, who he wanted to chat up.

I clearly saw that the performance we would make over the next few days needed to be about these bodies full of desire and their encounter with disaster, the aspiration to love and companionship surrounded by bombs without and within. I would gather together our newly mapped bodies, the recordings of our memories and imaginings, each man's story that he discovered on that map of his body, our lists of desires, and an encounter with an explosion. The piece would mark the men's stories of their bodies, their search for love, the challenge of so many bombs that the world tosses in our way. In the next days we would work very quickly to make space for each man's narrative and creativity, to conjure a full-evening performance called *Suck, Spit, Chew, Swallow*.

The Performance

As we prepared for our single performance, the intensity of our process hung around us like a dense fog. There was huge performance anxiety, interpersonal dramas, and the insane creative challenge of creating a full-evening performance work in two weeks. The chaos that ensued when two of the members slept together was our own little bomb that ate up much of two rehearsals. The torrential rain in Birmingham kicked us from space to space until I finally indulged one of my occasional righteous diva fits. Joseph couldn't find the proper projector for the visual material he had conceived, including close-ups of those body maps projected twenty feet tall on the scrim at the DanceXchange. The slings and arrows that performance art is vulnerable to!

In the hour before the performance I was afraid that Kuli, who was very nervous about his first time performing, would run for the hills. I seriously considered hiding his backpack. I worried that the two lovebirds would start snarling at each other again. I feared that this time I had pushed my luck too far, thinking I could gather five men at random, ask them to bare their most intimate selves, and work with them to make that into a performance for public consumption in only two weeks! But once the piece began, that forest fire in my head quieted down.

The piece began with five men "sleeping" in the space as the audience entered the theater at the DanceXchange. Outlined in a defined square of light, each man lay under a blanket surrounded by a haunting ambient audio score. Within a rich musical environment, a collage of snippets cascaded from each man's story about an intimate moment he had had with another man. Robert had made an aural space that was simultaneously comforting and scary, cozy and funereal. Were these men in their beds or their graves? Tucked in cozily or buried deep? The live-action video feed focused on parts of the men's bodies visible from under the blankets: a foot, a hand curled over the forehead, the gentle rise and fall of breath. The theater was alive with image, sound, and the embodied presence of these five men as the audience quietly entered a space that was already performative.

The audio score builds to a chaos of the men's voices, overlapping their desires and memories: *I want to be held. I want his touch. I want his dick. I want him to look into my eyes.* Finally there is a little movement from the performers. Very slowly, the curtain going up as it were, from under the blankets each performer, using a carefully concealed banana, slowly displays a tent rising up over his blanket-covered pelvis. The men regard their mysterious erections, seemingly having risen out of the cacophony of desire over the audio track. Then they reach down and pull the bananas out from under their blankets and proceed to energetically suck, spit, chew and swallow them. (Thus our title!) Giving the audience a moment to relax, the humor in the image introduces a sense of absurdity about the hyper-dramatization that surrounds the revelation of men's bodies, "the melodramatic penis," as Professor Peter Lehman aptly refers to it.

The question hanging in the air was "Are they naked under those blankets? When do we see some dick?" By frustrating that natural question with the summer-camp banana stunt, the space was cleared for us to go about our business unencumbered by the penis-searching gaze of the audience. The men shake out their blankets, fold them in a ritualistic manner, place them underneath a seat of the front row of spectators, then gather in a circle and perform a slow unison t'ai chi of gestures drawn from each man's story of an intimacy he discovered with another man. A breath is held full in the body and then exhaled into a mad game of cock-tag. This was drawn from Robert's narrative of how his friends would gather in a vacant lot by the grim council houses to play their version of tag which was an excuse to grab one another's cocks. The crazy exuberance of this disappears as quick as it arrived and we launch into the individual narratives of each man.

Carl is lying on his back, head tortured against the floor so he can see the audience. "I wanted SEX!" he begins, as he launches into a narrative of connecting with a man over the chat telephone lines then meeting him at the Birmingham train station. Carl's piece is full of the local specifics of how men connect in the Midlands of England. His narrative charts the dangerous DMZ where a sex hunt slowly begins to be about a search for greater intimacy. The audience in Birmingham recognizes a narrative of their own in Carl's words, a series of familiar spaces in their city that they also negotiate with their own bodies.

Kuli tentatively steps into the center and asks to be heard. "I need to tell you something." His journey through this two-week process has been his first-ever acculturation into a group of gay men: first gay tribe, first visit to a gay club, first gay sex. Kuli's body became the space for the Ur-queer narrative, coming out and into life! Kuli had literally been mutating in front of our eyes for two weeks, his body language and comfort level visibly altering by the second. His story in the performance is a reminder of this most fundamental step of claiming self. The story builds to a wild Trip Hop club dance as he describes occupying queer space for the first night in his life.

The whole group dances wildly with Kuli and then opens out into a circle as I take the space and tell the story of my hand. Each man slaps my hand as I tell the times I was discouraged from reaching. This leads to the central story of the bottle hitting me in the hand, flung by the queer-basher in Montana as I longed for the touch of my boyfriend Alistair, in Australia, kept out of the U.S. by my nation's homophobic immigration laws.

167

The group embraces and then from each of the hugs one man begins to fall as we hear Ken's harrowing imagination of the night of the bombing at the Admiral Duncan. The image of a fallen man from each couple echoes in the space as Robert sings about the Admiral Duncan blast and all the bombs that go off around us.

> Didn't I ever tell you, I'm not just zeros and ones
> Didn't I ever tell you?
>
> Didn't I ever tell you, I just wanted some respect,
> Yea that's right, didn't I ever tell you?
>
> And it felt like a lifetime had passed us by,
> Before our loves could walk by our side.
>
> But we were new born in the city lights,
> We were new born in those city lights.
>
> Then we walked in the darkness with a generation that
>   got no bloom,
> A whole fucking generation got no bloom.
>
> And didn't I ever tell you
> About the brothers and sisters that were blasted
> Into fragments across the surface of a Soho bar?
> Like pearls from a broken string.
>
> You said, my dear boy they're only queers, why oh why
>   all those tears,
> Why oh why all those tears?

As Robert finishes his lament, the fallen men are pulled in slow motion across the stage. We gather around Robert and place our hands, faces, on his body while the song echoes in the space. The performers face the audience. We check our bodies as if for injury, pressing and touching to make sure we are still there. One by one we speak out the affirmative statement, *I'm gay*. Slowly this segues to a more problematized question—*I'm gay?*—as each performer shifts from checking to make sure we're still breathing to madly feeling whether our hairlines are holding, our crows-feet spreading, our love handles showing. Panic about our male bodies builds to a peak, and then Ken parades out and shouts *I'm not gay!*

Ken slowly disrobes, regarding each revealed body part, as he performs a text explaining that his fifty-year-old body not only is no longer read as gay, but indeed compromises his claim on that identity:

> I'm not gay.
> I'm fifty years old.
> I'm not gay.
> The hair is gone. The face, oh God. I used to be a model. Was
>   it really that long ago?
> I'm not gay.
> The body, my body.
> Chest? tits? gone.
> Stomach? Twenty-eight no more — inches, years, what
>   the hell; gone is gone.
> Talking of gone . . . HELLO, DICK! ARE YOU AWAKE?
> I'm not gay.
> I want to be held, desired, loved.
> I am not gay.
> I want to feel skin upon skin. I want to lick his sweat, his
>   cock, his balls.
> I want to smell him.
> I want to wake to his breath on my neck.
> I want to feel him deep inside me.
> I am not gay.
> I am. I am. I AM A HOMOSEXUAL!

Ken's piece ends with that declaration, which claims a more complex, less colonized way of being exactly the queer man that he is. He then wanders through the audience, meeting and greeting, a naked man among the clothed public, fresh from having revealed his vulnerabilities from asshole to belly. There is a great sense of liberation in Ken's claiming a new way of seeing the embodied self. It makes the audience deliciously nervous and giddy at the same time with the new set of possibilities that Ken offers.

The rest of the performers wander the stage, regard each other, then face the audience. Each man offers a physical action, derived from their maps of their bodies, that taps into their deepest aspiration for themselves, and offers the act with one sentence as *Suck, Spit, Chew, Swallow* concludes:

> "I want to keep offering my heart to another man in
> my red, red hands."
> "I want him to respect me."
> "I want to feel safe to walk hand in hand."
> "I want my lover and I to grow old together."

Conclusion

As I climbed on the plane back to the States the day after the performance, I felt almost more jet-lagged than the morning I had arrived. The performers and I had gone into a deep inquiry of how we see our bodies, found some narratives that live there, and built a community with one another to share these tales of men's cocks and hearts. Not only that, we had also managed to create a complex, performative representation of these body stories that we could share with a larger community of people there in Birmingham, England.

I knew we had done something very difficult and very much worth doing. We had discovered that a man who becomes conscious of the narratives within his body is more ready to confront eye-to-eye the fucked up legacy of embodied experience. Through our struggle and drama with each other we had seen how the scarred and broken places on the body can also let a little light in. We jumped into the abyss of acknowledging the warfare that surrounds men's bodies, these bodies trained to fear vulnerability and each other. I think this inquiry just might prepare us for the raw activity of being more conscious, less colonized males of the species.

As I travel around the world performing and leading community-based performance workshops, I see the need becoming ever greater for theatrical, and experiential paratheatrical, spaces where people can explore the complex human life going on within their bodies. A rigorous and embodied participatory theater is one of the few ways these bodies can gather with one another in our increasingly disembodied culture. In the work I do with groups of artists and non-artists, I have learned that finding a way to be more present in our bodies and open to the narratives that we carry in our flesh and blood is the quickest route to discovering the revelatory material about what it means to be human.

References

"As G.I. Joe Bulks Up, Concern for the 98-Pound Weakling," *New York Times,* 30 May 1999.

Peter Lehman, "Crying over the Melodramatic Penis," *Masculinity,* ed. Peter Lehman (New York: Routledge, 2000).

Michaelangelo Signorile, *Life Outside* (New York: Harper Collins, 1997), 25–26.

Jesus and the Queer Performance Artist

Tim Miller wrote this essay for a collection of "stories of lesbian and gay faith." It incorporates materials from the performance art sermons he prepared and delivered with an Episcopal priest, Malcolm Boyd, in 1989 and 1990, as well as from journal entries discussing Miller's re-encounter with religion. The sermons at St. Augustine-by-the-Sea parish, where Miller attended services, began with alternating reminiscences: Boyd's primarily of his work in the civil rights movement, Miller's drawing on childhood memories as well as experiences during the ongoing AIDS crisis. Eventually the activist memories melded appropriately for the Easter season's commemoration of Jesus's arrest and execution, with Miller portraying a bullhorn-equipped civil authority arresting Boyd. As he notes in this essay, his creative activities with Boyd were hardly a radical departure for Tim Miller: his work always has had a mystical component, which he often humorously attributes to his upbringing in New Age California. The sense of religious awe is prominent in this essay, which ends with a remembered epiphany in the Sierra mountains. But perhaps most significant is Tim Miller's newly realized, delicately expressed sense of Jesus as performer, activist, and role model.

1990 was a very strange year for me. I am a performance artist, a gay man, and a member of the Parish Church St. Augustine-by-the-Sea in Santa Monica, California. This year, I found myself in two very different and intense situations, both pushing at each other in seeming contradiction.

I whirled around in the center of the nation-wide media circus controversy surrounding the National Endowment for the Arts. Unanimously recommended Theater Fellowships to Holy (ooops, that's *Holly*) Hughes, Karen Finley, John Fleck and myself were over-turned by NEA Chairman John Frohnmayer because of the content of our work. You see, three of us were gay, Karen Finley was an angry feminist, and *all* of us explore sexual content and refer in very different ways to Christian imagery and archetypes as a way of exposing and healing the lies and hurt of our society. We all exist in a highly ethical and moral framework of compassion for suffering. We were being fashioned as sacrificial lambs to the great slathering mouth of the lunatic right wing of Jesse Helms and his ilk. Our work was shown on network TV, misrepresented in the major press, and lied about in Congress. It became clear we were being hung out to dry. This was in order to soothe the nutso religious right who need to see gay men, lesbians and feminists censored and vilified for speaking the truth about the pain and hurt in our land to Caesar and King George.

Cross fade to a few weeks earlier. I was part of the Mass at St. Augustine, doing a performance art sermon with Priest Malcolm Boyd. This work, presented as the sermon for the 10:30 A.M. service on Passion Sunday, tried to interpret the intensity of Lent, Easter and the crucifixion in terms of social justice. Through humor, performance actions and audience participation we asked the congregation to search their hearts in order to identify the ways we crucify one another through racism, homophobia, economic injustice, AIDS, and environmental disaster. Building towards a powerful chaotic moment, the performers in the congregation began springing to their feet in the pews, hurling and receiving insults, being both crucified and crucifier. The craziness finished with a shout from a bullhorn, recalling a peace mass Malcolm had celebrated in the Pentagon during the Vietnam War. The policeman who arrested Malcolm said "You are disturbing the peace." I spoke over the cacophony: "This is my body, which is given for you. Do this for the remembrance of me." The sermon ended with Malcolm telling a story of an unexpected communion in a shack during the civil rights movement. I would break into the story with my genuine need to find the acts of love in this world. To find the gesture of redemption, whether that gesture is seen in an AIDS buddy or someone feeding the homeless. The point is that all of us put each other on crosses and are crucified. Malcolm and I asked the congregation to make the crucifixion personal; to acknowledge the sacrifices, miracles and evils all of us take part in. The performance art sermon was a charged event that moved and energized the audience who came that day to witness this happening and share in this fusion of liturgy and performance art.

Malcolm and I did disturb the peace that morning; but we also provided a journey for some folks through something strong. When the words "peace be with you" were spoken after the sermon, they carried a call and an urgency that was full of possibility.

I bring up these two events to pinpoint the strangeness of our time. The same year that I explore issues in my own faith as a Christian through a performance art sermon, I am also under assault from the Christian Right for being a visible gay artist. This might be seen as an interesting model of reality for gay people who are culturally Christian and trying to create a new relationship to Jesus and this complicated religious tradition.

OK. Honesty time. Enough with all the intellectual-cum-historical-slash-political-hyphen-contextual business. What is all this about? What do I actually feel about my Christian identity? I was raised with a lazy smattering of Sunday school, WASP spiritual cool, pro forma golden rule, confirmation, and then out the door into my intellectual artist self. At the time, my strongest experience within the church I grew up in, the Whittier Hillcrest Congregational

Tim Miller and Reverend Malcolm Boyd during the performance art sermon at St. Augustine-by-the-Sea parish, Santa Monica, 1990. Photo by Chuck Stallard.

Church, was that on a youth group field trip to the beach I managed to make out with one of the other boys in a cave. It was a kind of epiphany, without a doubt.

It is so confusing. . . . I feel that I was pushed away into exile from my Christian self. A whole part of my identity got left out in the rain. There I was devouring *Das Kapital,* Buddha's Four Noble Truths, teenage existentialism, and fellatio while ignoring Liberation Theology, the prayer of St. Francis, the love commandment, and the kiss of peace. *Oooops.* Why does this happen? It is certainly not uncommon. First, I was turned off by the blandness of organized suburban Christianity. Strike one. Then, I was driven away by the bloodstained history of inquisition, imagined heresy and conquest, those fucked up oppressive parts of the tradition and the exclusionary signals that are sent to gay people by the bigoted religious Right. Strike two. Finally, there seemed to be no way to incorporate my basically good feelings about Jesus into my post-adolescent intellectual/artistic/political hit parade. Strike three. You're out. Nothing personal, Jesus—I just can't stand the company you keep. It seemed to make more sense to chuck the whole thing. Get out of my face, Jesus.

A few tears—I mean years—later, the cultural crisis alarm bells start to go off. To go into hiding from my cultural and religious stuff is a tricky business for me. I clearly desired a spiritual underpinning to my life. This had led me to zazen meditation, Plato, and worship of Nature. Wanting the feeling of a higher power, I began also to search within my Christian self for the purpose of life and was moved by the message of compassion and social equality in the Gospel.

I have a desperate need to know who I am and to know where I come from. This means to snoop around the secrets in the attic and sift through your ancestors' faded papers that are stuck in a trunk somewhere in Kansas or Mesopotamia.

I am involved within a multi-cultural arts community where people from many different backgrounds and experiences are creating art that helps articulate identity. This search often leads artists to their deep spiritual roots, whether an African-American exploring a connection to Yoruban spiritual practice or a Celt tapping in to earth-based practices of the tribes of the British Isles. I need to understand why my heart and spirit are moved and illuminated by the need for renewal, the passion of sacrifice for social justice, the desire to find the way to love each other, the need to discover compassion as a building block for our culture. These are all spiritual needs that weren't really finding an answer in my art life and political activism.

In my work as a performance artist, themes that are clearly informed by a deep current of Christian identity keep coming up: crucifixion and rebirth, conflict and communion, epiphany and despair. The desire for moments of peace. Sorrow about the sadness in the world. A radical desire to ease suffering, my own and others'. For me, to finally comprehend these long-hidden emotions led me to look into my heart and soul, as well as into my culture, to see precisely what was there.

Journal Entry 3/14/89

Things have gone completely crazy . . . everything in this art-life terrain feels up for grabs. I've never been more excited. I'm collaborating with Malcolm on what we are calling a performance art sermon. This has been a great experience. Dealing with my whole confused Christian thing. The weird text of performance artist and priest. Vocation. Shamanism. Lesson through parable. The sermon is going to deal with AIDS, the love commandment and social responsibility. St. A's is a great liberation theology type place. After the service last week Malcolm and I rehearsed on the altar. Making plans. Talking about the big stuff. What we want this experience to be for ourselves and for the parish. What is communion? The kiss of peace? It's making me deal with my long suppressed Jesus stuff. Blood and body hey hey hey. Who is that guy up on the cross and what does he have to do with me?

I wanted to at least get on speaking terms with Jesus. This just seemed to make sense. But more important, it seemed to me that I *needed* to develop this relationship. The pressures of my world were pushing me into experiences of great spiritual challenge. The skinny guy up on the cross hits me stronger now after seeing so many emaciated friends wither away. *I.N.R.I.* over the cross has been replaced by *A.I.D.S.* over the hospital bed. The loss of so many friends and lovers to AIDS has pushed and aged me in ways I can't even begin to understand. The deaths of young men, whose bodies and spirits I had loved as much as my semi-retarded emotional abilities were able, have been an earthquake in the heart zone for me and my generation. Death scares me shitless. I have had to confront it at this early point in my life in a very powerful way. My friends and I have also had to create or rediscover rituals for burying our dead and marking their passing. This has thrown us back to our spiritual upbringing (if any) and meant a new call to recreate our relation to the universe and God/Goddess. For me, this also challenges me again and again with that question from my journal, "Who is that guy up on the cross and what does he have to do with me?"

Journal Entry 2/12/90

My first understanding of this Jesus guy is that he was a carpenter. This always made sense to me because I was always a carpenter, too. It just seemed reasonable to me that there was this dude long ago who made things: tables, chairs, useful things. When the church I went to as a kid was being built, I'd climb all over it with my friends, looking for metal slugs, saving them as treasure, climbing up plaster stairs, hiding in half-built steeples. It was like the holiness in the building was in the construction. The nuts and bolts of it, the nails and wood. I always felt good about the carpenter stuff since it was one of the few boy-type endeavors that I was really good at. That cutting and smoothing and building was a good thing and probably a holy thing—that rang true for me. And so it was good that Jesus was a carpenter and did those things too. I loved tacky biblical movies as a kid. There were those low-angle shots of chips of wood coming off of the hand planer as Ben Hur comes into sight on his way to the galley slave ships. Religious music, please. We would see Jesus only from behind, offering water to the sexy suffering Charlton Heston.

Later on, Jesus seemed to be much more something out of books. I was more comfortable with books because they were intellectual and appealed to my fat brain. Jesus hanging out with Alyosha Karamazov, trying to understand his brother's parable about Christ coming back during the Spanish Inquisition and then having to be crucified again by the Grand Inquisitor. Jesus in the bathtub with J. D. Salinger as Franny and Zooey battle about trying to turn Jesus into St. Francis, and then the final realization over the telephone that the fat lady with the big ankles is Jesus. All morality comes down to doing it for the fat lady, offering compassion and love. It was like these books, in my world that was built of such books, were the way to get at this thing. Alyosha and Zooey Glass became boyfriends, moved in together, and tried to make sense of the world.

Now, my hit on the Jesus thing, and the effort to try to get a sense of who he was and what it means now: I get this mostly through Jesus as activist. The ways the mad-dog message of love and social justice within the gospel Señor Jesus preached resonates politically in Central America, or through Gandhi's Satyagraha or Martin Luther King and the civil rights movement. Jesus as a member of ACT UP. The crucifixion as the ultimate civil disobedience. This guy building chairs. Trying to create a reality where people actually might love one another. Getting ready to go on a game show, offering love to the fat lady in the front row. The Jesuit priests killed in San Salvador. They could have been me and my friends.

I need to short circuit my intellectualizing a little. I need to find the way to be with and comfort the dying, feel the pain in the world, confront my own fears and faults, listen to my heart and soul. All of us in some way are trying to live up to this big challenge not to treat each other like shit. This is a tall order. And, oh, the sorrow that I feel at the impossibilty of the task.

So this is where I am now. I have opened up a line of communication with Jesus and even found some part of me that is able to pray. I talk to him. Say hello. I have begun to heal a place inside me that was alienated and adrift from a deep sense of my family and where I come from, these strange northern European Anglo-Saxon tribes finding the way to bring their forest gods into the new religion from the desert. We mark the birth of the man who sacrificed himself for others by bringing a cut tree into our living rooms at solstice time.

And, I am a carpenter. I have felt awe toward certain priests who have given their lives or labor for justice in El Salvador and other places, who display total commitment and faith and a willingness to work toward a world with a little less suffering and a little more compassion. This humbles my own well-meaning gestures. I approach Jesus as a friend and helper. He is someone I meet at an ACT UP action. He is there in the circle with us in my performance art workshop. He is part of the fellowship of my gay friends. I know his lips. He is around to help me find my way through the biggest challenges of understanding my own heart, the pain in my world, the Gospel as a social document, and the love commandment as an ultimate moral yardstick. We *must* love one another.

Meanwhile, I am still a performance artist. Still a sexualized gay man. Still a political activist working towards making this society start to work for the sick and poor, and to open its arms to diversity. I have found a way to incorporate the part of myself that is Christian into my identity and creative work. I try not to close my heart to feelings of grace, forgiveness, fellowship. The times of the year have become more layered and powerful: the birth of the light at Christmas and the planting and resurrection of Easter. I am part of a community of artists, social workers and political activists who are also Christian.

I felt that the two performance art sermons with Malcolm were the most controversial works I had done in terms of the community of artists and gay people. There was a strange sense of *Why is Tim doing this? This Jesus stuff makes me nervous! I just don't feel comfortable dealing with this Christian routine!* I had a feeling of simultaneous censorship: from the nutso Right—that I should keep my queer mouth shut—and from some people in the secular community of artists and intellectuals, that I should soft pedal the religion thing. Some people seemed to be saying: *It's bad enough if this is moving in your life, but can't you at least keep quiet about it, or at least have the decency to be a Tibetan Buddhist? Stick to Goddess worship, buddy, or else!*

Whew! I know these are real questions. I know there are no easy answers. I am a gay man yet I also am clearly connected to my self as a Christian. I love having sex; I am not monogamous. I believe in the healing power of sex and the role sex can play in creating communion in my body and spirit. It seems like Jesus and his friends were a passionate community of fellowship. Free from macho bullshit and focused on spirit energy. This is very familiar to the fellowships in my life. Jesus was ready to embarrass the idiots who wanted to stone the woman. This is a very important moment for me, the lesson where Jesus tells us to cut each other a little slack. This resonates for me as a gay man. It speaks to my heart as someone who has been vilified and attacked for being who I am. I love men. I love their bodies. I love their souls. I love their collection of characteristics, phobias and geniuses, all that makes them who they are. To be with a man physically is often to know him and value his personhood, and to create a communion and bond.

Journal Entry 10/18/89
In Minneapolis for an Arts Conference. Met a nice boy from Philadelphia who was way cute. He works at one of the artspaces there. He's also a performance artist and he's doing a piece where he cuts down a big tree and then puts it in the gallery. He called it "the ultimate Duchampian ready-made." He

was sweeter and dearer than this kind of art-school stunt would let on, and I felt a strong love for him. We were good to each other and had a sexy time. So strange: the last two men I've slept with (other than the boyfriend, of course): one cutting down a tree, the other the refugee from Peru who works planting trees on Martin Luther King Boulevard. One a boy in a leather jacket smoking cigarettes, the other tie died and recycling, and a faerie. I like them both. I love them both. A graceful and odd circle of styles and upper bodies, penises and souls, wardrobes and lifeforce. Between each other, between them and me. I know my body and spirit better from my time with them. I feel closer to the world with them both in my heart.

The first man I was ever in love with was Jesus. He was sweet. He was strong. He didn't play football or scream at me and he wore great clothes. This feeling I had for him from a very early age is part of my love for other men. I imagine him as a generous and sensitive lover, ready to give and receive pleasure. I see him there for the other person. Rubbing tired muscles with all those sweet smelling balms and ointments that they keep talking about in the New Testament. My relationship to Jesus is in a direct heartbeat to my gay identity. So for me there is not a contradiction. I feel firmly in line with the spiritual vocation gay men often feel, which has been an enormous influence on the church and toward the shamanic impulse in other spirit journeys.

The man I have loved and lived with longest is not Jesus, but my boyfriend Doug. Like Jesus, Doug is a Jew, a bit of a rabbi, and very much a troublemaker. We have shared the last cataclysmic eight years. His Jewish identity is very strongly defined both culturally and spiritually. Our connection is not challenged by the separation of our faiths. Neither of us excludes other metaphysical influences from our spirit lives, whether it be Jungian therapy, Sri Rama-krishna, Walt Whitman, or Earth worship. Our connection is not through what we don't share in specific cultural religious practice, but what we do share: the basic belief in a higher power and something outside ourselves that we can communicate with; that we find the way to honor the universe. It would be difficult if one of us had no kind of spiritual practice or foundation. That would be a conflict, a place with no dialogue. Our spirit journey is so intimate, so much a part of our relationship, that stereotyped ideas about a practicing Jew and Christian not getting along seem absurd. A moment where Doug and I recently waited to hear our HIV test results was an intense example of this. We were in about as existential a spot as I've been. Doug covered his head and prayed; I crossed myself and prayed. Our spirits were alive as these two queers called up Jesus/Goddess/Moses and anyone else who might help us at that moment, in that time of trial.

My identity as a spiritual person includes eucharist, zen meditation, sex between men, the Passover ritual, and planting my garden each year. The poetry and almost sexual intimacy of drinking the blood and eating the body of Christ connects me to the congregation, God, and the possibility for magic. The challenge of zazen, to just sit and breathe, tames my mind and craziness. The ritual meal of the Seder helps me understand my own liberation and flights from slavery. The miracle of planting seeds and harvest time tunes me in to the cycles of life and death. My compost heap is another resurrection. All of these are part of savoring the body I am blessed with and the universe I am part of. All challenge me to nurture growing things (including my soul), and to work to care for our world and to ease the pain that exists.

Journal Entry 4/1/90

I have had a certain dream my whole life, or at least as long as I can remember. I am with a bunch of other people. We are connected by a kind of bond, a bond built on a work towards justice. Sometimes it's like a concentration camp thing, sometimes it's like that Andreyev novelette *The Seven That Were Hanged*, about the friends who were rebelling against the czar and are taken out and hanged in the snow. Often it's set in Burbank or somewhere like that. The shit has hit the fan and people are being blown away. In this dream in all its forms, we are there about to suffer and die—but there is a feeling of purpose and reason, if nothing else than that we're trying to understand the world, why there is injustice and pain, finding a way to explain it, adjust, change.... I dunno.

I think this has informed in the biggest fattest way my search through all my religious/spiritual/mega-bigtime understanding of the world. Whether it's the years tuning in to cool Buddha here in my Southern California polyglot spirit heritage, or more and more my vibe on Jesus—teaching, working, forgiving, dying. Why do we do what we do? how do we respond to the horrors of our time? the particulars, the Jesuit priests' brains smeared on the wall by fascists in El Salvador.... Oh God.

I was climbing a mountain when I was about seventeen. I had hiked for about two hundred miles with my brother through the Sierras. We had heard gunshots and screams the night before. It was probably just people fucking around, though we hadn't seen anybody for days. I got real scared, as scared as I had ever been in my life. I was sure I was going to die. I stayed awake all night in my sleeping bag, waiting for some crazed lunatic types to blow us away after mutilating us or something. Well, it didn't happen and I finally greeted the day amazed that I was still alive.

My brother and I began to climb again before it was even light. Climbing step by step up a very steep trail up a two-thousand-foot rock face. I was feeling every molecule tingle and tune in to the miracle of being alive, reborn from my night of fear. I was ready for the big resurrection, the big satori, the goods were about to come my way! I was a great big satellite dish tuned in on God. Just send some my direction!

We got to the top of the pass. I expected some major chord epiphany, a brass band of the Virgin of Guadalupe, something. . . . But there were just more mountains, stretching as far as I could see, twelve-thousand-foot-tall mountains.

I was pissed off. I threw off my pack and began to climb some more, up the sides of this path, throwing rocks down as I climbed almost straight up. My breath exploding, I climbed up another five hundred feet. My brain pounding, almost bursting. Dizzy and angry and wanting, I got to the top and there was a big flat rock. I looked again and saw the mountains, and then *saw* the mountains, almost passing out. The big ecstasy, the big everything at once. Lying on this flat rock at thirteen thousand feet with Jesus, and Buddha, and the old mountain gods of my tribes of the forests.

Whew! it was all there . . . some kind of wordless thing . . . big voices, big feeling, and my heart getting as full as it has ever gotten, where my living and my dying were at the same time, my works and my death as one, the pain of Christ on the cross and a zillion acts of lovemaking through the ages as one . . . my life now and what is to come, long after my body is feeding somebody's California poppies. My breath quieted and I ate some peanuts and raisins, then climbed back down, ready to go back to the world.

It is not simple. The chasm that exists in my heart, in our society and between one another, is full of pain. I have experienced this firsthand as I debate crazed neo-nazis during this time of controversy around my performance art works. There are many wounds that need to be healed. The battles around inclusive spiritual practice have pushed and challenged our society for two centuries, over issues of slavery, the women's movement, civil rights, the war in Vietnam, and now lesbian and gay rights. The closer we can get to ourselves spiritually and find a generous place to include the diversity of our journeys, the sooner the hurts of our time may finally be healed.

For me, even as the hate mongering of the religious Right attacks me and my queerness, I still feel that I have my own relationship to God/Goddess and Nature. I will not let their hatred and racism and bigotry hijack Jesus to their polyester Bible Theme Park or make him a hostage in the Wedding at Cana water slide. Because I believe Jesus would be happier in bed with Zooey Glass and Alyosha Karamazov: planning to save the world, staying up late, talking philosophy. Making love.

Coda

The maw of Hollywood

From Tim Miller's journal, 1987.

Into the looming maw of Hollywood. I got a call from this casting agent at Columbia Pictures. She had seen my picture in the *L.A. Times;* she wanted to meet with me. I drove to Burbank and found my way to Trailer 36, walked past the Western town, New York tenement, ivy-covered college building, etc. She was casting this movie *Point Break* to be directed by Ridley Scott. There were a coupla people waiting to see her. . . . I instantly wished I wasn't wasting my time on this kind of thing, being object to their subject. I knew this was another scratch-n-sniff job where some casting person checks out the performance artist because they're "in" this year. I waited patiently, sitting on the reality side (the back) of some film set.

Finally I went in. She greeted me with "Well, the famous Tim Miller!" I said, "Oh boy, my favorite way to be greeted." We talked about what I did, why she was interested in performance artist/dancer types as opposed to actors. She was a bright handsome older woman. It looked like she could be the caretaker of a nudist camp, briskly dealing with problems. I liked her. She said I looked younger in my picture and asked how old I was. This movie seemed to be about surfers and the FBI. I think she wanted surfer-punk types. This was OK. I was so happy that my life is not about casting directors and pretending I'm younger than I am, and spilling my guts to be in some dumb movie. I felt such a relief that it didn't matter what she would say: I don't rely on *her* for me to do my work. . . . I practically danced to my car, past the film sets, wanting to get back to work in my life, having to battle my own demons and limits on *my* terms.

Part 5

Us

Tim Miller in *Us*. Photo by Dona Ann McAdams.

Oklahomo!

This short essay is specifically placed in time, June 26, 2003. Tim Miller was flying to Austin for an early performance of Us *when the Supreme Court in* Lawrence v. Texas *struck down all remaining U.S. laws outlawing "sodomy." Returning gay rights to the national agenda, the decision ignited the "gay marriage" issue that Tim Miller had been addressing, with increasing specificity, for a half-dozen years. Like* Us, *"Oklahomo!" uses Tim Miller's love of American musical theater as the starting point for reflections on his political activism. It makes an appropriate introduction to this concluding section. A shorter, somewhat different version was published in* American Theatre *magazine in August 2003.*

As I watched the Tony Awards broadcast a while back, savoring the folks singing and dancing their way through the numbers from the nominated musicals, I was struck by how cheerfully utopian it all felt. I never take for granted the sheer miracle of all these performers managing to cooperate and pull off something like the big final number from *Hairspray*. These shows and the people who made them seemed to manifest a clear alternative political vision of our country—one where gay couples are smoochingly visible; where the short fat girl wins; where people of different races boogie together;

where progressive politics are everywhere you look. The Tonys conjured an America that I wish actually existed and that we could all live in. For one moment during the broadcast segment from the beleaguered musical version of *Urban Cowboy,* I escaped from the grim realities of the Lone Star State, where the Texas Legislature had just outlawed gay marriage. The musicals on the Tony broadcast made me feel like I lived in a better world—perhaps Canada, where gay civil marriage was just legalized in time for June weddings!

It's easy for people, even theater folks sometimes, to malign musical theater as a kind of guilty pleasure, a bad habit like bingeing on bon-bons. Musicals can be bashed alternately as superficial fluff or as reactionary reinforcements of a colonized, court-jester status for gay people and communities of color. Maybe performers in musicals do become versions of Stepin Fetchit every now and then, but I believe the legacy of the musical theater canon is infinitely more complicated, subversive and admirable than that easy critique allows. Musical theater has been a primary site for generations of queer American kids to claim some kind of agency as they get out the hairbrush microphone and lip-sync to *Cabaret* or, more recently, the *Rent* cast album.

I was definitely one of those kids. These Broadway shows were a crucial finishing school for my nascent gay identity, offering me that rich tonic of diva agency and general fabulousness. I am not afraid to fulfill this stereotype. But musicals also provided my earliest political education: they were my crucial *Ur*-texts delineating social relations. I looked to musical theater for deeper, or at least more tuneful, guidance about how the world was organized and how systems of injustice were going to rain on my parade. *Gypsy, Carousel, Fiddler on the Roof, 1776, The Sound of Music, Camelot, Oklahoma, Man of La Mancha, Applause, Funny Girl, Oliver!, South Pacific, Hair:* these shows became the primary texts for how this boy I once was understood the world. A world full of strippers with gimmicks, dancing cowboys on beautiful mornings, de-frocked nuns fighting fascism, founding fathers and hairy hippies dreaming the Impossible Dream.

Climbing Every Mountain. Walking Through a Storm. Brave little queer Oliver daring to ask for more. Not a bad laundry list of the potential ways of claiming who you are supposed to be.

The first major production of a Broadway musical I ever saw was *1776* at the Music Center in Los Angeles. I was a small-for-my-age ten year old as I scurried with my oldest brother to our orchestra seats just as William Daniels, the actor playing John Adams, performed the speech leading into that much-beloved—at least by me—ensemble number "Sit Down, John!" As a small boy, I worshipped the musical *1776*. I will go further than that and risk enormous personal and professional embarrassment when I admit the persistent encouragement my political activism has received from this musical about the signing of the Declaration of Independence. *1776* inspired me profoundly then, as it did again in its Broadway revival a few years ago, for its frank political assessment of the darker contradictions present at our nation's birth. There is a song from *1776*, "Is Anybody There?," which John Adams sings as his idealism hits rock bottom when the Southern colonies at the Continental Congress refuse to vote for independence if slavery is abolished. On some level Adams is the archetypal activist, only one step removed from the pugnacious Larry Kramer-Ned Weeks character in *The Normal Heart*. John Adams' dark-night-of-the-soul song, whose lyrics were taken from Adams' own diaries, later echoed within me as I was arrested outside the Federal Building in Los Angeles with ACT UP. The song was with me when the Supreme Court ruled against my NEA Four First Amendment case. And Adams' song is definitely with me as my Australian partner Alistair and I struggle with our country's unjust laws that deny us the basic civil rights—and rites—of marriage and may soon force us to leave the United States.

There's a huge part of me that resents these musicals for filling me with too much hope. Sometimes I wish I could get these damn songs out of my head. Part of me wants to escape from the unreasonable expectation that my modest efforts as an artist and activist will meet the challenge of *climbing every mountain* and *dreaming the impossible dream*. It is still hard for me to really believe there will ever really be *a place for us* in America. Yet these musicals contributed hugely to my becoming an activist in the first place.

Maybe if I had never seen *Man of La Mancha,* I wouldn't be cursed with my Pollyanna political idealism.

Maybe if I never saw *Les Miz,* I wouldn't want to storm the barricades for justice and would instead be happy to count my ill-gotten capital gains.

Maybe if as a little kid I never cried my way through the show *1776,* I wouldn't be stuck with my ultimate baggage of wanting to make our country more just.

Maybe if I had never seen *Gypsy,* I wouldn't have become a performance artist and, in my own way, a stripper. Whether my clothes are actually on or not in my shows, on some level I have always been a stripper there in that hot white light, stripping away bullshit, lies, fear and political hypocrisy.

Maybe the "Sodomy" song from *Hair,* which ironically would lose the Tony as Best Musical that year to *1776,* planted one of those early seeds of the belief that our performing selves, our singing selves, our protesting selves could, indeed, change the world. From *Hair* long ago to *Hairspray* at this year's Tonys, I have never lost that faith.

I am writing this on my way to Austin, Texas, to perform at Vortex Theater my brand new show *Us,* which explores all this life, politics and musical theater material. This morning as I packed my bags for the gig, the U.S. Supreme Court declared six to three — with Justice Scalia doing a carpet-chewing performance of homophobic dissent — that Texas's sodomy law was unconstitutional because it allowed straight folks to do whatever they wanted in the privacy of their own homes but would arrest gay people for doing the same things! And the Supremes also overturned sodomy laws in the remaining twelve states that allowed the government to demean gay people's private lives and criminalize men's and women's bodies, straight or gay.

Once I get to Austin, I will go straight from airport to theater and dive immediately into a technical rehearsal, but I will make time to sneak out—after I have given lighting focus notes, of course—to a demonstration near the State Capitol to celebrate today's ruling. I can imagine my ideal production number there on the steps of the Texas Capitol. Cue on fade up of Ding Dong, the Witch is Dead! As I fly to Texas over the vast deserts of the southwest (Oklahoma, perhaps?), I am probably thinking to myself Oh What a Beautiful Morning! it is today in America. I probably feel a little bit vindicated for always being such an inveterate cock-eyed optimist. I can't help it; I clearly do believe in fairies, and these days I will count my blessings and my favorite things as I imagine the production number that a huge chorus will cheerfully perform as we sing and dance our queer hearts out there, deep in the heart of Texas.

Carnal Garage

TIM MILLER and ALISTAIR MCCARTNEY

Carnal Garage, *which ends with a symbolic marriage ritual, is Tim Miller's third collaboration with a lover. A happier, less conflicted work than* Live Boys *and* Buddy Systems *(both printed earlier in this volume), in tone it resembles the sunniest of Miller's solo performances,* Fruit Cocktail *(1996), which he was touring at the time* Carnal Garage *took shape. Tim Miller's teaching had brought him together with Alistair McCartney at a 1994 gay men's performance workshop in London. Three years later they performed* Carnal Garage *in San Diego and San Francisco. Anticipating the solo works that followed,* Glory Box *and* Us, *this piece intersects with the constellation of issues involving the legal status of same-sex relationships. Yet as in Miller's earlier partner works, danger in* Carnal Garage *resides mainly in personal and community issues, such as its discussion of safe sex against the death-haunted San Francisco background. The issues of commitment and fidelity that dominated the earlier duos seem to have been resolved, or at least put aside here, in the joy of affectionate erotic discovery. The work is gay-specific in its erotic language and its evocation of safe-sex decisions, but the humorous love story has appeal to a wide audience.*

[As the audience enters, Tim and Alistair sit naked in their grooming stations. On a white wall are projected huge images of them floating naked in blue water. They sit still for a while, then begin to measure the space and their bodies. Electric clippers come out and they begin to shave or trim hair. They lift weights facing each other and weigh themselves. They pick up flashlights and wander into the audience. Ask the audience to put sunscreen on their naked bodies. Tim and Alistair return to the stage and the show formally begins. They display large cards containing personal information about themselves. The cards are revealed one at a time.]

TIM: AMERICAN
      38
      MIDDLE-CLASS
      170 LBS
      PROTESTANT
      NEO-ESSENTIALIST RABBLE ROUSER
      HIV NEGATIVE
      TOP
ALISTAIR: AUSTRALIAN
      25
      WORKING CLASS
      158 LBS
      CATHOLIC
      HOMESICK NOMAD
      HIV NEGATIVE
      BOTTOM

[A pause and then they switch the last placard]

TIM: BOTTOM

ALISTAIR: TOP

> *[They set down the cards, face each other, and walk to-*
> *ward each other in a channel of light as they speak the*
> *text.]*

TIM AND ALISTAIR: His foot creaks.
His eyes are open.
His belly growls.
His breath closer.
His cock thickens.
His body.
His body.

> *[They are face to face. Their noses touch and they dance*
> *together, kiss and struggle, begin to roll their foreheads to-*
> *gether as the energy builds into a wild dance accompanied*
> *by intense electric guitars. The dance quiets and they move*
> *downstage, put on their pants, and begin the dialogue.]*

TIM: I wait outside of Customs at SFO two years ago. I wait for a man who has grown bright inside me. I know him only from some walks around the Eros Statue in London, many handwritten aerogrammes and a wet week in Glasgow. I wait at the airport in San Francisco.

ALISTAIR: I remember waiting in the Customs line behind a big group of German tourists, feeling like it was going to take forever. After a thirteen hour flight, all I want to do is see the man I want to see. I feel unable to contain my excitement. I feel like it is spilling out all over the beige walls and the German tourists. I worry whether the Customs officers will notice.

TIM: Each face seems to be his for a moment, then blurs into someone else. I want to run for the door and go back to LA. I also want to leap the barrier and see if I can find him waiting in the

Passport Control line. I stand there waiting, my feelings sending off dangerous sparks, confusing the Air Traffic Control Tower.

ALISTAIR: The Customs officer asks me whether I am here on business or pleasure, and of course without pausing I say "pleasure." All those hours on the airplane have made my anxieties about seeing this man low level. I pick up my luggage and even with its weight I feel intensely light.

TIM: There he was in his suede jacket right out of *Midnight Cowboy*. There he was, this man who has crossed an ocean and a continent to come and see what is between us. I panic. What am I doing? I already have a boyfriend. We move quickly towards each other and kiss surrounded by the balloon bouquets.

ALISTAIR: The first thing I see is his hair. It's curly and it's got traces of red henna in it. Then I see his face, which at that moment is his eyes and his smile. His beauty. He was, he is so beautiful. That red in his hair, that face. I hope that I am looking good.

TIM: I hold him close, smell the travel on him. Wonder what's going to happen. Kiss him again. Worry I have made a huge mistake. I have a hard-on. We walk towards the double doors. Together we begin a chemistry experiment.

ALISTAIR: He says, "Hi, Alistair," and smiles. I say, "Hi," and smile. As we kiss and wrap our arms around one another, the old trick that presence plays on absence happens. Six thousand miles and six months dissolve in the florescent airport light. There are several male couples reuniting this afternoon and we are one of them.

TIM: As the cab takes us to San Francisco, we talk about earthquakes. This man is an earthquake in my life. This man is shaking me. I want to fulfill six months of jerk off fantasies and fuck his sweet hole. I want this to happen soon after we arrive at the Pension San Francisco.

ALISTAIR: He holds my hand in the cab as we drive through the fog from the airport to the hotel. I look at him, his body, a lot. I look outside the window, my new surroundings, a lot as he holds my hand.

TIM: The Pension San Francisco is the cheapest hotel I have ever stayed in. I like it. Clean rooms perched over Market Street. Bathrooms in the hall. In 1990, before I had ever been tested, I spent a week here covered in a rash that I was sure was HIV related. Today, Alistair and I quickly check in.

ALISTAIR: We get to the hotel and check in. Or he checks in as I stand back and soak up the newness of it all. My first hotel on my first night in America. The exchange with the hotel clerk seems foreign and polite. I can't wait to take the elevator up to our room to have sex with him.

TIM AND ALISTAIR *[Tim speaks the first line of each couplet, Alistair the second]:* I have been fantasizing about his body for months.
    There is a smooth flow to our first sex time here in San Francisco.

I run the home movies of the skin to skin adventures we had on a big bed in Scotland.
Our clothes fall off our bodies as our bodies fall onto the bed.

I am a child on Christmas morning.
He fucks me, in which position I don't remember.

I unwrap, I mean undress, him and feel the long journey of his legs and sides.
His dick moves into me with an ease, a grace.

I had carefully placed the condom and lube in the outside pouch of my bag.
His ass tastes of the afternoon.

I need to get inside of him and I do.
I want to pull a rabbit out of it with my tongue.

TIM: Later, we wander out onto Market Street and walk to the Castro. We eat at a Thai restaurant that now is no longer there.

The waitress at the restaurant remembers my name from many previous Mee Krob sessions. We eat scalding curry over a mound of rice. I peer at him over a fork wound tight with noodles. He seems bigger than I remember him. It must be the push-ups.

After dinner we walk back from the Castro along Market Street. I am looking and he is talking. He has his arm around me, and I look at everything and I just want us to fuck again. As we walk, two men going into a sex club cruise us. Everything about the neighborhood this night seems potentially sexy—a man washing his clothes in the Laundromat, an all-night supermarket. The air is warm and everything I breathe on turns to sex. I just want to touch him again. I want to touch everything.

We have sex once again before bed. As I sleep, I feel like I am lying in a frying pan, like the pan the fish cakes were cooked in at the Thai restaurant. Our bed is burning up. My back is in flames. I discover the mattress is covered in a thick plastic sheet—perhaps the Pension is wary of water sports. We peel it off and stash it under the bed. I sleep.

ALISTAIR: On my first morning in San Francisco I wake up early, 4 A.M., and walk quietly through the corridors on the third floor of that empty hotel. I wake up early because my body is still not quite here yet, it's somewhere between London and here, not sure whether it should be sleeping or eating. I am sure that I want him, but he's still asleep. I feel turned on and jet-lagged, dehydrated and alive.

TIM: We take the bus to Land's End and walk where I have walked many times before. I remember other lovers. I remember walking there with Vernon and his dog. I remember other stories. We are at the edge of the world. There is a sign here that says *Caution! People Have Been Swept From These Rocks and Drowned.*

ALISTAIR: We take the cable car to catch the Geary bus for Land's End, gripping the steel, leaning into the wind as pigeons fly into our faces, our mouths. I have never been here. I have no memory of here. My memories of this place are from here on. I can write anything I want into the sand. I have never seen the Pacific. "Want to touch the Pacific?" he asks. I take off my black and white Converse sneakers and dip my feet in.

TIM: Alistair and I walk, discovering the world, looking for the source of the Nile. The day is Biblical in its beauty. I expect Adam and Eve to walk down the path in spite of the *Breeders Keep Out* graffiti on the wall. The sun comes out and we take our shirts off.

ALISTAIR: There is a house that has fallen down a cliff, sitting precarious and lopsided on the slope. Its roof has blown off, it doesn't have any windows or doors. It's covered in graffiti like *Scandalera* and *Less is More.* I could see us living there.

TIM: I hold his long slender waist between my hands. We kiss with the Pacific Ocean under our feet. There is a circle of people up on a bluff. It is either a bunch of radical faeries or a white supremacist group. What are they doing up there?

ALISTAIR: At first I think it's a car rally. Closer, I realize it's a group of people. They are holding hands. They're standing very close to the edge. I have never seen anything like this before. My only point of reference is an old horror movie I saw once, where these little pagan kids gleefully throw themselves one by one off a clifftop that looks vaguely similar to the one standing before me now.

TIM: We gingerly climb along a narrow cliff path to a tower of rocks surrounded by the sea. I begin to freak out. I feel like the spinning earth is going to fling me to outer space or smash my brains on the rocks. How did I get into this precarious place with this man?

ALISTAIR: I begin to reveal my fears to him slowly, a slow, tentative undressing, at first only by looking at him. I let him know and he begins to let me know and we both kind of laugh through our fear. Undressing for real now, we begin to make out like mad on this exposed rock. I lick the sunrays and salt water off his skin on this exposed piece of rock that feels somehow as private as our hotel room. A beautiful scary bed, the hardest mattress ever.

TIM: I cling to the rocks so tight that I get tiny cuts on the tips of my fingers. Up on the bluff, one man leaves the Fairy Circle/Nuremberg rally and tosses a handful of white ashes into the wind. The ashes falling let me know what the gathering is. Several of the mourners at the memorial have skirts on or are naked.

ALISTAIR: As we make out some ashes fly over us, out of the palm of someone's hand into the air and from there into the Pacific. We make out in the fallout and I think of confetti at a wedding. Below us half naked men are cruising each other. And above us half naked men are mourning each other. What are we doing? I want to go back to the hotel.

TIM: The white puffs of ash and bone are swept away on the wind. We carefully crawl back to firm land. I feel like I have been given a reprieve, a new lease on life. We go back to the hotel and fuck wildly. I fantasize his ass lips drinking my cum.

ALISTAIR: Is language a map? Is a story a map? Is each word we speak a kind of map, an attempt at mapping? Is it possible to map love, desire, sex, trust, fear, time, feelings, memory? And as I resort to words, am I attempting to map out this time between us? Why am I attempting to map a time where I would happily have fallen off the face of the earth?

[They move upstage and—very slowly, as sand trickles out of paper bags in their hands—begin making a large circle of sand on the floor.]

TIM: The next day we wander through the Castro and talk. I float out the unprotected sex subject, tossing it like a paper airplane into the brisk off-the-bay wind. The camouflage of this homo intellectual discussion *du jour* allows me to fool myself that we are just talking about other gay men, not us. We are both HIV negative.

ALISTAIR: What began as an intellectual discussion, if it ever really was that, rapidly transformed into something else. My intellect left me, dissolving in the late afternoon sunshine. My hard on rose in time to our words, straining beneath my Levi jeans. It began here. And it ended here, here and here.

TIM: As I continue discussing the "Australian Model" of negotiated safety with this man from Australia, I am not aware that I am hoping he'll say I can fuck him without a condom. All I know is that something inside me wants to get inside of him, wants to get closer yet.

ALISTAIR: At least two things are happening at the same time. As my body walks around, explores the spaces of this city—this city that is so new to me that I know few of the street names—this desire that is so new to me, so new that I couldn't name it for you, begins to walk around, to explore the spaces of my body.

TIM: We walk to the drugstore at 16th and Mission. In a gesture of compromise, I have thought I would buy these new polyurethane condoms that promised a flesh-like feeling. *Avanti* they were called: that means "come in" in Italian. The drugstore is all out. There has been a run on the condoms, as if there was a stock market crash.

ALISTAIR: We leave the drug store empty-handed and my mouth feels dry, in need of lubrication. He points out different places to me and we talk. I tell him many things, but I'm not really telling him what I need to. That thing—I want him, his dick inside of me, my ass, without a rubber. I want our flesh to brush past one another's, and if he asks me why, I will not be able to tell him.

TIM: We walk up Mission Street past Rainbow Grocery towards our hotel. I remember my friend Reynaldo, who worked at Rainbow long ago. Reynaldo long dead. We discuss the inner life of gay men like academics at a conference. Why is it so hard to tell him what I want?

ALISTAIR: We reach the hotel. Just as we step off the pavement into the blur of traffic, I tell him what I've been holding back from telling him all afternoon. "You can fuck me without a rubber if you like?" I blurt out, feeling that in the very saying of these words I'm taking some kind of risk.

TIM: In the middle of Market Street, he tells me this. Bells and buzzers, three cherries in a Las Vegas slot machine. For once, words fail me. I am frozen in time, a sitting target for the cab racing downtown. I want to feel the grip of him. I want to get upstairs to the hotel room quick.

TIM AND ALISTAIR *[Alistair speaks the first line of each couplet, Tim the second.]*: I said go for it, go on. He said, are you sure?
   I ask, are you sure you want me to do this?

   I said Yeah. He said, are you sure?
   I say, I'll just put it in for minute.

   I said, uh huh. He said, are you sure you're sure?
   I tell him I won't cum in him.

   I said, I'm pretty sure.
   I slip my dick inside him without a rubber.

   It was the safest I'd felt in years.
   His body so alive under my touch.

   Our words give in to a big silence.
   I'm off the edge of the map.

   Just two bodies trusting.
   I am finding my own way.

   Three floors above Market Street. No more talking.
   I am making it up as I go along.

   Our tongues, brains thoughts quieted in trust.
   I am hot to the touch.

Switch off and we let our skins begin to speak—
I am looking for the secret.

to one another, flesh talk and the sound of that.
A siren on Market Street inside of my head.

Above the noise of the traffic I can tell you now.
My heart pounding in my ears.

It's deafening.
It's home.

It's open.
It's shelter.

It's noise.
It's warm.

It's more.
It's sky.

It's touch.

*[Tim pulls Alistair's pants down and blindfolds him with
a belt. Tim lights a candle and begins word improvisation.]*

TIM: G-G-G-G-Gotta walk ahead.
   W-W-W-W-Wanna know my shit.
   H-H-H-H-Hopeta move from here.

*[Tim lies Alistair down, removes his pants, and places a
large burning candle on his chest. Tim reaches for the*

Alistair McCartney and Tim Miller performing *Carnal Garage*, 1997. Photo by Mary Milelzcik.

candle and gets it very close to Alistair's skin. The hair be-
gins to burn. Tim waves: "Hi dad."]

TIM: I can open myself up like a window. I can get close to the heat.
I can let it in. I can burn myself up. I can find my vulnerable
places. I can put that heat in the places that can melt and change
and consume themselves into something new.

I can change my life.

I can make it new.

I can blow up my house.

I can burn the garage down.

I set my garage on fire when I was eleven. I love garages. They
are places where you can hide. Garages are places where mysterious things are always just underneath an old surfboard. It's where

I rehearsed having my own life. Like a one-man three-chord punk band. My garage is where my father lived. The garage is where my father kept things hidden from me.

[As Tim speaks the following text, he is putting arms, legs, and testicles close to the candle flame, burning hair off his body. The theater fills with the smell of burning hair.]

In my father's garage he kept his tools.
In my father's garage he kept his paint.
In my father's garage he kept his pain.
In my father's garage he kept his silence.
In my father's garage he kept his jumper cables.
In my father's garage he kept his son . . . he kept me.

I had my laboratory in my father's garage. I was into science. I was trying to turn lead into gold. All the others who had tried this were amateurs: I was going to make it happen. I was going to turn lead into gold. I was the lead. While I kept working on this problem I thought I would try something easier, so I was making a pipe bomb instead. I had found the recipe in a battered copy of the *Anarchist's Cookbook* that my brother had brought back from Berkeley. I had my sulfur, my potassium nitrate, and my charcoal from the briquets from last weekend's barbeque. I jammed in the gunpowder, then the broken glass, then the metal fragments, then the fuse, and screwed on the cap. During one of my tests on the fuse, something went wrong, very wrong. Maybe the sulfur had been too close to the potassium nitrate. The bunsen burner was still on. There was an explosion and flames licked up an old mattress against the back wall of the garage. The fire wouldn't stop. It climbed up the walls of the garage, set the Christmas ornaments ablaze, headed for the rafters. I tried to put it out. I had started a fire I just couldn't stop. I took off my Macy School sweatshirt and waved the flames. I ran for the hose just as my dad drove up, finally home from work.

He saw the orange glow and jumped out of his mustard colored Datsun. He said "OH MY GOD," sounding like Charlton Heston at the end of *Planet of the Apes,* and grabbed the hose from me. Dousing the flames with one hand, he whisked his jacket off with the other and tried to suffocate the fire, cursing me all the while. I huddled numb and frightened in the corner.

When the flames were out, my dad looked at me like he was going to kill me. He glanced around for the closest thing he could whip me with. He picked up jumper cables off the top of a smoldering fifty-gallon drum and began to whip me. Chasing me all over the backyard, he beat me and shouted:

[Tim whips the floor with jumper cables as Alistair flails at Tim with a leather belt.]

You could have burned the house down!
You could have killed all of us!
You could have killed your mother!
You could have killed your brother!
You could have killed your sister!
You could have destroyed everything we have!
You stupid, stupid boy!

I ran away. It hurt so bad. I thought he might kill me. I kept running, hoping I could avoid the worst of it, though knowing I deserved whatever I got. I was a bad boy. I deserved whatever I got. I had done something wrong. I was ready to be judged.

My dad lost interest and got embarrassed: the neighbors might see.

I lost interest in science at this point. It seemed too dangerous. Perhaps I'll take up art instead.

My dad just didn't understand, I had to be willing to change. I needed to see if I could turn lead into gold.

My whole life I have been willing to take the chance of burning the garage down. The place where things are kept hidden.

The place where the past gets dusty. I still feel the welts on my back and ass and legs where my dad whipped me with those jumper cables.

I left my father's garage and I started my own fire. I can make a garage for myself inside my body. A place I keep things.

In my garage I keep my memory.

In my garage I keep my sex.

In my garage I keep my sorrow.

In my garage I keep my pleasure.

In my garage, my heart.

In my garage I keep my tears.

In my garage, jumper cables are good for more than connecting one Chevrolet to another. The jumper cables can start my motor.

These jumper cables can link heaven and earth.

Can connect my heart to my head.

Can connect me to another man.

[Tim and Alistair begin to hook the jumper cables to different parts of their bodies, making different potential electrical connections.]

TIM: I lick his balls. I pinch his tit.

ALISTAIR: I fuck his ass. I stroke his dick.

TIM: I suck his cock. I bite his neck.

ALISTAIR: I tongue his ass. I fuck his mouth.

TIM: I cum in his heart. I ground my feet.

ALISTAIR: I put my pain into his head. I place my teeth in his thigh.

TIM: I remember the past. I stand here now.

[Tim and Alistair walk toward each other, disconnect the cables. Tim takes the jumper cables and places them along the stage line, then walks the tightrope as Alistair puts on his pants full of coins. Alistair begins to flip coins.]

ALISTAIR: Heads. Tails. Heads. Tails. What's going to happen? Hey Tim, want to play a game?

TIM: What kind of game? What are we flipping for?

ALISTAIR: Heads. Tails. 1981. In 1981 I was ten years old. Little boy in Catholic Boys school, wearing short pants.

TIM: In 1981 I was twenty-three and I visited my boyfriend John in the hospital at Bellevue, one of the first people sick with AIDS in New York City.

ALISTAIR: Heads. Tails. 1990. In 1990 I didn't know you. I had no knowledge of you.

TIM: I didn't know you. I had never met you in 1990. In 1990 Jesse Helms started hassling me on the floor of the Senate and I began having sex with a lot of men.

ALISTAIR: Heads. Tails. 2002.

TIM: I . . .

ALISTAIR: Shhhhh. . . . . What's going to happen to me, to you? Heads or tails, Tim?

[Alistair plays heads or tails a few times as he moves to Tim and covers him with coins.]

In the absence of memory, his body becomes my memory. When we fuck, your body becomes my memory. When we fuck something happens. So come to me, in the face of not knowing. Let me cover your body with accidents. Kisses. Risks. Amnesias. Let me fill your mouth, your ass with treasure.

[Tim drags Alistair by his pants to center stage. Alistair backs upstage to scales, steps on and weighs himself. Alistair does a gesture dance for about three minutes, heading downstage as Tim sends paper airplanes across the space. He ends up downstage center as the music finishes. Tim approaches Alistair and begins to mummify him in plastic.]

ALISTAIR: I wrap plastic around memory.

My mother's lover was a butcher.

My mother's lover was a butcher, he wraps plastic around meat.

My real father by occupation was a fitter, a turner, for British Petroleum. As a husband, he was a butcher, a butcher to my mom's memory and creativity. He butchered her and then wrapped her in a wedding dress. My mom, to get back at him, overcame her Catholic femaleness and began fucking Giuseppe, our handsome local butcher.

That's a lie. I wrap words around memory.

It's 1980. I am eight years old. I love going to the butcher with my mom. I love holding her hand in the butcher's shop. It's where I feel closest to her, my floppy hand entwined around her hand covered in sunspots. It's so cool inside there. The butcher wears a blue and white stripy apron. He knows everyone's name, even mine. I love waiting to see what my mom will choose for my dad's dinner tonight. What will it be? Will it be chops, sausages, steak, mince, veal, corned beef, chicken—or fish, even though it isn't Friday? What is she going to choose? The suspense is too much for me. The sexual tension between Giuseppe, our handsome brute of a butcher, and my mother is apparent to everyone's eyes, even mine. My mother—this woman whose cunt I came out of, fell out of into this world, slipped between her legs, covered in blood only to be wrapped in a blanket. What will she buy for my father's table, for my father's mouth tonight?

That afternoon she chose steak. Expensive. Maybe out of guilt, because as she gave Giuseppe her order, she stared right at the hard on beneath his apron. So did I.

I wrap my mother around my body.

I held her hand very tightly, as if it might be the last time I would get to hold that hand. I came out of her hand, not her cunt. As if the palm of her hand might protect me from the all too many fears I had already gathered up into my child's body. I held her hand, unable to take my boy child eyes off the crescent-moon-shaped knife the butcher used to cut the exact amount of meat my mother required for my father. The butcher weighed the meat, drained it of its blood and looked at my mother as he wrapped the steak very tightly in plastic.

I wrap my body in plastic to protect it from memory. I begin to unwrap.

[Tim and Alistair look at each other. Tim lifts Alistair, wrapped in plastic, and carries him upstage. Alistair emerges from the plastic. Tim covers himself. He goes to get water and prepare a fire in a large metal bowl.]

ALISTAIR: Tongue. Some things are worth tasting—tongue, flesh, air. Tongue—like something's worth tasting, leads me to flesh. Flesh. I love his flesh, his body, his ass. I love the taste of his ass on my face—my finger-dick-tongue, speaking in-out of my tongue. I used to be a vegetarian, but since I met him I love to eat meat—blood—I love meat in my mouth, flesh on my tongue. I love flesh—fat, muscle, gristle, tissue, dick, asshole, tongue. . . .

[Tim lights the fire, walks to Alistair with a bottle of water, drinks.]

TIM: Want a drink?
ALISTAIR: Yeah, I'm thirsty. Thanks. Do you want a drink?
TIM: Yeah, I want a drink. Is there anything else you want?
ALISTAIR: I want your presence.
TIM: I want my head to be connected to my body and I want to see you naked.

[Alistair takes off his pants and shows his butt.]

ALISTAIR: I want you to make yourself vulnerable to me.
TIM: I want to drink your tears.

ALISTAIR: I want to really see you.

TIM: I want to see the man you keep becoming.

[Tim and Alistair continue this for a few more exchanges: these requests—these promises—these wedding vows. They wash each other with water from the bottle. The bottle is now empty.]

TIM: Is there anything else you want?

ALISTAIR: I'm still thirsty. I'm still thirsty.

[The fire burns. Tim and Alistair cover the fire. Darkness.]

Tokyo Tim

During the period when he was composing Us, Tim Miller traveled to Japan for the 2002 Dokkyo University Performance Conference, where he gave his first performance in Asia. For the Tokyo appearance he compiled segments from several previous works—including, as he reports here, his walk into the audience to sit naked on someone's lap, from My Queer Body. Miller also worked with Japanese collaborators to create new elements for the Tokyo performance, giving rise in the essay that follows to thoughts about cross-cultural communication within common areas of gay experience. The film from which Miller's voice-over text was translated by a Dokkyo University student was originally done for a PBS station in Minneapolis (which declined to show it). "Tokyo Tim" was published in The Drama Review in 2003.

Hello.
Konnichiwa.

My name is Tim.
Watashi no namae ha Timu desu.

I come from America.
Watashi ha amerika kara kimashita.

I love Japan.
Nihon ga daisuki desu.

Do you come to this bar often?
Kono bar ewa yoku kimasuka?

Let's take off our clothes.
Fuku wo nugimashou.

I walked naked through the audience in a theater in Japan trying to scope out whose lap I would plotz my sweaty butt down on for a section of my performance. I knew I was in trouble when I saw a young Japanese woman hiding her eyes to avoid my nude, Western, *gaijin* body! She was not just covering her face with a few fingers, but rather burying her head as far as possible in her armpit under a tangle of elbows and forearms.

I was performing in Tokyo at the Dokkyo University International Forum on Performance Studies. This remarkable conference was organized by Professor Yuichiro Takahashi, a leader in Japanese inquiries into performance theory and practice. I was fortunate to be invited to perform my work at the forum, along with performer Denise Uyehara, my colleague from LA, and Japanese installation artist Yoshiko Shimada. The conference was subtitled "Resistance, Mutation and Cultural Hybridities," and definitely all three of those things were happening as I gamboled without clothes through the aisles and the Dokkyo student's gaze crept further and further inside her armpit. Now admittedly, I have made young ladies—as well as young men—all over the English-speaking world shrink into their seats with eyes gazing heavenward when they encounter my queer narratives on stage and my even queerer body in the orchestra seats. Sure, dismantling the unfamiliarity, the ick-factor and general invisibility of lesbian and gay embodied experience is one of my main jobs as a performer wherever I travel and perform, but there was something quite unique about approaching my first audience in

12/15(日) 14:00 ソフトウェアとハードな真実
パフォーマンス、グローバリゼーションと情動のネットワーク　ジョン・マッ

15:30 東アジアの/をめぐるカルチュラル・フ□
パフォーマティブな発明と「想像」の東アジア
キャロル・マーティン（ニューヨーク大学）/内野儀（東京大学）/C・J・W・L・ウ

18:00 BODY BLOWS by Tim Miller

会場…獨協大学（入場無料）
分科会を含むプログラムの詳細、参加方法、発表要旨、アーティスト紹介などは、http://ww
またプログラムは郵送も致します。下記までお問い合わせください。
獨協大学国際交流センター：phone 048-946-1918〜1920 fax 048-943-3259 e-

獨協大学インターナショナル・フォーラム&

Japan, indeed my first audience in Asia! Though I have performed in many countries, cultures and languages—and even allowing that this was an international conference sponsored by the English Department at Dokkyo University—I felt a particular challenge with this first performance in Japan. My inner self-doubt monologue was fast and furious: how will this Japanese audience make sense of my homo-centric world view? Why should they give a shit about the travails of an American gay performance artist? In my text-heavy U.S. performance, how are they even going to understand a word of what I say!

We can coolly theorize about the pitfalls of cross-cultural dialogue, but the specificity of the live performance is a much more gnarly, real-time communication challenge. On the upside, there is a kind of freedom that comes to the performer when the audience is not necessarily understanding every word you say on stage. (As if we can assume that even with an English-speaking audience!) My performance in Tokyo felt set free in some ways by the problematizing of language. It gave me opportunity to understand the piece in a totally different way, to literally make sense of it anew. I have had this experience before when performing in Sicily or Belgium or Austria, but in Japan I felt a fresh set of performance possibilities come forward. Of course, as I performed the piece I indulged that universal human tendency to negotiate language borders by beefing up my idiosyncratic sign language, a post-modern semaphore of gestural commentary added to my already high-energy, kinetic performance style. But I knew I wanted to come up with some fun, wild but simple translation devices to make my nonstop English work for this mostly Japanese audience.

In Japan this need I had to translate not so much the show's English, but my own experience of performing the show, created interesting opportunities for collaboration and juicy two-way pedagogy. Many e-mails zipped over the Pacific between Yuichiro Takahashi and me, discussing strategies for how the performance could pack the best wallop for this audience in Japan. With Prof. Takahashi's assistance one of his students at Dokkyo, Masashi Shiratori, translated my voice-over text of an extremely homoerotic film of myself and another fellow cavorting, and performed the text real time as a kind of duet aria with my own performance. Not only did Masashi get to have a bravura full-throated, sexy monologue that seemed to be a great performance experience for him, but he also got a translation extra-credit!

For another section, my longtime Japanese friend in New York, Gen Watanabe, translated and recorded a goofy Berlitz-style Japanese-English gay language lesson that I had written for the Tokyo performance. This brand new section gave me a chance to learn how to say "Suck my dick" in Japanese—*Shakuhachi shite,* if you're interested—and ended up being the comic highlight of the performance. Gen and I had long phone calls trying to figure out translations of colloquial English expressions for sex and love, to untangle the very different ways U.S. and Japanese culture experience and name such things. As Gen and I rehearsed the piece, I came to realize how ethnocentric my work's assumptions are about nudity, the body, and the language of desire. But as we worked on this piece, I also gained a deeper understanding from Gen of just how charged it might be for me to be doing a piece like this in Japan. Gen shared with me how much it would have meant for him a few years ago, as a young Japanese gay man in university, to have such an out, sex-positive, queer performance happen as part of an international conference. I thought of Gen's words many times during my adventure at Dokkyo University.

As I worked with Gen and Masashi on these simple translations, these gestures of understanding, my psychic and soulful relationship to the performance plan was immeasurably deepened, and I hope I also returned the favor by offering an interesting creative runway for both of these Japanese men. This kind of private, human-scaled, before-the-performance exchange is as important to me as whatever happens onstage.

Back to the show in Tokyo—I have left the young woman hiding her eyes and am looking for my victim for audience participation. One of the things I have learned over the years of performing is that I always eventually end up sitting naked on the lap of the person I need to meet in a new city or country. While in Japan, I had been hearing a great deal about the most self-identified gay theater in Tokyo, Flying Stage, and I wanted to meet the folks making that theater happen. As I walked naked through the audience, I was pulled with a huge wash of intuition toward the lap of a particular Japanese guy. I sat my butt down and—with my limited Japanese on display—we performed together this intimate dialogue about presence and sweat and the encounter of real humans in these theaters and performance spaces. After the performance I would learn that for this sweaty butt-on-the-lap moment I had picked Shin-ichi Sekine, the playwright of the Flying Stage. It is such encounters, serendipity and translations that renew my faith in the potential of performance, and the heart-held hope that we do have a fighting chance to communicate across oceans, languages, and even the footlights.

Us

"*I don't want to be* forced *to leave my country,*" *Jim Miller says at the end of his 1999 performance* Glory Box, *facing exile from the United States due to his partner Alistair McCartney's lack of American citizenship and the refusal of U.S. law and immigration policy to recognize their relationship. The prospect of exile is much closer in* Us, *which was performed during the extraordinary historical period ranging from the Supreme Court's 2003 decision against sodomy laws through the war in Iraq, thousands of gay marriage ceremonies (most subsequently invalidated by courts), and into the aftermath of the 2004 election, when eleven states voted to define marriage so as to bar gay and lesbian relationships and when the United States narrowly retained in office a national administration pledged to write that exclusionary definition into the U.S. Constitution.*

Us *begins with Miller packing a suitcase with mementoes of an American life. As if to stave off that final departure, the performance that follows is filled with other, metaphorical journeys—first, in memory to the always-potent world of his childhood, with its love of Broadway musicals and* National Geographic *magazines and its fear of the Vietnam War that, a generation ago, forced thousands of other Americans into exile in Canada. Later in* Us, *Miller and McCartney wear matching tuxedoes to the middle of the Rainbow Bridge separating the U.S. and Canada, marking the northern country's recent granting of marriage rights to same-sex couples. Tim and Alistair don't yet step over the border into exile, but on the south side of the line their situation seems more intractable than ever. Us has perhaps the most muted conclusion of Tim Miller's major works, but it still, characteristically, ends with an expression of hope.*

> [*When the audience enters the theater, they hear the loud, campy, throbbing beat of the Ethel Merman disco album. Around 8:05 P.M.—a bit late so folks can park, go to the bathroom, etc.—Tim enters from the back of the house, lugging a huge suitcase down the stairs. Tim shouts over Ethel Merman.*]

Hi. It's time to start the show. We've been enjoying the Ethel Merman disco album, but now it's time to get to work. Turn cell phones off, or at least set them to vibrate and sit on them. The show hasn't started yet. You'll know it's started when I throw this suitcase into the theater. Here it comes! 1 . . . 2 . . . 3!

> [*Tim throws suitcase onstage.*]

I'm packing my bags. We don't have much time left and there are a lot of decisions to be made before you go into exile.

Do you take the thirty-nine garage-sale fluorescent drag wigs I got three for a dollar in Pico Rivera? What about my Broadway cast albums from childhood? I have thirteen hundred of them! Do I take *South Pacific* and leave *Sound of Music?* I can't face a choice like that. You get Mary Martin either way. How many *National Geographics?*

> [*Tim grabs American flag from suitcase.*]

And what about this flag? Do I bring that with me? Y' know, I've been thinking about the flag lately. What mad queen in Philadelphia circa 1776 designed this thing? Betsy Ross was probably some founding father's drag name. I can see him thinking, "I see stripes . . . AND STARS! IN THREE COLORS!" It's so busy! I have to rethink this flag. See, up here on stage is the flag for the country I wish we lived in!

[Tim gestures to a huge American flag backdrop made from Broadway albums.]

I want to live in an America where the flag is made from Broadway musical cast albums. *Godspell* the red stripes, *Gypsy* makes the white, and *Oliver!* is the starry field! I want America to be a country where Jesus is not Bush's bigoted freak but is like the kind, hottie hippie Jesus in *Godspell,* who wants to hang out backstage with the cool strippers and looks after the future gay boy activists like little Oliver!

But meanwhile we're stuck with this flag. Do I put it in my baggage? Speaking of baggage . . . I got plenty. Okay, let me get this over with: we're not having to leave the US because one of us got a great new job or a time-share in Switzerland. As you smart audience members know, here in America gay couples have not one single Federal right respecting our relationships, and since Alistair is from Australia and we can't get married so we could get Alistair a green card and stay together in the US, we have to leave this fucking country. OOPS, don't want to seem too angry!

Okay, maybe I'm not angry, but I am bit peeved. I mean what's wrong with US? With Alistair and me? We're nice guys. We recycle, religiously! We watch *Animal Planet*—especially the Pet Psychic! We adopted a dog from Malibu Pet Rescue, a small red dog named Frida who looks like a cross between a fox and a wombat and identifies as a Latina lesbian. We're good guys. I mean, what's wrong with US?

When I think of what Al and I are going through, I've stopped trying to figure out what's wrong with "us." Me and Alistair, I mean. The question we should all be asking is "What's wrong with US?" Yes, you got it, the United States. What's wrong with America, that she has such a hard heart toward gay people? I want to figure it out before we go. I don't want to travel with that in my baggage, either as checked or carry-on. I want to leave that old shit here where it belongs.

You can't take everything, though. My Broadway musical soundtracks alone would fill a dozen suitcases. Look, I CLAIM the stereotype proudly. Fulfilling all the gay clichés, I've been into musicals ever since I was a little kid. They're crucial texts—the way I figured out the world and where I fit in it.

Let me tell you a little fairy tale. There once was a boy who would play inside a lot. He would put a stack of twelve musical shows on the turntable, stacked up like his mile-high pancake stack for his birthday at IHOP, and then spend the whole day listening to the Broadway shows and playing with his Lego. What would be on the playlist? *Gypsy. Cabaret. Man of La Mancha, Funny Girl, My Fair Lady, Fiddler on the Roof, West Side Story, Carousel, The Sound of Music, Hello, Dolly!, 1776, Hair, Godspell, Oliver!, Jesus Christ Superstar.*

These Broadway shows were his finishing school as a future queer boy, his political education as a crazed leftist. They were the light bulbs going on over his head and they made a great light . . .

[Tim is abruptly caught in an incredibly bright follow spotlight. The rest of the stage is dark.]

I'm surrounded by light. I can taste it. It surrounds me. It burns my fingers. It sizzles my skin. It's the light that defines me. It makes my boundaries that hold me in . . . the boundaries that I push past. I'm surrounded by light . . . shining . . . from my brother's desk lamp shining from his top bunk bed . . .

[We hear a scratchy phono recording of the overture from
Gypsy begin to play loudly.]

. . . as I do a striptease for my brothers. I was seven, maybe eight.
Gypsy was my favorite album. *Gypsy*—the great musical by Stephen
Sondheim, Jules Stein, and Arthur Laurents, about the famous burlesque stripper Gypsy Rose Lee. *Gypsy* was my favorite musical when
I was a little boy. I wanted to be Gypsy Rose Lee when I grew up. Escape from my family. Find your voice. Take off your clothes onstage
in front of strange men all over America. See, a boy's dream can
come true! I would perform my numbers from the show when no
one was home because I was afraid to have people hear me sing:

"Let Me Entertain You"
"I Had a Dream"
"Ya Gotta Have a Gimmick"

—and I had a doozie: to be the youngest boy burlesque stripper on
my block. This was my "Gypsy Rose Lee" game that I mostly played
with my friends, but once my brothers, after my parents went to
sleep, had me do a striptease for them between our double bunk
beds. I would play the Gypsy Rose Lee game for them. Because you
are a smart audience, I know this may seem like a *Citizen Kane*
"Rosebud"-type revelation that explains the psychological motives
behind my work. But it's much more complicated than that.

They would shine their light on me and I would do my striptease. They made their striptease mouth trumpets "WAH, WAH,
WAAAAH." . . . Off went my mis-matched pajamas, the flannel
astronaut tops and the cotton cowboy-themed bottoms. I must have
looked like a freaky Hummel figurine stripping, taking it off, taking
it all off. This was my first strip for other boys. I loved the heat of
that light, the light of their eyes, the heat of their gaze. The light I've
always been surrounded by. It defines me. It makes my boundaries
that hold me in, the boundaries I push beyond. I'm surrounded by
light.

[The music fades out.]

But ever since, I have always been a stripper . . .
There in that hot white light.
I strip away bullshit. I strip away lies. I strip away fear.
Let me entertain you. I had a dream. You gotta have a gimmick.

I learned everything I needed to know from these shows, about love, politics and America. Who needs Marx and Engels when you have Rodgers and Hammerstein!

[Tim makes stepping-stones out of the soundtrack LPs as he shares his vision of the message of the musicals.]

Fiddler on the Roof is all about gay marriage. Well, at least the consistent expansion of the definition of marriage! There was a high school production in South Carolina a couple of years ago that had two boys play the final couple. The usual nuts freaked out. Thousands were killed and the National Guard was called in! *Fiddler* made me want a Jewish Commie boyfriend like Perchik. I had a couple of those during my NYC years. *Fiddler* taught me to disobey my parents and marry for love even if it challenges Tradition's taboos. *Fiddler* prepared me for exile, whether from Cossacks, storm troopers or George W.

1776. I suspect if we polled the audience we would find that it is everyone's favorite musical about the signing of the Declaration of Independence. *1776* won the Tony in 1969. This show actually has a hard-hitting left-of-center perspective. *1776* taught me that America was founded by merchant-capitalist hypocrites who dared to write about human freedom while most of them owned human slaves!

The Sound of Music showed me that it was crucial to leave organized religion behind, get laid, and fight Nazis through festive song and dance.

Applause gives us the first image of a cheery gay bar in a musical. Based on *All About Eve,* this show came just a few months after Stonewall and had all the gay chorus boys dancing with Lauren Bacall at the gay bar singing the hit "ALIVE!" I got the cast album for my eleventh birthday, and these were the first images of gay people I had ever seen. These photos of the gay bar scene in the cast album let me know my future as a gay boy included silk scarves knotted at the neck and long leather-fringed vests.

Cabaret helped me expand my fashion sense with its world of gay men, Nazis, and Liza. When I was twelve I had cobbled together my Liza Minnelli outfit from the movie soundtrack and was singing "Mein Herr" along with Liza. My sister snuck in with her instamatic and shot a photo of me dressed as Liza. (Perhaps this is the origin of my internalized drag phobia!) I freaked and chased her, grabbed the camera, and smashed it with a heavy garden gnome. Think what I would pay for those photos so I could use them to promote this show!

My Fair Lady showed me the perfect library—I still want that rolling ladder and globes and skull—a library shared by two men in smoking jackets who sang songs about how they would never let a woman in their life.

Hair taught me that we can confront the government, take drugs, and be in theater projects where the attractive young cast takes their clothes off and has sex with one another backstage at theaters like this one!

South Pacific—the great anti-racist Rodgers and Hammerstein musical! It was banned across the South because of the interracial romance between hottie Lieutenant Cable and the Tonkinese girl Liat. *South Pacific* showed me you could fight bigotry while being surrounded by hunky, naked sailors and drag queens.

These shows became a bridge to the future, the script, the primary text for how this boy understood the world. A world full of strippers, sexy Jewish Communists, founding fathers, de-frocked nuns, gay men dressing badly, hairy hippies, humpy sailors, brave little queer Oliver daring to ask for more.

[Tim holds Oliver! *cast album high.]*

Not a bad laundry list, all in all, of ways of claiming who you are supposed to be.

I think maybe I'll keep this one with me.

Since I was a little kid, like Oliver, I could see when things were unfair, when there wasn't enough gruel, and gay people are ready to settle for a miserly bit of gruel. I've always known there was something wrong with US, with America. There was something that would try to mess with me. Even as a kid I knew this. I was going to have to be very clever to survive. That as I looked for love, I was going to be fucked with as I tried to find the answer to that five billion dollar question . . .

[Tim sings along with Oliver's plaintive song "Where is Love?"]

> "Wh-he-he-he-here is love?
> Does it fall from skies above?
> Is it underneath the willow tree,
> That I've been dreaming oooooof?"

When I was nine I was enraged that I had not been cast as Oliver Twist in the 1968 Academy Award winning film version of the musical *Oliver!*

How could they have given the part to that little English boy-bitch Mark Lester? That part was mine! Don't you understand, IT WAS MINE! Home alone, I would practice singing Oliver's tuneful lament "Where is Love?" again and again in the living room of our house in Whittier, California, when no one could hear me. I even choreographed that excellent dance. Did you see the tree? The sophisticated use of levels?

I was so mad at Mark Lester for stealing my part from me. I wanted to hit him and kick him and gouge him and tickle him and kiss him and hold him and lick him and undress him and sleep next to him for the rest of my life in a designer garret in London. I watched the movie *Oliver!* not long ago on AMC and it's the most homoerotic movie ever made. No wonder I loved it so much when I was a kid. All these sweet naughty English adolescents with hair hanging in their eyes sharing beds with each other, pimped out by the irascible older man Fagin and in love with a Judy Garland–type torch song singer named Nancy played by the incomparable Shani Wallis in the film.

I loved Mark Lester, but I hated him too. He was getting in between me and the true object of my desire: Jack Wild playing the Artful Dodger. Jack Wild—who would later fill my Saturday morning cartoon-time with homosexual desire on the acid-trippy children's show *H. R. Pufnstuf*—was a dark teenage beauty, full of danger yet capable of love and affection. He knew how to make community, as witnessed by his hit song from *Oliver!*, "Consider Yourself One of Us"—which is clearly a coming-out anthem.

Why had Mark Lester gotten that part instead of me! If I had gotten what was mine I would have felt Jack Wild's arm draped seductively over my shoulder as we danced our hearts out there in that mythical back-lot London. I would have found where love is! I would be somewhere safer than I felt growing up in America. See, it was clear to me that all people with English accents were gay and camp and slept in beds with other boys and were nice to each other and sang and danced in the street and had hair hanging in seductive fringe over their eyes!

Maybe they didn't cast me because I didn't have an English accent? That can be easily remedied. So, in fifth grade I carefully— almost as if it were a science project—began to assume an English

Tim Miller in *Us* with *Oliver!* cast album. Photo by John Aigner.

accent in my daily life. It started creeping in slowly: emphatically pronouncing both my *t*s in the word "little." Speaking with exaggerated politeness to grown-ups, saying "yes, please" and "thank you very much." Displaying my vast *Oxford English Dictionary* vocabulary to anyone who would listen. I was never happier than when one of my classmates asked during dodge ball, before hitting me in the head with the ball, "Hey, Tim, you talk funny. Are you from England?" and I, a good queer boy, would primly reply, "Well, my mother's family does come from Dutton, England." (I neglected to mention that they had come from there in 1754.)

Okay, I know I'm not alone in this. I know a lot of people do accent surgery, a little nip-n-tuck or Botox on the vocal cords as a way of escaping from vocal markers of class, race, or regional dialect. I happen to know lots of gay men who went through a period as kids where they took on some kind of English accent and tried to live as little English gentlemen in Tulsa, Oklahoma. Somehow the refined English, Noel-Coward faggy other maybe gave us an escape hatch from some harsher realities of homophobic America. It seemed like somehow it might be safer in England for boys like me who listened to showtunes while playing with Lego!

Things only got worse the following year when yet another part was stolen from me, the part of Tiny Tim in the movie musical *Scrooge,* based on *A Christmas Carol.* Growing up in suburban California as a "Tim," Christmas always carried a particular resonance for me because the yuletide pity-puppy poster boy that I most related to had the same name as me! As a ten- or eleven-year-old boy, I was deeply in love with Tiny Tim. He was the first boy I wanted to get married to, if I could just get him out of England and the nineteenth century and the world of fiction! I fantasized that Tiny Tim would be my "special friend" when we grew up. I imagined that if Tiny Tim and I were best friends, I would knit Tiny Tim a brand new scarf, feed him Vitamin C, and find a physical therapist for him in Beverly Hills. We would grow to be strong young men. We would run together in romantic slow motion on the beach in Santa Monica. He and I could create a special world of "Tims" at Christmas time. We would leave our tastefully decorated condo in West Hollywood as we negotiated our families. We would exchange that subtle, knowing smile that lovers share with one another as we noted that the Cratchits seemed so much more functional as a family than the Millers.

This obsession I had with Tiny Tim knew no bounds. In sixth grade it wasn't enough for me to have affected an English accent, so I took on a "Tiny Tim solidarity limp" as soon as December rolled around in Los Angeles, and insisted on seeing the film musical *Scrooge* dozens of times. The love affair with Tiny Tim Cratchit was finally consummated the year I broke my leg right before Christmas. There I was on crutches and wearing my Dickensean scarf as I hobbled into the dining room. I made everyone lift a flagon of Christmas punch—I had mulled it from cherry Hi-C and a hard rock of carbon-dated cinnamon I had found on the spice rack—and join me in a toast over the Butterball turkey: "God bless us, every one!"

My profound love and attraction for things English reached their peak with my production in fifth grade of *Hamlet*. My teacher Mrs. Bush—one of only two positive associations I have with that four letter word "bush"—encouraged me in my desire to direct and star in a sixty-minute adaptation of Shakespeare's play. I had an ulterior motive, though: I was in love with my desk mate David Suggs, and I figured if I staged *Hamlet* I could cast him as Horatio and he would have to follow my direction and hug and kiss me at the end of the play!

Which came first, the chicken or the egg? The desire to play the Prince of Denmark and speak those killer lines, or the desire to wear tights and be cradled by David Suggs as Horatio with his long blond hair falling over his forehead? I don't know. Maybe they came at exactly the same moment. Art and sex? The word and the deed? Everyone got in on the act to help ten-year-old Tim do *Hamlet*. Mrs. Bush gave us vast amounts of class time for my increasingly despotic rehearsals. My brother nixed *my* choice for incidental music for the play—the overture from *Hello, Dolly!*—and found the right bit of Purcell for the court processional at Elsinore. My Mom sewed the costumes for the production, including my elegant black-belted tunic, which went over my sister's tights from modern dance, and a frilly white shirt from one of my mom's pantsuits. My mom finished it all off by ripping a shiny metal medallion off a huge holiday gift box bottle of Seagrams and then hanging it on a bathtub chain around my neck. (Thus teaching me at a young age how crucial it is to accessorize.)

Finally the great day of the show arrived and I got to English accent up a storm, have a sword fight, and swoon into David Suggs' arms: "If thou didst ever call me friend, live to tell my story! Oh I die Horatio. . . . The potent poison quite o'ercrows my spirit. The rest is silence." My head fell face down into Horatio's lap, only a thin layer of tights separating my lips from the Suggs family jewels. (I told him he couldn't wear underwear cause it would ruin the line of the costume.) I breathed hot air into his crotch and I felt a stirring within. As directed, David Suggs held me close, stroked my hair, and kissed my forehead as he flatly intoned the closing lines: "Now cracks a noble heart. Good night sweet prince, and flights of angels sing thee to thy rest."

"Where is love?"

I don't know what ever happened to Mark Lester after his role in *Oliver!* and I don't even know the name of the boy who played Tiny Tim in *Scrooge*. As for David Suggs, I tried to Google him last night but couldn't find anything. But I do know where love is. Because in my story Oliver Twist-Tiny Tim-Hamlet found the thing they wanted.

For more than ten years I have lived with Alistair, a man I met in London, spitting distance from where Oliver picked a pocket or two. He no longer has hair fringing far down his forehead—Alistair is going for a butch-er, shaved-head hip-hop look—but we do share a small bed which before long is likely to be in an over-priced London garret somewhere south of the river.

Alistair's beautiful voice, his soft Australia-meets-London-meets-L.A. accent, has finally given me permission to pronounce both my *t*s in "lit-tle" (at least around the house).

And we both know where love is.

God bless *Us*.

God bless Us, every one.

[Tim walks back to suitcase.]

Well, I guess there's no question. I'll have to take my *Oliver!* soundtrack, *Scrooge* LP, and definitely my *Hamlet* costume. I don't think I can fit everything in my suitcases, though, if I take most of my musicals. I'm going to have to get rid of some other stuff. I need to get rid of some really heavy stuff—like perhaps my rock collection? Or maybe I should lose my twenty-eight years of *National Geographics?* That would make a dent. It's a scientific fact that they are the heaviest objects on the planet Earth! If we piled in Tierra del Fuego all the world's *National Geographics* they weigh enough to throw the earth off its orbital axis! I can't give these up, though. These magazines are where I learned about the world! They are where I discovered cultural difference. They were my first porn magazines!

Not long after my triumph with *Hamlet* and David Suggs' lap, I came home from school one day. My parents both worked, so I got the key out from the garden gnome's wheelbarrow, grabbed the mail and let myself in. I cracked open the just-delivered *National Geographic.* I spread it open, sniffed the delicious inky crotch of the magazine. I breathed in the world from between the pages of the new *National Geographic.* I sniffed the ink on the pricey chrome coated paper that distinguished *NG* from all the competition. Opening a *National Geographic* and breathing it in was like sniffing glue. . . .

[Tim walks down left sniffing the National Geographic.*]*

If you breathe it in long enough you can get stoned—a cheap good-boy suburban buzz. Then I would sneak the magazine into my bedroom and, as had millions before me, I pulled down my pants, pulled down my underwear, and began to touch myself as I leafed through the pages to see if there were any photos of scantily-clad Third World people. Come on! How do you think this magazine has been around for so long? Do you really think in the 1950s all those bachelor insurance men subscribers in Des Moines were obsessed with the monarch butterfly? Of course not! They were checking out the topless New Guinea native babes!

For us queer boys there was also plenty in *National Geographic* to keep us busy while our pants were around our ankles. You open any page at random, like in this one, and suddenly you have a two-page spread of naked Japanese men in a "ritual" bath. This cute Japanese guy is showing the other positive association I have with the word "bush"! There are so many images! Handsome naked Brazilian rain forest youths with those weird sheaths over their dicks. And to prove that I can objectify and erotically colonize white folks, there was a cover of a rosy-cheeked Laplander tending their reindeer. Man, you don't get whiter than that! I just bought that one on e-Bay. There was a photo of a bunch of fifteen-year-old Siberian youths in their tiny underwear and goggles standing before the sun lamps. If you held up the photo to the light you could clearly see the hooded heads of their Soviet penises poking against the thin fabric of their Evil Empire tighty-whities. Apparently the air-brush maestro at *National Geographic* had the day off when the Siberians came through.

See, I'm not shallow. I didn't just rely on movie musicals for archetypal love objects or political instruction about the world. I read *National Geographic* too! I learned from the *National Geographic* that the world was full of potential young men to have adventures with and hug and kiss as we shared a sleeping bag in a youth hostel in Portugal or Uzbekistan. It's why I still subscribe. Anyhow, back to my bedroom where my pants are around my ankles. On the cover of the issue that day was a small story about Vietnam. The cover featured a cute naked slippery Vietnamese youth surrounded by rushing water with a silver-scaled fish clenched between his teeth.

While I had been staging *Hamlet* in 1969, the US was staging a whole other show in Southeast Asia, there in the war "theater" in Vietnam. Weird how they use our word! The US military even had its own "Hamlet" in the form of the notorious Strategic Hamlets program. This was not a traveling Shakespeare program; it was a harebrained scheme to force friendly South Vietnamese farmers off their rice fields and into barbed-wire-surrounded militarized con-centration camps, I mean villages, so we could "protect" and keep control of them. This program had the usual result of most US foreign policy in that it managed quickly to turn lukewarm friends into complete enemies of the USA. Right after my *Hamlet* produc-tion, the conflict was at its peak. War criminals Nixon and Kissinger invaded Cambodia, America was exploding in protest, US National Guard had slaughtered American students at Kent State. Our tax dollars at work. Then, just like now. Something was definitely rotten in the State of America.

While I was reading *National Geographic* imagining the young men around the world I wanted to hug and kiss, the US had other plans for our white and Asian, and black and Latino, bodies. Thou-sands of young American men, just ten or so years older than me, were being sent home in body bags. Every night in the flickering light of our black and white TV I saw the image of the plastic body bags being loaded on the helicopters. Unlike now, we were actually allowed to see those images then. They reminded me of the mystery-meat sandwiches my mom would pack in sandwich bags and put in my *Lost in Space* lunchbox that I took to fourth grade. Just what was I being fed?

I was a smart kid. By 1970, you didn't have to be a brain surgeon to know the war was wrong, immoral, doomed. You just needed to be a reasonably smart sixth-grader who read the *L.A. Times* every day and watched Walter Cronkite on the news to know the war was idiotic and wrong. I knew where my sympathies lay. They lay with the lanky, long-haired androgynous protesters with the booty-enhancing bell bottoms. I knew the war was wrong. I knew that I didn't want to go, but mostly I knew I didn't want to die. I knew the war would go on forever. I knew that I would turn eighteen and would be sent to die by Nixon or one of his vile protégé spawn like Donald Rumsfeld. I became so afraid of turning eighteen in eight years that I decided to try to stop growing up. I asked my family to stop celebrating my birthday. I won't grow up, and I'll never turn eighteen and be drafted and forced to kill the Vietnamese boy on the cover of the *National Geographic* that I wanted to kiss.

I know you are a clever audience and you are on to my musical theater through-line in the show tonight—that I'm connecting these musical theater texts to my life narrative—and you probably think that during this period when I didn't want to grow up, my favorite Broadway show was *Peter Pan* so I could sing "I Won't Grow Up." No! Even though I love *Peter Pan* and it is one of the great lesbian roles in the American theater, the show I especially loved during this Vietnam time was *Man of La Mancha,* the great musical theater war-horse about Don Quixote and Cervantes and the Impossible Dream. *Man of La Mancha* was perfect for a self-important ten year old with an English accent. So overblown with its utopian idealism of the hit song "The Impossible Dream." As I listened to *Man of La Mancha* I could relate to everything. One moment I'm Cervantes–Don Quixote tilting at windmills. The next instant the sultry scullery whore Aldonza. The next, one of the hottie chorus-boy Muleteers! I used to draw the *New York Times* Hirschfeld cartoon image from the record cover obsessively onto all my schoolbook covers. To me, "To dream the Impossible Dream" could mean only one thing—that we could do something about the war in Vietnam.

Man of La Mancha opened on Broadway at the Martin Beck Theater in March 1968, during the Tet offensive, the worst fighting of the war in Vietnam. I got the soundtrack for my birthday and I would listen to the soundtrack imagining the well-heeled audiences going to see the show, but I started to worry that "The Impossible Dream" could mean different things to different people. Maybe there is some working-class Polish boy from New Jersey who didn't have the wealth and connections of George W. Bush and was actually gonna have to go to Vietnam. Maybe his family was going to take him, before he shipped out, to his one Broadway show and Times Square steak dinner, to see *Man of La Mancha*. Maybe that soldier boy had his own impossible dream, that he would fight the Viet Cong and come back in one piece? But come on, in 1968 people knew this song was really about fighting injustice and racism. This song is about the good guys—the recently-slaughtered Martin Luther King, and Bobby Kennedy, who would be assassinated in the first weeks of the Broadway run. I knew what the Impossible Dream was. I could personally stop the war.

And if *Man of La Mancha* wasn't enough, a few months later the musical *Hair* would open and we would have singing, dancing, Vietnam-protesting hippies on Broadway. Of course, I wasn't allowed to see this show at the Aquarius Theater in Hollywood or even to have the Broadway cast album, but a friend's brother brought the record down from Berkeley and he and I secretly listened to it over the headphones, each of us with just one headphone coconut-shell half of the stereo recording pressed to a single ear. "Sodomy" was my favorite song in the show. I wasn't sure what sodomy was exactly, but I knew it was for me. Which, indeed, it would prove to be.

Anyhow, I had played with myself for about fifteen minutes while looking at the Vietnamese boy with the fish in his mouth, spending much of the time fantasizing that I was the fish being clenched between his teeth. Since I wouldn't go through puberty for about four more years, this was more process than goal-oriented self-love. I was starting to chafe, so I finally gave up and took a final few more sniffs of the magazine. Then I shook the *National Geographic* to see what special treat was in store this month. Better than any prize at the bottom of the Cracker Jack box, the map-of-the-month fell with a slap to the floor. This month, it was a map of the west coast of North America. That's where I come from! I opened up the map—gave it a sniff to try to keep my high going, but it wasn't quite as narcotic as the magazine itself, more porous paper apparently—and then followed my nose up the whole scratchy coast of the US. From Mexico to California to Oregon to Washington. My nose reached the top of the map and my eyes saw the word CANADA. I knew what I would have to do. I knew at the age of ten that hell no I wouldn't go, and that when I turned eighteen I would burn my draft card. I would have to join the hundreds of thousands of other young Americans who had gone to Canada to seek asylum and escape America's madness and murder.

See, maybe the Broadway musical can't stop American imperialism after all. Go with me on this, okay? I know the musical is a strong cultural force, but maybe not that strong! Maybe show tunes could still save me, though. Maybe I needed to adjust my "Impossible Dream." My dream would have to become that I would escape to asylum in Canada where I would meet a boy like me!

I became obsessed with all things Canadian. My mom and dad began worrying about my sudden interest in Canada—a clear character flaw in a young American. Having a child who had assumed an English accent was one thing, but excessive interest in things Canadian seemed somehow unwholesome to them, like taking up taxidermy or Satan worship. They were even more troubled by my insistence we shift from Farmer John to Canadian bacon, my sudden interest in ice hockey, and especially by the huge poster I had hung over my bed dedicated to the "Men of the Royal Canadian Mounted Police." Strange to grow up in a country like ours where little American boys have to go to such lengths planning how they escape their own country's craziness?

[We begin to hear the overblown, stirring, tumescent chords from the Man of La Mancha *overture, as Tim*

moves into a pathway of golden light and performs the following text in time to the "Impossible Dream" theme.]

I began planning my escape from the US at the age of ten. I put the map that would lead me to Canada over my bed, right next to the map of the US that my oldest brother had up, that showed all the likely thermonuclear war targets in Southern California. I outlined in red magic marker my route north to Canada. I figured out how far I could take a bus to get to a good freeway on-ramp for Interstate 5 to hitchhike. I saved money from my lawn mowing and car washing jobs to finance my trip. Squirreled it away in my American Savings Bank account. I planned what I would wear to cross the border. I decided on a Mormon missionary look. I got all the books about other young people who fled America to find freedom in Canada, African-American slaves trying to get to Canada and freedom, Native American tribes fleeing the US army massacres, half a million war resisters right now. I would make a triumphant entrance to Canada right there at the Peace Arch, where Paul Robeson—the star of the musical *Showboat*—had done his concerts in the '50s when the US State Department wouldn't let him leave the country, to try to stop him from telling the truth about American apartheid.

[The music is louder.]

I stand with Paul Robeson! I would cross over the border into British Columbia, cameras flashing, reporters asking me questions. Maybe I won't even wait until I'm eighteen. I walk hand in hand with Paul Robeson. At ten I would be the youngest war resister to ever seek asylum in Canada. I had achieved my impossible dream and became one of the half million Americans who fled our country for freedom in Canada. I dreamed the impossible dream. I beat the unbeatable foe. I reached the unreachable star!

[The music ends.]

Well, the war ended freshman year. We left a huge mess, like bad kids who break all the toys before they go home for dinner. But this was not child's play, because we left two million Vietnamese dead, three million Vietnamese maimed and wounded, and sent fifty-eight thousand Americans home in body bags never to be hugged or kissed by anyone ever again, including one ten-year-old in Southern California. I would not have to go to Vietnam. In fact, as it turned out, I didn't even have to register for the draft. But I never threw that map away. I kept it around for a rainy day and I will definitely be packing it in that suitcase. I always had an intuition that our country would sooner or later get up to some new kind of mischief and that would mean I would need a map to freedom once again.

Our war is not over.

[A narrow corridor of sharply focused red and white light comes from stage left and right. One side of Tim is in over-exposed white light; the other is blood red.]

My body is a BRIDGE!

My body is at the border. My body at the red border. Maple Leaf red over here, bloody stripe red over there. I am standing in the middle of the Rainbow Bridge that crosses over the Niagara Falls. There is an American flag to my right—naturally—and a Canadian Flag to my left. The bridge makes a graceful leap, rainbow-like I suppose, over the rushing torrents of the Niagara River. There are lots of tourists who want to be photographed with one leg in Canada and one in the US. They want their legs spread wide; they want to be ripped, opened up by that hot throbbing US-Canadian border. Well, I should just speak for myself, I think.

I'm here to plan my wedding with Alistair, here in the middle of the Rainbow Bridge. We'll be married just two inches over onto the Canadian side, where gay people have rights. What place could be better to get married, right? The scene of the crime, Niagara Falls, all those millions of weddings and honeymoons over the decades! It's

240

the prime locus for unjust heterosexual marriage privilege! Niagara Falls on the Rainbow Bridge! Who knew they had made a homosexual bridge between Canada and the US? For moi, it seems. It's so culturally sensitive!

When you're at the Falls you can't help but imagine all the bad things that could happen. The Maid of the Mist might hit a rock, sink, sending the yellow-slickered tourists plunging to their deaths. The plump white observation balloon from the American side over Goat Island pops a panel and spills everyone into the Niagara River heading over the American Falls onto the rocks below. We can witness the meltdown of the heterosexual family unit as husbands push their wives over the falls; wives shove their husbands. Fed up parents throw their children over the wall into the torrents below. There goes Bobby and Suzie! Anything can happen at Niagara Falls!

Everywhere I look at Niagara Falls I see recently married straight wedding couples walking in rented tuxes and wedding gowns. The straight couples promenade down the path, gracefully receiving smiles from all who pass. They look like shabby Balkan royalty—okay, the one mean line in the show. Now, Alistair and I have already bought our matching Prada tuxes for our wedding—we maxed out all our credit cards on them—and we put on the tuxes and take them out for a test drive as we walk hand in hand along the Falls promenade. It was weird how when we walked past the American tourists no one said anything nice to us. In fact a woman from South Dakota who was smoking *two* cigarettes actually spit at us! Where are all the other gay couples?

I'm here on the Rainbow Bridge for a very good reason. I'm getting ready to take the plunge. No, I'm not going to fling myself off the bridge. I'm not that much of a drama queen, but there is a plunge coming. Alistair and I are planning our future marriage here in Canada, here in Niagara Falls, Canada. Even though we are planning this wedding day, there is a huge clock hanging over our heads ticking down to when we have to leave America. For a gay couple like us, the Rainbow Bridge is the perfect spot to really see how we are treated in the US. We can do the math here. Over here to my right in America, lesbian and gay couples don't have a single federal right respecting their relationships—plus we have a freak in the White House who wants to amend the US Constitution to deny gay people marriage rights forever. Over here to my left in Canada, they have re-written hundreds of laws to include gay couples in the definition of spouse, and gay couples have complete equality of civil marriage rights. See, for a gay person, when you leave the US and step into Canada, that's when you enter the free world! I am balanced between the Maple Leaf Candy and the Kentucky Fried Chicken, feeling all existential and ripped in two. And as so often happens in moments like this, I start to hear some bagpipes. Scottish bagpipers arrive. Oh God, it's Alistair's Scottish father come to stop our wedding! One of Alistair's sisters must have tipped him off. He's going to come up with all his drinking buddies from Glasgow to stop me from marrying his youngest son. He's going to rush out onto the Rainbow bridge waving his highlander broad sword and shouting, "Ach, you dirty devil, you'll not have me wee bairn Alistair Duncan McCartney."

But wait—it's not Alistair's dad. It's a Canadian bagpipe orchestra! About thirty people in kilts with bagpipes. It's the Niagara Falls, Canada, Police Department Bagpipe Orchestra! They are being led by some guy in eighteenth century town crier costume, He steps onto the middle of the Rainbow Bridge, pulls out an elegant scroll, and rings his bell. "Oyez! Oyez! Oyez!" he cries as the bell clangs. "On this Victoria Day in honor of HRH Elizabeth II of the United Kingdom and the Dominions of Canada and Australia, I welcome you to the forty-second annual tug of war between the police of Niagara Falls, Canada, and the police of Niagara Falls, America." Three dozen buff and hunky Canadian cops march out on to the bridge dressed all in black, with neat berets. They look like sleek sexy otters—I mean *ot-ters!* They are carrying a huge rope over their shoulders, thick as an anaconda. The US police department team arrives a moment later. They're working a whole other look, sort of a sky-blue, polyester-jumpsuits, doughy—too many doughnuts for these cops—changing-planes-at-Memphis-International-Airport kind of look.

At this point, 138 Boy Scouts from Troup 883, Wexford, Pennsylvania, suddenly surround me, and the crazy synchronicity of what is happening becomes a bit too much for me. Let me do the checklist: I am standing here at Niagara Falls, historical heterosexual marriage destination, as I ponder gay marriage, balanced at the very edge of being tipped off the edge of the United States and forced to leave with Alistair, and feeling tugged in two, watching the US and Canada have a tug of war on the exact borderline between the nations on the Rainbow bridge, surrounded by Boy Scouts from Wexford, PA, yet another organization that—only in America—discriminates against gay kids. What comes next? Jesse Helms on a broomstick spelling it in smoke?: "SURRENDER, TIMOTHY!"

BANG! The game is on. The US makes an immediate move and almost drags the Canadians over the line; but the humpy Ontario cops dig their feet in, every Canadian sinew tensing, and slowly pull the US team closer, closer, and finally over the line. Canada has won the first round. It's going to be the best two out of three. It takes them a while to get set up for the second match. The rope is straining so tight it looks like it's going to snap and decapitate the sunburned head of the Scoutmaster of Troop 883, Wexford, PA. And I realize that I am the rope, being pulled to the breaking point.

Oh God, I realize something scary about myself. I realize I want Canada to win this tug of war. Oh, aren't I naughty? Aren't I being such a bad American? But I don't just want America to lose this little game of tug of war. I want all our huge outstanding bills to be paid. Just a few little debts we owe. Like for 250 years of human slavery that created the nation's wealth. Our huge overdue debt to the native people whom we took North America from. That we are five percent of the world's population and use thirty-five percent of the world's natural resources. Like the bill to be paid for the eighty-five countries we have invaded in the last century or so. I don't know about you, but I'm sick of our country's racist, sexist, homophobic, gun-loving, faggot-hating, red-baiting, health-care-denying, sodomy-criminalizing, gas-guzzling, war-mongering, carbon-dioxide spewing, wealth-grasping shit!

I realize I have become a daytime TV cliché—I'm stuck in an abusive relationship with the US. America slaps me and I say, "thank you Land of the Free." The US slugs me and I say, "I'll have two lumps please." She kicks me and my partner Alistair out of the country and I say, "you're too kind." I'm so fucking sick of America's racist, sexist, homophobic, gun-loving, faggot-hating, red-baiting, health-care-denying, sodomy-criminalizing, gas-guzzling, war-mongering, carbon-dioxide-spewing, wealth-grasping shit, and I don't know what I feel anymore.

The US was slowly pulled over the line and lost. The Canadians on the bridge roar as they win the best two out of three. The Americans do what Americans do when we lose, have an out of body experience, pretend it never happened, slink off and look for a country much weaker than us to beat up on. The bagpipes cry out as everyone marches back to their side of the border.

I look to the US and see the departing, defeated US police team. They march back to the US, which will not be my home much longer. When I look back to the Canadian side, I see a huge billboard for Planet Hollywood and a Hershey's Kiss the size of the Goodyear Blimp draped over the façade of a fine old Canadian hotel. There is no escape.

[We hear some very beautiful, mournful bagpipe music fade up.]

Alistair takes my hand; soon it will be our wedding day, but not in America. We will have to find a free country. Surrounded by bagpipes, I turn and walk with him back on the Rainbow Bridge. For a moment I indulge one of my not infrequent Barbra Streisand fantasy moments. I am suddenly dancing and singing my heart out with Barbra in either of the big parade-themed numbers from *Funny Girl* or *Hello, Dolly!* With Alistair's hand in mine, Barbra Steisand in my head, the drums and bagpipes swirling around us, and rain definitely falling on my parade, we walk slowly back to Canada.

> *[As rain falls on his parade, Tim walks past the suitcase and picks up the flag. Fast actions with flag: washing, cradling, being strangled. Through that pressure around his throat, Tim struggles to find his voice, wrestles intensely with the sound of a "V."]*

V-V-V-V-V-V-VOICE! VOICE!

It's all about voice. Losing it. Silencing it. Dampening it. Smothering it. Finding it. Raising it.

I might have done a striptease for my brothers that one time, but I was always afraid to sing out, to tell the truth, to raise my little queer voice. I'd hide my voice in the closet. Would only sing out when no one was around. That's what I love about these musicals. They're not afraid. They helped me find my voice. These voices from the records fill my head; I don't even need a record player to hear them. I just put that vinyl to my ear and they sing to me. They fill my memories and most sentimental nooks and crannies. All these people, singing, shouting, crying out for love, equality, justice, more and better sequins on their costumes. Bringing on home their truth.

> *[The music changes to the horribly scratched LP of the overture to* Gypsy. *During the following, a freeway collision of quotes from the many Broadway musicals mentioned accompanies this stripper monologue until Tim is naked.]*

Stripping it down to the body and the voice.

Let me entertain you. I have a dream! You gotta have a gimmick. Because I have always been a stripper . . . there in that hot red light. Stripped down to the bone and heart and still bright-red pumping, shouting, singing and dancing, all music, all the time.

I have always been a *Gypsy* stripper—I strip away bullshit. I strip away lies. I strip away hypocrisy. I strip away fear. How ya like them eggrolls, George Bush? I am a big cock-sucking, ass-fucking Gypsy Rose Lee with a 4th of July American Flag as the fan for my dance.

I have always been a *1776* stripper—because we need to smell the stinky socks of our history, stripped down to the hard not-pretty truth that when those founding fathers in Philadelphia wrote "all men are created equal," that didn't include women, black people, and definitely not gay folks—and my pursuit of happiness is being royally fucked with.

I have always been a tilting-at-windmills *Man of La Mancha* Don Quixote stripper, and I do still have an impossible dream that America's hard heart will finally soften and America will stop shitting on gay people's lives. I can't help it, but I do still believe America could be less screwed up and live up to its promotional materials. We ain't even close. Not even in the ballpark. Just watch the news every night this week.

I have always been a *West Side Story* stripper, pissed off that on that some enchanted evening when we meet someone we love, faggots still have to kiss in the shadows to find a place for us . . . somewhere . . . somewhere . . . somewhere! Someday Riff and Tony won't have to die and can get married without going to Canada and instead will be able to love each other and grow old together, get fat and remember their salad days of tenement fights and street ballet that made their butts look so good in the movie.

I have always been a little *Oliver!* English boy stripper, me and all those Hummel figurines taking it all off. There go the lederhosen. There goes the alpine hat. There go the neck scarves. All those Hummel figurines sing and dance looking like underage Rockettes with the Artful Dodger's arm around my shoulder and goddamit I want some more. Fuck that bowl of gruel. I want some more respect. More freedom. More hope. More love. Where the fuck is more love? I found it already.

I have definitely always been a Barbra Streisand drag-queen stripper with a huge swooping wig and high heels that will hammer out shit. Even though I have always been just a teensy-weensy bit drag–phobic, I thought this show might be the one where I finally do drag, but then I chickened out. These black Calvin Klein under-wear making that swooping Barbra late '60s hair swoop will have to do! I still have that wig like an aura around me and her high heels in my hand, to hammer out injustice and bigotry and war. I want those people to stop raining on my parade, before that parade passes by.

I have always been a *Fiddler on the Roof* stripper. I admit it. I want that sunrise-sunset wedding. I want that glass breaking underneath my foot as I marry the boy my father doesn't approve of. I don't want to go into exile. I don't want to be forced to leave my home. I don't want to be forced to leave and go far from the home I love.

I have always been a *My Fair Lady* stripper. The day I was born into this world, Julie Andrews and Rex Harrison were performing that show in London at the Drury Lane Theatre. A few months ago I was wandering around Covent Garden looking for a London sublet for Alistair and me before I saw the *My Fair Lady* revival. Why did I weep twelve times before the intermission as I watched the show?

I have always been a stripper . . . there in that hot red light. Stripped down to the bone and heart and still bright-red pumping, shouting, singing and dancing, all music, all the time.

And when will it be Tim's turn, all queer people's turn? When will everything come up big fat queer roses? Big fat, sunrise-sunset, climb every mountain, dream the impossible dream, there's a place for us queer roses? For me and for you.

[The show tune collage slowly cross-fades to mournful Celtic bagpipes. Tim takes a while to put his clothes back on, gather his props, and pack them in his suitcase. He is about the leave the American flag behind on the floor, but at the last moment goes back, brushes it off, and hangs it over his shoulder, then moves downstage.]

Well, I'm just about packed. Alistair and I don't have too much time left before we have to leave the country and there's only so much you can fit in one suitcase. I mean you can't take everything. Maybe just a Broadway cast album, a *National Geographic* or two, an imagined photo from my wedding in America that maybe we will one day be allowed to have.

And on our wedding day in America—even though Alistair thinks it will be corny—there will be bagpipes.

And this . . .

[Tim holds up the U.S. flag.]

Ya know, I wasn't gonna take this flag with me, but there's just no getting away from it. It's part of me. It's in me. It's in us. And I guess I hope that some day that flag might get a little bit clean. That our country might finally open its heart to me and Alistair, might open its heart to us. That there wouldn't be so much fear in our country, in US and of us.

But for now, this flag is coming along with me.

[Tim picks up his suitcase.]

I can't help it. I still have hope.
I still have hope for US.

[The lights slowly fade to black.]

Making Us

An Interview with John S. Gentile

Us *was a work in progress when Tim Miller was interviewed by John Gentile, a member of the editorial board of* Text and Performance Quarterly *(* TPQ *), during performances in Atlanta early in 2003. Typically, Miller continues to shape his works during their early performances; as he indicates, one key segment of* Us *had been conceived only three weeks earlier. That immediacy produced in this interview his most extended discussion of the creative processes through which his works take shape. The interview also significantly addresses Miller's techniques for making political material acceptable, while still challenging, to an audience. The text that follows is edited from the original transcript; a longer version of the full interview was published in* TPQ *in 2004.*

JOHN S. GENTILE: You've said that your work grows out of whatever is most urgent in your life at that time. Would you say that's generally true throughout your solo career?

TIM MILLER: I think so. I respond to what's going on in my life. That's a big totemic burden to put on creating work, but I think it is a good one. If you make work from that autobiographical conceit, if you have this notion that our lives matter, then that's what you're going to make work about. For the last three to four years, the biggest presenting problem, as the therapists among us would call it, is this drama around my situation with Alistair and the spooky ticking clock on us having to leave the U.S. There is part of me that is just so annoyed that I have to busy myself with all this stuff now. Which may keep me from making pieces about other things that really intrigue me, like "what is it to be forty-four?" If I weren't making this piece, that's a piece I might be interested in making right now.

GENTILE: So, once a particular aspect of life is pressing forward a need to create a piece, what happens next?

MILLER: Well, with this piece *Us,* the question I ask myself, and I say it in the show, is, "*What's wrong with us?*" The double meaning of that. "What's wrong with us?" Meaning Alistair and me. Why can't we do after nine years of a committed relationship what a straight couple could do after a day? That's a big question, an existential question, but the larger question there is: "What's wrong with U.S.?"—meaning America. I knew I wanted to make a piece that took a larger view of American culture and our journey and struggles as a society, and the way I'm feeling it impact my life.

Then, what began to be interesting to me—and this is a way of finding that delight amid the political content of my work—I started noticing, "man, I'm talking a lot about Broadway musicals in this show!" They were just coming up, unintentional and intuitive. It was that fun thing that happens with intuitive creativity. So then I started finding it a hoot to beef up that musical theater material: these musicals that I was raised on and that formed my identity as both a gay boy and an American. It's a very appropriate crucible to look at, since the piece is about these clashing identities of my experience, as a gay person, as an American, and as a gay American being forced to leave my country. That became a structuring principle. And also knowing that if you make highly politically-contexted work, you enter a minefield of people's interest in it, but also their resistance to political rhetoric and topics and information. So, finding the fun thing for

me as a performer in the Broadway musical through-line, but also
a vernacular that the audience can connect to, seemed quite important to me. The fun and the joy in the piece needs to be there
for me the performer if it's going to be there for the audience.

GENTILE: How do you select the different narratives that comprise
a show?

MILLER: With this new piece I wanted to explore early core moments where my identity as an American was formed. It's probably not surprising that the musical theater thing really kicked
in, because at the age of ten there was no cultural material more
important to me, as someone who loved musicals, or as someone
who loved history. I loved the Broadway show *1776,* which amazingly had a successful revival three or four years ago, which I
saw—twice—and I have the CD. (Laughter.) As I note in the
show, it has a fairly hard edge critique of the contradictions and
hypocrisies of our Founding Fathers, most of whom were owners
of human slaves.

I was curious about other moments in my life, like when I realized, "oh my God, Americans are fleeing our country," and
when I realized exile was part of my life also. That's in the section
about *Man of La Mancha* and Vietnam: how aware I was when I
was in fifth and sixth grade that half a million young Americans
were seeking asylum in Canada to escape from the insane policies
of our government in Southeast Asia. I felt panicked about that—
that I was going to have to go to war; I was only ten and I was
worried about it already. That became the real first core piece for
the show: "OK, this is interesting. Here at the age of forty-four, as
I face having to seek asylum in the United Kingdom where my relationship will be respected—when else have I felt that?' I think
that many, if not most, lesbian and gay Americans feel exiled in
some way from America. We are not welcome here. We're not
treated fairly. Our work as a country is so unfinished in terms of
really welcoming difference; it's so horrifically unfinished. That

Tim Miller in *Us*, Atlanta, 2003. Photo by Yvonne Boyd.

was a narrative of how to explore the feelings of exile, whether you go into exile or not. Going back and finding that narrative, which felt like a core to start configuring other things and, then, constellating out from that. Such as the funny story of my assuming an English accent when I was ten years old so that I would be cast in a potential sequel to the movie musical *Oliver.* Which is about how pretentious those smart, teacher's-pet gay boys are, who assume cultural materials that aren't theirs. But that was also another gesture towards otherness, toward trying to find an identity that fit better, which is played for humor in the show, but is actually quite poignant.

GENTILE: "When else have I felt this way?" Is that typically an important question for you as a performer?

MILLER: Oh, yeah! As a teacher, too. Anything that connects. Almost doing what I think of as "life dramaturgy," seeing the ways the themes in your life develop, change, grow. How something that happened when you were nine connects with something that happened when you were thirty-nine. A therapist may say, "What is it about what you're going through right now that reminds you of when you were a child?" But to me, this is more of a political act than a therapeutic act. Both artists and therapists are interested in childhood as a source of the primary texts, of our life narratives. That's why we mine and explore childhood and connect through the filmy gauze that can obscure it sometimes.

GENTILE: Is your process literary? Do you write it out? Or is your process oral?

MILLER: Both, but much more oral. This show is so about voice. And teaching gives me the opportunity, when I'm working on a show, to tell the stories and to work on the structure of the show. Every section of *Us* began as an improvised spoken performance; it didn't begin on the page. "Okay, this is what came up." I trust that a lot. For tens of thousands of years our species didn't use paper; we just had the stories inside of us. It's good to have a period where paper isn't coming into it. Instead we can focus on the breath and body and presence and the moment. I do a lot of workshop exercises about how to re-negotiate a relationship to words on paper and how words arrive there. Actors really like these exercises, because usually they're tortured by their papers, their scripts, being "on book," "off book," all that. For me the best stuff comes when I work improvisationally around a kind of inquiry I've done, around the kind of narrative I'm interested in.

Three weeks ago when I was in Chicago teaching at Roosevelt University, I was thinking about the light in this show, and I suddenly remembered the light of my older brothers' desk lamp when they once had me do a striptease for them, when I was seven and so into the musical *Gypsy*. I hadn't thought of it before, although I don't believe I had put any big energy into repressing it. If I weren't improvising and intuitively finding, I don't know if I would have dredged it up. My intuition pulled me to this funny, a little bit kinky, story about my older brothers encouraging their youngest brother do a striptease in the light of their desk lamp. So that's where the process pays off. Trusting your intuition and improvising it orally a couple of times gives you a chance to discover it.

Then usually right after I improvise a story, I write it down. While it's still fresh and still sweaty on your skin, the words are still there, and they're words that live as you speak them, shout them, chant them, sing them. They're in breath meter already because that's where they came from. Since I know any stories that I tell in performance are going to be real time, spoken breath, it's much better if it begins with breath, with spoken voice.

GENTILE: When you are first working on a story, before it goes down on the page, are you telling it to another person? Do you ask someone to listen to you?

MILLER: Always. Usually my students. That is how teaching feeds back into my creative process. If you are a good teacher, and like teaching, you probably have figured out how to make sure that it feeds you, and that's part of how that works for me. It's a way for

me to keep exploring things. It also means I get some of the experience of an ensemble in my creative process, because most of my
finished work is solo. In a way, I feel like the students co-created
my solos because they heard a story the first time when it was still
sizzling on the griddle.

GENTILE: Once you have the individual stories, how do you discover the structure of a solo piece?

MILLER: Well, I'm a Virgo, so I seek order and cosmology and man-
dalas. Certainly my images are constellational and mandala-like.
I see how they weave, what hooks up, what's the core, the heart of
the themes, where are the outer rings. In this show *Us,* there's the
core narrative of American identity, gay identity, voice, this sub-
theme of stripping from the *Gypsy* stuff, stripping away memory,
fear, the denial about our condition in the U.S. I look for the big
narrative and metaphorical glue that links things and, obviously,
in this show the musicals became a glue to help link the stories. I
make fun of it in the show, and kind of trick the audience. I find
metaphorical structures and through-lines rather hysterical, too,
because on a certain level, they're so artificial. If you ironically
criticize your own structure, you actually immunize yourself to
criticism, which I think of as an insurance policy. The quota-
tional, italicized making fun of yourself gives audiences permission to exhale, especially with something that's as over the top as
this Broadway canon.

How does someone who's not a gay man in a bi-national relationship pay attention to this piece? That's what I mean by "connecting the dots." Even though I am not an African-American
whose brothers have been killed in non-stop gang violence in
South L.A., if I see a performance work by an artist who has had
that terrible experience I may be able to find the way to connect
the dots and open that empathy window and relate. I'm assuming people do that with my work. But you want to help them
along. And for me the structure is the way of helping the audience understand what the issues of the piece are, what its quirky

logic is. Giving them a window to enter in and relate to the piece. The structure of *Us* has given me enormous pleasure. The linking of themes and the cultural materials—using these sentimental cultural materials as sacred stuff. For me, the structure is finding the deeper, metaphorical artesian wells that live inside me that might also connect to different audiences, and organizing those into a theatrical language that serves the piece.

GENTILE: You once said that you found solo performance to be "a quintessentially American form."

MILLER: The idea that our stories count, are worth telling, is one of the best American characteristics that I can identify in myself. I perform in England and Scotland, and that notion of telling your story, spilling the beans, is fundamentally counter to those cultures' temperaments. I sometimes think it gives them the creeps even as they're fascinated by it. The idea that you talk about your private details, toot your own horn, reveal your dirty laundry are to me very positive American characteristics. I can get on a plane in Memphis—this happened to me just recently—and a woman with big hair will sit down next to me, and literally within twenty seconds she's telling me that she's on her way to L.A. because she has inoperable ovarian cancer and there's some new treatment at UCLA Medical Center. I'm a story magnet, people tell me these things. That would be impossible in England or Scotland. Nosiness about each other, I think it's a really good thing about Americans. It's one of the hopeful ways we might actually deal with some of our denial about our political actions.

The ability to tell the truth is a very good quality, even with its dangers of narcissism or self-involvement. You have to imagine you matter, to think that you should be doing this. And Americans do imagine that we matter. Growing up, certainly for boys, there's a huge value put on public speech, claiming your space. Whether it's in front of the class, or in the pulpit, or among your friends, or on the playing field, there are all these sites where public speech is valorized in a very particular way. It's an interesting fact that most solo performers did forensics at some point in junior high or high school. It's more common than having done theater, I've been finding. The horrible oral dramatic interps I would do of *A Clockwork Orange* in junior high were links towards knowing that the act of speaking matters. It's also informed hugely by African American homiletics and preaching, which is probably our strongest public speaking model right now. And it's communicated through our national systems, such as our public education. That's partly why there is so much American solo performance.

In 1986, I started coming to the Alternate ROOTS (Regional Organization of Theaters South) Annual Meeting. That had a huge impact on me. Living as a New York performer, there wasn't a huge value put on the mechanics of just telling a story; you need smoke and mirrors and video projectors and stuff. And suddenly at these ROOTS gatherings in the woods at Black Mountain, North Carolina, I was seeing all kinds of other things. There are some really good storytellers here in the South. It has protected the form, which is now, of course, newly vital. We're a story-obsessed, life-narrative obsessed culture. That had a big impact on me and was a real lucky thing for me. I was telling stories, but in some ways I wasn't clear as to how that connected—not to an ancient lineage, because we are a new country, but to a deep cultural river, a way of telling stories and looking at people and being present. I don't really think of what I do as "performance art." I tell three or four stories and try to link them with some kind of metaphorical glue, and then share that with people.

GENTILE: Dance informed your early solos very significantly. Why has storytelling become more important than dance?

MILLER: Dance did launch me. I liked that training because I was being encouraged to make pieces. Virtually every dancer choreographs pieces, whereas most actors don't write a play. It's a flaw in theater training: actors should be encouraged to see themselves as primary creators as well. I was given much more permission in dance settings. It opened up my ideas, and I started making dance pieces which included words. Over time, I knew I wasn't really that great a dancer; what I was good at was writing and storytelling. But I was also developing a sense of the body as a site of narratives. A lot of the stories I tell are about physically being alive, being physical, being in our bodies. It's physical performing, but it's really my mouth, me telling the story and hopping around some. My twenty-two-year-old self would look at my work now and believe that I ended up doing incredibly conventional narrative-based theater. But my younger self would be impressed with the content. The queer and political content in my work is consistent with my earlier goals and what I wanted to make work about.

GENTILE: Elsewhere you've said that the explosion of diverse life narratives and performances has changed how this country sees itself.

MILLER: Solo performance is legislative theater, is representational activism, creating the images that are out there. For solo performers who have a strong community connection—to the gay, or the black, or Latino, or Asian, or homeless, or disabled communities—it's one of the most effective ways, maybe the only way, that non-corporate voices can actually speak up. Especially now when corporate media conglomerates increasingly control us.

For me, it's gay life and politics. Through solo performance I can reach a wider audience, and I know my work has been marked, in an interesting small-scale way, as an articulation of gay identity. In the issues I'm working around these days—the denial of civil marriage rights for lesbian and gay Americans, and this immigration stuff—I'm the only American theater artist traveling work extensively on either of those issues. Considering how huge the gay marriage discourse is right now, and that it's being debated in every state legislature, it's surprising theater has not responded in any kind of dramatic way. It gives me the performer a voice to speak. But it also gives the audience, whether they're straight or gay or in-between, a chance to sit with some of this material and create a relationship to it, sift it around inside themselves.

GENTILE: You've said that you tell your stories to change their endings. How do you hope to change the ending with *Us*?

MILLER: As I said in my essay about memory and the future, I've had this notion, ever since I started writing in my journal, that the act of telling is an act that imagines you have some kind of agency or power, because it means there's something worth telling, and also that it's worth listening to. It means you want to shape events, shape your story. You tell stories to claim greater agency rather than to have less, to have more integration and wholeness rather than less.

I certainly have this idea—and it has been true—that speaking my narratives of my life as a gay person around the emotional, sexual, political topographies that I've explored has deepened my sense of who I am, deepened my social relations, transformed aspects of American political life, raised hundreds of thousands of dollars for AIDS or for freedom of expression, founded the two main art centers in the U.S. for new performance, gone to the Supreme Court with a freedom of expression case. Again and again, speaking up has affected, challenged, troubled the status quo, the stuff that strikes me as unfair. I see the ways that it's happened. There's the part of me that really believes it can ultimately change the ending of the story, and I know it does in small ways.

At the age of forty-four, I no longer assume that certain kinds of progressive change will happen in America in my lifetime. But we have to remember America kept human slavery three generations longer than any other Western country. That reminds us how slow our progress in human rights tends to be in this country. That's a helpful reality check.

I assume that sometime during the course of performing *Us*, Alistair and I will have to leave the country. I don't think there's going to be a positive political change in the next ten years in America around stuff like that. However, I think the deeper ending of the story is about how our interior lives are changed, and that absolutely is do-able and happens. You can change the laws and still feel weak, disempowered, scared. Just like the laws can be as bad as they currently are and you can nevertheless feel powerful, claiming your voice, all that. Certainly as artists, we have much more control over that interior landscape, that inner theater, of what it feels like to be human. I have enormous confidence in our ability as artists to create those spaces in our hearts and to tell, and to retell, and to reframe our life narratives, our social narratives, our social relations as well, at least within certain microcosms. Even as I get more skeptical about the larger social, political, legal kind of change, I grow more and more confident about how we can change how the stories turn out inside us.

Epilogue

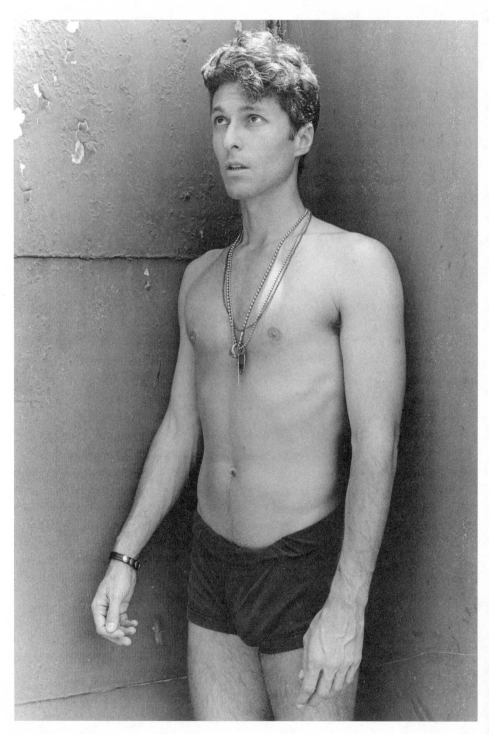

Tim Miller on the road in New York City, 1994. Photo by Dona Ann McAdams.

1001 Beds

Travel is work. I mean that statement literally, because I am one of those grunts who make their living out on the road performing. My life as an artist and activist is built around constant travel, twenty-five to thirty weeks a year doing gigs all over the world. Tokyo one week. Cincinnati the next. Glasgow right after. My life is that of the wandering queer performance artist minstrel, or a Johnny "Fag" Appleseed. Believe me, this constant schlepping takes its toll: time-zone confusion, sleeping on the floor at O'Hare International during snowstorms, the permanent sinus condition I share with all flight attendants, having to ask myself "if it's Tuesday this must be Tennessee?" On the plus side, I can see myself as a fierce culture worker out there nurturing those ever-crucial Whitmanic leaves-of-grassroots. But on the downside I sometimes feel exactly as one "friend" once referred to me, I thought insultingly, as "Tim Miller, the Willy Loman of performance art." As the son of a traveling salesman dad and a mom who worked for years behind the wristwatch counter at May Company department store, I took slight at that!

I did the math recently and figured that I sleep in a minimum of twenty-five different beds each year as I travel and perform. If I continue to tour for another twenty years as I have for the last twenty-one, I will end up sleeping in at least 1000 hotel beds in my lifetime. For maximum poetic oomph, let's say 1001 beds. This scary statistic seems important, but we do the math on our lives at our own peril. What seems pleasurable in week-by-week doses can add up to an exponential horror show, an endless phalanx of beds extending as far as the eye can see.

I was thinking about these metaphorical 1001 beds tonight as I checked into the Vernon Manor Hotel in Cincinnati for a gig at the Cincinnati Playhouse. The Vernon Manor is a huge old sprawl of a hotel. Designed with a Gothic-cum-Tudor confidence, it's like the set for a well-funded touring production of *Camelot*. The hotel was built in 1924 as a retreat for wealthy Cincinnati residents from the busy downtown riverfront district. That part of Cincinnati was referred to as "Porkopolis" in acknowledgment of the squeals of protest from pigs that were becoming hot dogs at the many pork processing plants of sharp-knifed Cincy. Over the years the Vernon Manor Hotel has hosted everyone from President Kennedy to Judy Garland, the Beatles to "Barney," Bob Dylan to Kevin Bacon—returning us to the pork-theme of Cincinnati.

I checked into Room 626, right next to 624, The Beatles Suite. There's a huge sparkly star on the door of 624 in honor of the two times the Beatles stayed there in the '60s. The Vernon Manor is very popular with performing artists who tour to Cincinnati, our guild-hall tavern in a way. It's used by many road shows and by Cincinnati Playhouse actors, directors, and designers. I sometimes think that there is no real difference between some actors' bar in Athens during the fourth century B.C. and the late-night bar at the Vernon Manor, where we can order our third Jack Daniels and Coke and the Beggars Purse appetizer plate. Those ancient Greek actors getting ready to head out to Samos for some Euripides premiere are in a direct genealogical line to me gearing up for my show tomorrow night at Cincinnati Playhouse. I like feeling that deep historical link, just as I do the more recent histories of the Vernon Manor. Certainly the Beatles-who-are-lost-to-us haunt this hotel. John Lennon at the ice machine. The young George Harrison in 1966—a real look alike for my partner, Alistair—running from the screaming teens outside the hotel.

How many stories the five hundred or so beds that I have already encountered could tell if they hadn't agreed to the confidentiality clause! Just as every hotel is haunted, every hotel is a sex hotel. Certainly a good percentage of my already-slept-in hotel beds have been sex beds. There was a time in my life when the main perk of the road was savoring the local brew of the boys of Edinburgh or San Antonio or Palermo. Finally, in 1994 in a hotel bed in South Kensington, London, I met my partner Alistair—and that put a stop to those sexy shenanigans with boys of the world!

But it's not just the hotel as erotic vortex that I'm interested in here. These 1001 beds have become my symbol for the burden of these endless journeys. Each of those beds means I have to face the ordeal of prying myself out of the bed I have shared for many years with Alistair in our home in Venice Beach. Peeling my limbs out of the sheets and bedclothes, I then fling myself somewhere in the world far from my man. I am doing this partly because on the practical level I need to make a living, but mostly because I have a deeper calling to run around the world and create queer space in small Southern colleges or fading industrial cities in the Midwest of America or the Midlands of England. I believe that real, face-to-face culture is retail not wholesale. (Back to my traveling salesman motif.) It relies on us being near each other, in the same room.

My mission—and I have decided to accept it—is to be always ready to run around doing my lean-and-mean homo-drenched performances, my cultural agitating and teaching—and offering myself as a way-out gay role model and/or target. Whenever I need to hop on a tiny plane for Des Moines or Chattanooga to show the rainbow flag, I am ready. Sure, I usually feel blue on a Sunday night nested with Alistair, knowing that the next morning I need to hit the highway. But I know that whatever cultural agency and visibility I have accrued over twenty years as a performer and sparring partner, duking it out with American homophobia, make me a useful cultural provocateur. This doesn't make me dread the nuts and bolts of travel any less. In the two days before a trip I begin to feel depressed and anxious. The tribal anxiety-attack drums gear up as the stress and challenge of my travel schedule begins to undermine any sense of a "normal" life Alistair and I try to have together.

I make a very unlikely traveler. I love my domestic patterns and I am incredibly disorganized in my travel preparations. I have never had that glacial travel cool that Joan Didion—my personal uberdiva of California first-person narrative—describes in *The White Album*. La Didion tells us of her precise check-lists for travel and how she always has a bag packed ready to go to Viet Nam or Cannes. Not me. I am always scrambling at the last minute through the dryer for my costume, or wondering where I put my passport, or have you seen my mini-disc with the show's sound cues?

These days there is another spotlit irony as big as the Hollywood sign in my situation. I force myself into these two dozen annual mini-exiles from home and love to perform a piece about a larger exile that haunts Alistair's and my household. Since Alistair is a U.K. and Australian citizen and we are gay men, I am unable to sponsor him for a green card in the U.S. even though we have been together for more than ten years. Contrast this with any straight American, who can meet their foreign sweetie for the first time today in Las Vegas, head on impulse to the Elvis Marriage Chapel, and tomorrow have provisional immigration status in the U.S.

This issue obviously provides lots of fuel for performance art interventions, and I am confident that the hundreds of traveling gigs I have done exposing this injustice have contributed in a huge way to public awareness and incremental political progress. Just "Google" the issue and you will see how much focus I have brought to the subject. But what a big, fat contradiction, that I have to leave my partner constantly to decry the injustice and exile we face—and meanwhile we are apart for close to half the year. Well, back to that Johnny Appleseed, Walt Whitman part of myself: "You say I contradict myself—well then, I contradict myself!" The truth is, each time I pry myself out of our home to hit the highway and raise awareness about the human rights violations gay Americans face, it is really a tribute to the depth of love I feel for Alistair and the longing I have for home. It is exactly because it's so hard for me to be away from him that I must travel, agitate, and educate to try to make our country grow up. And each time I get on a plane I enact the exile that Al and I together face, from our home and my country.

The comfort I can find in that scary statistic of 1001 beds lives strongest in the knowledge that those beds have meant something. They symbolize a life and art dedicated to reaching out toward folks from Bozeman to Tampa. A life and art that has traveled widely and, I believe, reached a couple hundred thousand people with my stories of queer life and love. My journeys are dedicated to nurturing that spark of vision, that someday American gay people won't be second-class citizens in our own country. Connecting to other lives and communities is the only way I can avoid seeing those 1001 beds as a Sisyphean hell. Is that really me carrying the plush Simmons double-king Posturepedic on my back up a steep hill—only to have it roll back down again and again? Not entirely: that endless parade of beds marking the journeys of my life instead becomes my own personal Boy Scout merit badge, for a life that has a strong sense of service and mission.

Acknowledgments

We are happy to acknowledge the many people who helped and encouraged us in preparing this book. Among them are:

Tim's collaborators in the pieces collected here: Rev. Malcolm Boyd, Linda Frye Burnham, Steven Durland, John S. Gentile, Thomas Leabhart, Dona Ann McAdams, Alistair McCartney, and Douglas Sadownick. We are particularly grateful to the mother and sisters of John Bernd: Mrs. Dorothy Williams, Sarah Durkee, and Kate Bernd-Barnett.

Others whose work with Tim could not be included in the space we had: Jill Carleton, Lizbeth Goodman, Michael Kearns, Linda Montano, George Rios, David Román, and Darrell Taylor.

For illustrations: John Aigner; Yvonne Boyd; Paula Court; Alan Crumlish; Johan Elbers; the Chris HA Theatre Museum Collection, Victoria and Albert Museum, and Dr. Jim Fowler for the photo by Chris Harris; Dona Ann McAdams; Mary Milelzcik; Chuck Stallard; Thomas Strand; William D. Ward and the UCLA School of Theater, Film, and Television; John Warner; Billy Weeks on behalf of the *Chattanooga Times Free Press;* and Maryette Charlton and Paula Court on behalf of the estate of Kirk Winslow.

At the University of Wisconsin Press: Raphael Kadushin, Andrew Sawyer, Adam Mehring, Sheila Moermond, Benson Gardner, and Carla Aspelmeier.

For various contributions: Robbie Allen; Roberto Bedoya; David Cole; Chris Doggett; David Gere; Richard Harrison; Mary Helms, Suzette Rainey, and the Local History staff of the Chattanooga Hamilton County Bicentennial Library; Ann Law; Alistair Livingstone; Jordan Peimer; Alan Pulner; Jack Ricketts; Jan Rothschild; Richard Schneider, Jr.; and Jason Weidemann.

Grateful acknowledgement is made to journals and monographs where items in this book were previously published:

"An Anarchic, Subversive, Erotic Soul: An Interview with Tim Miller." With Steven Durland. *The Drama Review* 35, no. 3 (Fall 1991): 171–78. Copyright 1991 by New York University and the Massachusetts Institute of Technology.

"The artist becomes really woven into the community as a worker" originally appeared as "Tim Miller: Interview with Linda Frye Burham." *Art Papers* 14, no. 1 (January/February 1990): 10–15.

"Jesus and the Queer Performance Artist." In *Amazing Grace: Stories of Lesbian and Gay Faith*, ed. Malcolm Boyd and Nancy L. Wilson, 57–66. Freedom, CA: The Crossing Press, 1991.

"Memory and Facing the Future." *Harvard Gay and Lesbian Review* 6, no. 2 (Spring 1999): 32–37.

"1001 Beds." In *Wonderlands: Good Gay Travel Writing*, ed. Raphael Kadushin, 241–46. Madison: Terrace Books, University of Wisconsin Press, 2004.

"Professional Autobiography" originally appeared as "Tim Miller." *Mime Journal*, ed. Thomas Leabhart (1991–1992): 123–42.

"Suck, Spit, Chew, Swallow: A Performative Exploration of Men's Bodies." In *Masculinity: Bodies, Movies, Culture*, ed. Peter Lehman, 279–300. Copyright 2001, reproduced by permission of Routledge/Taylor & Francis Group, LLC.

"Making *Us* " originally appeared as "A *TPQ* Interview: Tim Miller on Autobiographical Storytelling," with John Gentile. *Text & Performance Quarterly* 23, no. 3 (July 2003): 271–87. http://www.tandf.co.uk.

"Oklahomo!" *American Theatre* 20, no. 9 (November 2003): 91–93. Published by the Theatre Communications Group.

"Tokyo Tim: A Report from the Dokkyo University Performance Studies Conference, January 2003." *The Drama Review* 47, no. 3 (Fall 2003): 143–48. Copyright 2003 by New York University and the Massachusetts Institute of Technology

GLEN JOHNSON and TIM MILLER

September 2005

Bibliography

Major Performances

Paint Yrself Red/Me & Mayakovsky. 1980.
Live Boys. With John Bernd. Three episodes: *We Had Tea We Ate Cashew Chicken,*
    Live Boys, Live Boys: I Hate Your Guts. 1980–81.
Postwar. 1982. Earlier version: *Survival Tactic.*
Cost of Living. 1983.
Democracy in America. Brooklyn Academy of Music, Next Wave Festival. 1984.
Buddy Systems. With Douglas Sadownick. 1985.
Some Golden States. 1987.
Stretch Marks. 1989.
Sex/Love/Stories. 1990.
My Queer Body. 1992.
Naked Breath. 1994.
Fruit Cocktail. 1996.
Carnal Garage. With Alistair McCartney. 1997.
Shirts & Skin. 1997.
Glory Box. 1999.
Body Blows. 2002.
Us. 2003.

Published Scripts and Performance Texts

Body Blows: Six Performances. Madison: University of Wisconsin Press, 2002.
Civil Disobedience Weekend. In *Sundays at Seven: Choice Words from a Different
    Light's Gay Writers Series.* San Francisco: Alamo Square Press, 1996. Also in
    Dona Ann McAdams, *Caught in the Act: A Look at Contemporary Multimedia
    Performance.* New York: Aperture, 1996.

"The Maw of Death" [from *Some Golden States*]. In *Out of Character: Rants, Raves, and Monologues from Today's Top Performance Artists*, ed. Mark Russell, 259–66. New York: Bantam Books, 1997.
My Queer Body. In *Sharing the Delirium: Second Generation AIDS Plays and Performances*, ed. Therese Jones, 310–36. Portsmouth, NH: Heinemann, 1994.
Naked Breath. In *O Solo Homo: The New Queer Performance*, ed. Holly Hughes and David Román, 51–92. New York: Grove Press, 1998.
"Spilt Milk" [from *Shirts & Skin*]. In *Extreme Exposure: An Anthology of Solo Performance Texts from the Twentieth Century*, ed. Jo Bonney, 155–63. New York: Theatre Communications Group, 2000.
Stretch Marks. The Drama Review 35, no. 3 (Fall 1991): 143–70.
"Vigil/Manifesto" [from *Stretch Marks*]. In *Blood Whispers: L.A. Writers on AIDS*, ed. Terry Wolverton. Los Angeles: Silverton Books, 1991.

Essays and Personal Narratives

"An Artist's Declaration of Independence." July 4, 1990. Reprinted in *Culture Wars: Documents from the Recent Controversies in the Arts*, ed. Richard Bolton, 244–45. New York: New Press, 1992.
Democracy in America. With photos by Dona Ann McAdams. New York: The Next Wave, Brooklyn Academy of Music, 1984.
"How to Grow Fruit" [narrative version of opening part of *Fruit Cocktail*]. In *Boys Like Us: Gay Writers Tell Their Coming Out Stories*, ed. Patrick Merla, 204–13. New York: Avon Books, 1996.
"Jesus and the Queer Performance Artist." In *Amazing Grace: Stories of Lesbian and Gay Faith*, ed. Malcolm Boyd and Nancy L. Wilson, 57–66. Freedom, CA: Crossing Press, 1991.
"Memory and Facing the Future." *Harvard Gay and Lesbian Review* 6, no. 2 (Spring 1999): 32–37.
"Oklahomo!" *American Theatre* 20, no. 9 (November 2003): 91–93.
"1001 Beds." In *Wonderlands: Good Gay Travel Writing*, ed. Raphael Kadushin, 241–46. Madison: Terrace Books, University of Wisconsin Press, 2004.
"Out of the Box: A Performance Art Call to Arms." In "How Do You Make Social Change?" *Theater* 31, no. 3 (Fall 2001): 89–90.
"'Preaching to the Converted.'" With David Román. *Theatre Journal* 47 (1995): 169–88. Reprinted in *The Queerest Art: Essays on Lesbian and Gay Theater*, ed. Alisa Solomon and Framji Minwalla, 203–26. New York: New York University Press, 2002.
Shirts & Skin. Los Angeles: Alyson Books, 1997.
"Suck, Spit, Chew, Swallow: A Performative Exploration of Men's Bodies." In *Masculinity: Bodies, Movies, Culture*, ed. Peter Lehman, 279–300. London: Routledge, 2001.

"Tar Pit Heart" [narrative version of a segment from *My Queer Body*]. In *His: Brilliant New Fiction by Gay Writers,* ed. Robert Drake and Terry Wolverton, 36–44. Boston: Faber & Faber, 1995.

"'Til Death Do Us Part." *Los Angeles,* May 13–26, 2001. Pp. 54–55.

"Tim Miller." With Thomas Leabhart. *Mime Journal,* California Performance, vol. 2: (1991–1992): 123–42.

"Tokyo Tim: A Report from the Dokkyo University Performance Studies Conference, January 2003." *The Drama Review* 47, no.3 (Fall 2003): 143–48.

Miscellaneous

Body Blows. Video documentary by Charles Dennis. 2002.

"Performance Artist." *The Larry Sanders Show.* Episode 215. Chris Thompson, John Riggi, and Drake Sather, writers. Brillstein-Grey Productions/Home Box Office. August 19, 1993.

Tim Miller: Loud & Queer. Video documentary by Richard L. Harrison. 1992.

Selected Interviews

"Tim Miller." Interview with Linda Montano. *Performance Artists Talking in the Eighties: Sex Food Money/Fame Ritual/Death,* comp. Linda Montano, 100–105. Berkeley: University of California Press, 2000. Interviewed in 1986.

"Tim Miller: States of Art: An Interview with Michael Kearns." *Edge* [Los Angeles], April 27, 1988.

"An Anarchic, Subversive, Erotic Soul: An Interview with Tim Miller." With Steven Durland. *The Drama Review* 35, no. 3 (Fall 1991): 171–78.

"Bodies and Stages: An Interview with Tim Miller." With Lizbeth Goodman. *Critical Quarterly* 36 (1994): 63–72.

"Tim Miller Exposed." Interview with Randy Shulman. *Michael's Entertainment Weekly,* Washington, D.C., April 7, 1994. Pp. 30–36.

"Miller Time." Interview with Randy Shulman. *Metro Weekly,* Washington, D.C., August 10, 1995. Pp. 28–34.

"The Naked Truth: Catching Up with Tim Miller." Interview with William J. Mann. *Frontiers* [Los Angeles], November 14, 1997. Pp. 69–73.

"Narrative and Nudity: An Interview with Tim Miller." With Glen Johnson. *Lambda Book Report* 6, no. 5 (December 1997): 35.

"Tim Miller." Interview with Linda Frye Burnham. In *Interventions and Provocations: Conversations on Art, Culture, and Resistance,* ed. Glenn Harper. Albany: SUNY Press, 1998. Reprinted from *Atlanta Art Papers.*

"Exploring the Culture War: A Journey with Tim Miller." Interview with Darrell Taylor. *Iowa Journal of Cultural Studies* 17 (1998): 63–67.

"The Naked Truth." Interview with Randy Shulman. *Metro Weekly,* Washington, D.C., July 29, 1999. Pp. 24–31.

"Boxed In." Interview with Randy Shulman. *MW* [previously *Metro Weekly*], Washington, D.C., July 11, 2002. Pp. 30–34.

"Critical Relations: Tim Miller and David Román in Dialogue." *Theater* 33, no. 3 (Fall 2003): 119–25. Adapted from a public conversation at the University of Minnesota, April 2002.

"A TPQ Interview: Tim Miller on Autobiographical Storytelling." With John S. Gentile. *Text & Performance Quarterly* 23, no. 3 (July 2003): 271–87.

Selected Criticism

Banes, Sally. *Subversive Expectations: Performance Art and Paratheater in New York, 1976–85.* Ann Arbor: University of Michigan Press, 1998. Pp. 104–13, 133–36. [Reprints "Men Together/Bloolips" (*Dance Magazine* 1981); "As, I Like It" (*Village Voice* 1982); "The Politics of Performance and the Performance of Politics" (*Village Voice* 1982).]

Brustein, Robert. "The War on the Arts." *New Republic,* July 7, 14, 1992. Reprint in *Dumbocracy in America: Studies in the Theatre of Guilt, 1987–1994.* Chicago: Ivan R. Dee, 1994.

Burnham, Linda. "Making Family: Tim Miller, Douglas Sadownick, and the New Buddy System." *High Performance* 36, 9.4 (1986): 48–53.

Carleton, Jill M. "Embodying Autobiography: A Lesbian Performance of Gay Male Performance Art." *Women & Performance: A Journal of Feminist Theory* 19 (1999): 73–83.

Corey, Frederick. "Gay Life/Queer Art." In *The Last Sex: Feminism and Outlaw Bodies,* ed. Arthur and Marilouise Kroker. New York: St. Martin's, 1993.

———. "Tim Miller's Body (of Work)." *Text and Performance Quarterly* 23, no. 3 (July 2003): 253–70.

Gere, David. *How to Make Dances in an Epidemic: Tracking Choreography in the Age of AIDS.* Madison: University of Wisconsin Press, 2004.

Goldberg, RoseLee. "Art After Hours: Downtown Performance." In *The Downtown Book: The New York Art Scene, 1974–1984,* ed. Marvin J. Taylor, 97–115. Princeton: Princeton University Press, 2005.

———. "Performance Art: In and Out of the Mainstream." In *The American Century: Art & Culture, 1950–2000,* by Lisa Phillips. New York: Whitney Museum of American Art/W.W. Norton, 1999.

Goodman, Lizbeth. "Death and Dancing in the Live Arts: Performance, Politics and Sexuality in the Age of AIDS." *Critical Quarterly* 35, no.2 (1993): 99–116.

Heddon, Deirdre. "'Glory Box': Tim Miller's Autobiography of the Future." *NTQ: New Theatre Quarterly* 75, 19.3 (August 2003): 243–56.

Johnson, Glen M. "Performing Access: Tim Miller, Larry Sanders, and Jay Leno." *Text and Performance Quarterly* 18, no. 2 (1998): 137–44.

Phelan, Peggy. "Tim Miller's *My Queer Body:* An Anatomy in Six Sections." *Theater* 24, no. 2 (1992): 30–34.

Román, David. *Acts of Intervention: Performance, Gay Culture, and AIDS.* Bloomington: Indiana University Press, 1998. [Extended discussions in chapters "Solo Performance and the Body on Stage" and "Negative Energies."]

———. "Performing All Our Lives: AIDS, Performance, Community." In *Critical Theory and Performance,* ed. Janelle G. Reinelt and Joseph R. Roach, 208–21. Ann Arbor: University of Michigan Press, 1992.

Ryan, Katy. "A Body's Mind Experience in Tim Miller's Workshop." *Theater Topics* 7, no. 2 (September 1997): 205–7.

Taylor, Darrell. "Tim Miller's *My Queer Body:* Performance of Desire." *Journal of Medical Humanities* 19, nos. 2–3 (Summer 1998): 225–34.

Wolford, Lisa. "Oppositional Performance/Critical Pedagogy: A Report from the Penn State Symposium." *Theater Topics* 7, no. 2 (September 1997): 187–203.

LIVING OUT
Gay and Lesbian Autobiographies

Joan Larkin and David Bergman
SERIES EDITORS

Raphael Kadushin
SERIES ACQUISITION EDITOR

The Other Mother: A Lesbian's Fight for Her Daughter
Nancy Abrams

An Underground Life: Memoirs of a Gay Jew in Nazi Berlin
Gad Beck

Surviving Madness: A Therapist's Own Story
Betty Berzon

You're Not from Around Here, Are You? A Lesbian in Small-Town America
Louise A. Blum

Just Married: Gay Marriage and the Expansion of Civil Rights
Kevin Bourassa and Joe Varnell

Two Novels: Development *and* Two Selves
Bryher

The Hurry-Up Song: A Memoir of Losing My Brother
Clifford Chase

In My Father's Arms: A True Story of Incest
Walter A. de Milly III